3RPrep
The Unofficial ACT
Solutions Manual

Complete Solutions for Six Real ACT

Official Practice Tests

First Edition

Phil McCaffrey
Jay Hadfield
Dr. Robyn Satty
William Meyer

3RPrep
Ambridge, PA

ISBN: 9781690619697

Any references to historical events, real people, or real places are used fictitiously. Names, characters, and places are products of the author's imagination.

The ACT is a registered trademark of the ACT which is in no way affiliated with this book, its writers, or publishers.

Front cover image by Samantha Zemanek.

Printed by KDP Amazon in the United States of America.

First printing edition 2020.

3RPrep
PO Box 509
1400 Church St.
Ambridge, PA 15002

www.3RPrep.com

Table of Contents

Introduction

3RPrep is a private tutoring company based in Ambridge, PA with over twenty-five years of experience in the test prep field. We use a tried and tested method with our students that encourages reflection and critical analysis in order to become a better and more successful test-taker (See "The 3RPrep Method," p. 7). Furthermore, we have categorized and coded the ACT content so that students can focus their efforts on the particular content area that they are struggling in (See "The Concepts," p. 10).

We have taken the time to solve all of the questions on six real ACT practice exams. These tests are all written by the ACT. They were used by the ACT as their official practice test, included in the booklet "Preparing for the ACT Test." These booklets are published every three years or so. Here is the complete list of official ACT practice tests by year and test number:

1. 2018:   1874FPRE
2. 2015:   1572CPRE
3. 2012:   1267C (67C)
4. 2009:   0964E (64E)
5. 2006:   0661C (61C)
6. 2003:   0359F (59F)

All six are available for free download at www.3RPrep.com. Every question in this booklet has an answer, the concept or concepts that the question is testing, and an explanation. Some of the concepts are very simple, while others may take some practice to become second-nature. In our experience, it is the student who practices that makes the biggest difference in her score.

Improving Your Score

Improving your score is fairly simple, though it's not always easy. It's not enough to simply *do* the work.

After working with thousands of students over the past 25 years we've observed some common traits among those students who were able to achieve a significant score improvement (4+ points) on the ACT.

Students who improve the most tend to have these things in common:

1. They *plan* before they practice. They pick a target test date, set a goal score, and plan backwards. Students with a specific goal in mind—even if that goal is arbitrary—improve more than students who simply want a "better" or "higher" score. If your goal is to improve 4+ points, you will need at least 40 hours of practice. If you can practice 5 hours per week, you'll need to begin 8 weeks before the test. Adjust as needed.

2. They practice *a lot*. There's no shortcut here. Getting better at anything—chess, field hockey, violin, coding—requires practice. This is no different. The further away from your goal you are, the more work you have in front of you.

3. They practice *deliberately*. Sitting down for 30 minutes, answering some questions, and just checking them is not nearly as effective as sitting down with the specific intention to work on hard math problems for 20 minutes and then reviewing comma rules for 10 minutes.

4. They practice *consistently*. Even though you know how to read and do math, that doesn't mean you know how to do the reading and math *the way it's tested*. Think of preparing for this test as learning a brand new skill. The more consistent you are, the faster you'll learn. If you practice in starts and stops, you can still improve, but it will take longer.

5. They practice *frequently*. It's better to practice one hour, five days per week than it is to practice for 5 hours straight every Sunday. More frequent short practice sessions are better than one or two longer sessions, even if the total times are the same.

6. They know when (and where) to ask for *help*. Using this book is a way of asking for help, but if you need more, visit 3RPrep.com for more resources.

The 3RPrep Method

1. **Test**. Go to www.3RPRep.com to find the practice test. Print out and take the test. I know that you're used to reading on a screen, but the ACT is still paper and pencil, so paper and pencil are the best way to practice.

2. **Check**. When you're finished, check your answers and mark any that you got wrong, skipped, or were unsure about (even if you chose the right answer).

3. **Reflect**. This is absolutely the most important part. For each question you missed, you should look at your answer and at the correct answer and try to figure out why you missed the question. I can hear you asking, "Well if I missed it, how do I know what I did wrong?" The idea is to focus on what part of the question you missed. In many cases you'll be able to tell what threw you off.

4. **Adjust**. Make adjustments based on your reflections. If you are misreading questions, for instance, focus on underlining key words in the question. If you're a little fuzzy about math formulas, plan some time to work on memorizing the formulas you need.

5. **Repeat**. Keep doing it until you get it right.

The Three Stages of Practice (3:2:1)

1. **Accuracy**. Always put accuracy before speed. If you can't get a question correct in 10 minutes, it's unlikely that you'll be able to get it correct in 60 seconds. Spend half of your time practicing your accuracy at answering questions.

2. **Speed**. Once you've hit your score goal *untimed*, you can begin to work on speed. While continuing to be accurate, now work on timing. This should be about one-third of your overall practice.

3. **Endurance**. Finally, you'll need to be able to maintain your accuracy and speed across the full (175 minute) length of the test. The test is one of endurance; one-sixth of your practice time should be doing it all at once.

ACT Scoring

The scoring on the ACT can be a little confusing at first, but it's important to know how the test is scored.

When you get your score report, you'll notice that you receive eight separate scores.

	Composite	Math	Science	STEM	English	Reading	Writing	ELA
Score	1-36	1-36	1-36	1-36	1-36	1-36	2-12	1-36

Students who are using the ACT for college admissions and financial aid should only focus on the scores for the four major sections of the test—English, math, reading, and science—and the composite. In fact, your focus should be on increasing your composite score. Your composite score is calculated by *averaging* your English, math, reading, and science scores.

Remember that in most cases, for most colleges, the composite is all that matters.

ACT Goal Sheet

	Scale Score Goal	Raw Score Goal		Percent Correct Goal
English			Raw/75 x 100	
Math			Raw/60 x 100	
Reading			Raw/40 x 100	
Science			Raw/40 x 100	
Composite				

To determine the sum of your subscore goals, multiply your composite goal by four.

ACT Goal Sheet Example

Let's say your goal is a 26 composite. The easiest way to get a 26 composite is to get a 26 in English, math, reading, and science. Of course most of us will do better in certain sections than others, so adjust your English, math, reading, and science goals accordingly. Just make sure the four numbers average to your goal score.

After some soul searching, you decide to shoot for a 28 (English), 24 (Math), 25 (Reading), 27 (Science).

	Scale Score Goal	Raw Score Goal		Percent Correct Goal
English	28	63	Raw/75 x 100	84
Math	24	35	Raw/60 x 100	58
Reading	25	27	Raw/40 x 100	68
Science	27	23	Raw/40 x 100	58
Composite	26			

In this example, any increase in any of those areas would mean a marginal increase in your overall score. However, your overall score can only increase by gaining four points in your scale scores, so figure out your strengths and play to them!

Now, it is important to keep in mind that some tests are harder than others. For example, on the 1572 you can only get a 36 in English by getting 75 questions correct, whereas on the 1874 you can get one question wrong and still get a perfect score. However, the goal sheet should give you a good idea of what you should shoot for in each section.

The Concepts

English Concepts

Code	Concept	Description
E100	Grammar & Mechanics	Grammar in all of its glory!
E101	Verbs: Agreement/Tense	Ensure that verbs agree with the subject in number (singular/plural) and that the tense is correct given the context.
E102	Commas	Identify correct comma usage.
E103	Independent Clauses: Period, Semicolon, Comma and FANBOYS	Correctly punctuate independent clauses.
E104	Nonessential Information: Commas, Dashes, Parentheses	Identify and correctly punctuate nonessential or appositive clauses.
E105	Pronouns: Agreement/Case	Ensure that pronouns agree with their antecedents
E106	Apostrophes: Possessive, Plural, Contractions	Correctly use apostrophes to indicate possession or a contraction.
E107	Colons and Dashes	Correctly use colons and single ("em") dashes.
E108	Adjectives and Adverbs	Distinguish between adjectives and adverbs.
E109	Relative Pronouns	Correctly use and distinguish among relative pronouns.
E200	Reading/Rhetoric	Methods of reading, rhetorical devices, and tones.
E201	Relevancy: Adding, Deleting, and Replacing Information	Choose the correct addition, deletion, or replacement given the sequence of events and agreement of grammatical elements.
E202	Word Choice: Correct Word	Pick the correct word based on meaning or usage.
E203	Word Choice: Tone	Pick the correct word based on the tone of the passage. Wrong answers are often too informal or casual.
E204	Short and Simple	Eliminate redundancy and overly wordy answer choices.
E205	Transition	Pick the correct word or phrase that transitions between

	Words/Phrases	sentences or paragraphs.
E206	Modification: Dangling Modifiers	Identify and correct dangling modifiers.
E207	Modification: Moving Modifiers	This question type asks students to ensure that modifiers are modifying the correct sentence element.
E208	Moving Sentences	Move a given sentence to the correct place in the passage.
E209	Moving Paragraphs	Move a given paragraph to the correct place in the passage.
E210	Writer's Goal	Identify whether or not the stated "writer's goal" is correct or not, and why. These are essentially main point questions.
E211	Parallel Structure	Ensure that all verbs used in a sentence to describe the action of a single subject retain the same structure as well as agreement and case.

Math Concepts

Code	Concept	Description
M100	Numbers & Operations	Basic math operations (mostly pre-Algebra level).
M101	Word Problems - Translation & Vocabulary	Translating words to math. Sum means add. Product means multiply.
M102	Operations - Order of Operations; Number Theory	The order of operations: PEMDAS.
M103	Properties of Integers	An integer is a whole number or negative whole number - no fractions or decimals.
M104	Fractions	One integer divided by another.
M105	Number Line	Numbers plotted on the number line.
M106	Sequence	Arithmetic and geometric series and sequences.
M107	Sets - Union and Intersections; Venn Diagrams	A set is a grouping of numbers or things. Things in BOTH sets are almost always a Venn Diagram problem.
M108	Ratio & Proportions	Comparing a part to a part, or a part to a whole.
M109	Rate	The rate at which something happens (usually means multiply).
M110	Percent	Percent means part of out of 100. Always involves multiplication or division.
M111	Units: Time & Money	Units can be tricky, write them out.
M112	Logic	If P then Q.
M200	Algebra	*Most* of Algebra I & *Some* of Algebra II, but not much.
M201	Algebraic Operations: CLT, in terms of	Combine Like Terms. When a problem states *"x in terms of y"* solve for *"x"*.
M202	Solving Equations	Solve for the variable or expression.
M203	Inequalities	Less than or greater than. Always on the test.
M204	ABS Absolute Value	A number's positive distance from zero.
M205	Exponents & Roots; Scientific Notation	The number times itself or its root.
M206	Logarithm	The inverse of an exponential function.
M207	Linear Functions: y = mx+b	Lines, slope, y-intercepts and other linear functions.

M208	Coordinate Geometry & XY plane	Anything that is tested in the xy-plane the standard coordinate plane. Though it says geometry, it is mostly an algebra topic.
M209	Variation: Direct, Inverse	Varies directly means y=kx. Varies inversely means y = k/x.
M210	Systems of Equations	Comparing two functions or equations in the xy-plane.
M211	System Word Problems	Using words to solve for two or more variables.
M212	Linear Function: Rate	A constant rate using algebra.
M213	DRT Distance/Rate/Time	Distance = rate (velocity) multiplied by the time.
M214	Functions $f(x)$	Functions in all of their glory: evaluation, tables, graphs, and compound functions. $f(x)$
M215	Equation of a Circle	A circle plotted in the xy-plane.
M216	Quadratics and Parabolas	A second degree polynomial.
M217	Factoring & Foil	Manipulating quadratics.
M218	Rational Functions & PLD	Advanced Algebra II with polynomials and rational functions.
M219	Complex Numbers	i = square root of -1; i^2 = -1
M220	Matrix	An array of numbers.
M300	Geometry	Planar and three-dimensional geometry.
M301	Lines & Angles	Lines connect two points in a plane. Intersecting lines form an angle. The point of intersection is the vertex.
M302	Triangles	Three-sided figures. Angles (180 total), area, and perimeter.
M303	Quadrilaterals	Four-sided figures. Angles (360 total), area, and perimeter. Squares, rectangles, trapezoids, etc.
M304	Polygon	Figures with 3 or more sides. Usually pentagons and hexagons.
M305	Circles	Area, circumference, radius, diameter.
M306	Sectors & Arcs	A section of a circle. Arc, sector angle, and sector area.
M307	Solids	Boxes, balls, and cans: rectangular prisms, spheres, and right cylinders. An occasional pyramid or cone.
M308	Multiple Figures	More than one geometric figure, usually in a plane.
M309	Rotate a Figure	Translation of a planar figure or rotation of a solid.

M310	Geometric Rate	Rate at which a three-dimensional figure is filled.
M400	Trigonometry	Breaking up the world into triangles.
M401	SOHCAHTOA	Right triangle trigonometry. Sine, cosine, and tangent.
M402	Unit Circle	Degrees and radians.
M403	Trig Function	Sine, cosine, and tangent functions.
M404	Laws of Sines/Cosines	Finding a missing side or angle of a non-right triangle.
M500	Probability & Statistics	Central tendency & aspects of Probability and Statistics.
M501	Mean, Average	Calculated average of a set of data.
M502	Median, Mode	Median is the middle point of a set of data. The Mode is the point that appears the most.
M503	Probability	Random probability.
M504	Counting, Permutations & Combinations	How many subsets can be made from an array of possibilities.
M505	Charts & Graphs	Reading data off of a chart or graph.
M506	Tables	Data arranged in rows and columns.
M507	Standard Deviation	Calculating standard deviation as an equation and on a bell curve.
M508	Sampling	Random sampling from a population.
M600	Solving Techniques	Using the answers or a technique other than straightforward calculation to find a multiple choice answer.
M601	Plug In Your Own Numbers	Plug in your own numbers for Algebra.
M602	Backsolve - Use The Answers To Solve The Question	When there are numbers in the answers but algebra in the question, it is often easiest to simply use the answers to solve the equation.
M603	Estimate	Rationally thinking through a list of multiple choice answers to "see" which ones could possibly be the answers. Often useful when using process of elimination.
M604	Measure	Most figures are drawn to scale. Use your answer sheet to measure points on a line or an angle.
M605	Last Digit Math	A very advanced technique using only the last digit to solve arithmetic.

Reading Concepts

Code	Concept	Description
R100	Reading: Find	All R101-R104 indicate how or where to find the answer in the passage.
R101	Line Number	Read around the line numbers indicated by the question.
R102	Paragraph Number	Read the paragraph indicated by the question.
R103	Keyword	Read around the key word or phrase from the question.
R104	Big Picture	These questions refer to the whole passage and may ask about the main point, the tone, or chronology.
R200	Reading: Question Type	Recognizing question type and what is being requested of the reader.
R201	Detail	Find a specific detail in the passage.
R202	Vocabulary in Context	Identify what a word means *within the context of the passage.*
R203	Inference/Assumption	These questions ask about inferences, but the correct answer will only be an inference that *must be true* given what the passage says.
R204	Main Idea/Function: Paragraph	Identify the main idea or function of a given paragraph.
R301	Main Idea/Function: Passage	Identify the main idea or function of the whole passage.
R302	Organization of the Passage	Correctly identify how the passage is organized thematically.
R303	Chronology	Identify when an event occurs *chronologically* in the passage, as opposed to when the event is *told.*
R304	Both Passages	These questions ask you to compare or contrast different elements from two passages.
R401	Literary Device	This question asks students to identify the author's use of rhetorical devices and techniques (compare, contrast, provide an example, etc.)
R402	Rhetorical Device	This question is specific to a literary device, such as allusion, metaphor, simile, and personification.
R501	Least/Not/Except	This question type asks students to identify the incorrect or least correct answer.

Science Concepts

Code	Concept	Description
S101	Find in Text	The answer is explicitly in the text.
S102	Experiment Design/Parameters	The answer is explicitly in the text and relates to the design of an experiment. The answer may relate to independent, dependent, or controlled variables (constants). The answer likely includes the same units provided in the text.
S103	Argumentation and Evidence	The answer relates to using scientific or textual evidence to make an argument.
S104	Inference	The question asks you to infer the reasoning behind a given statement or section within the passage or in the question.
S105	Text to Data	The question asks you to find information in the text and use it to interpret or find data in a chart, graph, or figure.
S106	Conflicting Viewpoints (Agree/Disagree)	The question asks you to evaluate a viewpoint as it relates to the passage. Of the six ACT science passages there will always be one that conflicts viewpoints.
S201	Reading a Table	The answer can be found by reading a table.
S202	Reading a Graph	The answer can be found by reading a graph.
S203	Reading a Figure	The answer can be found by interpreting a figure. Information can be found by reading figure labels, in a similar way to reading graph axes.
S204	Trends	Use the numbers in a table, graph, or figure to determine whether there is an overall increase or decrease. Note that there can be outliers (points that don't fit) from general trends.
S205	Extrapolation	Use the numbers in a table, graph, or figure to identify a trend, then use that trend to predict the next highest or next lowest number that fits the trend.
S206	Correlation	Compare the data in two or more different data sets to determine whether there is a correlation. Note that there can be outliers (points that don't fit) from general trends.
S207	Infer from Data	Use the numbers in a table, graph, or figure to infer additional information.
S208	Conversion	Convert data in a table, graph, or figure into another form, such as taking the data in one column on a table and plotting it on a line graph.
S301	Inquiry Process	The question requires knowledge of the inquiry process, such as how to craft a hypothesis.
S302	Science Math	The question requires the use of science-related mathematics skills, such as scientific notation or basic statistics.

S303	Biology	The question requires knowledge of basic biology.
S304	Chemistry	The question requires knowledge of basic chemistry.
S305	Physics	The question requires knowledge of basic physics.
S306	Earth/Space Science	The question requires knowledge of basic Earth science or astronomy.

ACT 1874 (2018)

English 1874

1. Answer: A.

Concept: *E201 Relevancy: Adding, Deleting, and Replacing Information*

The keyword in this question is a single word: "complexity." The answer is a synonym for "complexity." Alternately, words can be eliminated that don't mean "complex." Also, options **B**, **C**, and **D** are synonyms for each other (e.g. Superb! Impressive! Terrific!), so **A** is the obvious outlier.

2. Answer: G.

Concept: *E206 Modification: Dangling Modifiers*

Look carefully at **F**, **H**, and **J**: in each of these answer choices, it is the sculpture that is delighted. The correct choice (**G**) is the only option where the subject is doing the action of the verb.

3. Answer: A.

Concept: *E202 Word Choice: Correct Word*

"To dub" is to give a name. It can be gathered from context that something is being named, not "honored," "adorned," or "specified."

4. Answer: F.

Concept: *E102 Commas*

> ### Big 3 Comma Rules
> 1. No commas between subject and verb
> 2. No commas before or after prepositions
> 3. No commas between describing words and the things they describe

"At Edinburgh's Filmhouse Cinema" is a prepositional phrase (or an introductory clause), so it always gets a comma after it: that eliminates **H** and **J**. Answer **G** is incorrect because there is a comma between the adjective "sculpted" and the noun it modifies: "scene."

5. Answer: C.

Concept: *E101 Verbs: Agreement/Tense*

There are actually two concepts being tested here: apostrophes and verb agreement. **B** and **D** are incorrect because the apostrophes are wrong. There is no possession occurring here. Both "horse" and "theater" should be plural, not possessive. **A** is incorrect because "horses" does not agree with the verb "leaps." Whenever a verb is underlined, immediately look for the subject doing the action.

6. Answer: F.

Concept: *E102 Commas*

Remember: *commas have very specific purposes! They separate clauses - they aren't there for "pauses!"*

G can be eliminated because a dash would turn both clauses around it into dependent clauses and there would be no sentence. **H** is incorrect because we can't remove the phrase between the commas without the sentence breaking down, and **J** puts a comma before the preposition "of."

7. Answer: D.

Concept: E204 Short and Simple

Each of these answer choices says essentially the same thing, but notice how wordy **A**, **B**, and **C** are. In situations such as this, pick the shortest and simplest answer.

8. Answer: G.

Concept: *E205 Transition Words/Phrases*

Look at each of these words in context. "Therefore" indicates cause and effect. So, **F** is wrong, as is **H** since there is no evidence in the text that this is obvious. **J** is wrong because these sentences do not contradict each other.

9. Answer: C.

Concept: *E101 Verbs: Agreement/Tense*

This is a common trick on the ACT. When a verb is underlined, look for the word "of," since it's often used to separate the correct subject from the verb. The subject here is "creator," not "sculptures." So, the correct subject-verb agreement is "the creator *is*."

10. Answer: J.

Concept: *E204 Short and Simple*

F can be eliminated since "Whatever" doesn't serve any purpose and is too informal in this context. That leaves three answer choices that are all grammatically correct: **G**, **H**, and **J**. Just pick the shortest and simplest.

11. Answer: C.

Concept: *E105 Pronouns: Agreement/Case*

Pronouns replace proper nouns. When a pronoun is used, it is often replacing a proper noun from the preceding sentence. In the previous sentence, the phrase "reveals her gender" indicates the pronoun should be "her."

12. Answer: F.

Concept: *E204 Short and Simple*

Note: the ACT loves to sneak in redundant answers!

Each of these answer choices says essentially the same thing, but three of them are redundant. The wrong answers either repeat "gratitude" or "thanks" in some way.

13. Answer: B.

Concept: *E201 Relevancy: Adding, Deleting, and Replacing Information*

Answer choice **B** is correct because the previous sentence answers *why* she created the sculptures. "Because" she wanted to express thanks for "libraries books, words, ideas." **A** is incorrect because there is no indication the author knows who the sculptor is. **C** is incorrect because it proves nothing. **D** is incorrect because there is no proof that the artist is a librarian.

14. Answer: J.

Concept: *E104 Nonessential Information: Commas, Dashes, Parentheses*

Whenever a dash is underlined, always look for another dash somewhere else in the sentence, indicating there is nonessential information. (For a single dash, the rules are different.) Since there are two dashes here (after "elaborate works of art"), take out everything in between the dashes and plug in the answers to make an independent clause. **F** is incorrect because it is actually a dependent clause when the word "who" is added because the subject never actually *does* anything. **G** is incorrect for the same reason but "whom" turns the subject into an object. **H** has the same problem. **J** is correct because it is the only one that is actually an independent clause when the nonessential information is removed.

Tip: *parentheses, a pair of dashes, and a pair of commas function in the same way - they offset a nonessential clause between them. This means that all of the information between the punctuation marks and the punctuation can be taken out without affecting the rest of the sentence.*

15. Answer: B.

Concept: *E202 Word Choice: Correct Word*

Identify the correct conjunction. Only "and" properly joins "cutting up" and "refashioning."

16. Answer: G.

Concept: *E104 Nonessential Information: Commas, Dashes, Parentheses*

As with all nonessential information, **G** is correct because "Pollack is likely to point out" can be removed and a grammatically correct sentence will remain. The other three options will create either a run-on sentence or a grammatically incorrect sentence.

17. Answer: C.

Concept: *E104 nonessential Information: Commas, Dashes, Parentheses*

This question tests two things related to commas. Answer choice **A** properly sets off the nonessential information between two commas (" , 165, 231 in all,"), but adds an extra comma at the end next to a preposition. **B** improperly puts parentheses around the number of corks, but not the entire nonessential clause. **D** adds an unnecessary comma after the number. Answer choice **C** correctly uses dashes to offset the

nonessential clause *and* doesn't include any other unnecessary punctuation.

18. Answer: F.

Concept: *E102 Commas*

> # Big 3 Comma Rules
> 1. No commas between subject and verb
> 2. No commas before or after prepositions
> 3. No commas between describing words and the things they describe

Answer choices **G** and **H** are wrong because they put commas before the preposition "from." The reason to eliminate **J** is a bit more complicated, but the reason it is incorrect is that the phrase "based in Portugal" is modifying the "company," and simply doesn't need a comma to offset it.

19. Answer: C.

Concept: *E202 Word Choice: Correct Word*

This is the beginning of the explanation of how Pollack constructed the boat. Every answer choice other than **C** indicates that he had already begun.

20. Answer: G.

Concept: *E202 Word Choice: Correct Word; 106 Apostrophes: Possessive, Plural, Contractions*

Remember that "than" is used for comparison. (E.g. "I'm better at this *than* him.") "Then" is a pronoun for a specific time. This is a comparison question so "than" is necessary and eliminates **F** and **J**. The noun doing the possessing is singular ("a year") so the apostrophe comes before the "S."

21. Answer: D.

Concept: *E201 Relevancy: Adding, Deleting, and Replacing Information*

Because the question asks which answer "most effectively *introduces* the paragraph," the whole paragraph must be read. The paragraph is about Pollack's "strategy," not piles of corks, convincing people, or his fears.

22. Answer: G.

Concept: *E201 Relevancy: Adding, Deleting, and Replacing Information*

This is a tough one! The clue here is the phrase "most *specific*." Although the passage never states *how* he assembled the corks, the point is to answer the question. "Hexagon" is the "most specific" answer.

23. Answer: C.

Concept: *E211 Parallel Structure*

"Binding" and "shaping" need to be parallel—that is, they need to have the same form—because they are joined by the conjunction "and."

24. Answer: H.

Concept: *E201 Relevancy: Adding, Deleting, and Replacing Information*

Look for the key word(s)! The question asks for the choice that will indicate how "challenging" the process was. Out of the four answer choices, only "rigorous" (**H**) fits the description the question is looking for.

25. Answer: B.

Concept: *E101 Verbs: Agreement/Tense; E109 Relative Pronouns*

For answer choices **A** and **C**, the verb does not agree with the subject. Both "he had saw" and "he seen" should sound very wrong! **D** has a verb that could be correct (saw), but the sentence indicates that he is looking at "himself," not someone else.

26. Answer: F.

Concept: *E102 Commas; E103 Independent Clauses: Period, Semicolon, Comma and FANBOYS*

Big 3 Comma Rules

1. No commas between subject and verb
2. No commas before or after prepositions
3. No commas between describing words and the things they describe

The word "of" is a preposition, so **G** can be eliminated. It's also helpful to know that "But at a length of twenty-two feet" is an introductory phrase, which needs a comma—that eliminates **J**. Answer choice **H** is wrong because semicolons can only separate two independent clauses.

27. Answer: C.

Concept: *E202 Word Choice: Correct Word*

Answer choices **A** and **D** are both wrong because "with" and "as" cannot be used as prepositions after "suited" in this context. **B** is wrong because "most well suited to" is a superlative, which would indicate that more than one thing is being compared.

28. Answer: F.

Concept: *E109 Relative Pronouns*

Answer choices **H** and **J** are incorrect because the noun is "company" and a company is not a person. "Which" is used to introduce nonessential information or a dependent clause, but the clause began by the "the company" is the independent clause, or main idea, of the sentence. So, **G** is incorrect.

29. Answer: D.

Concept: *E204 Short and Simple*

Remember: if unsure, check for redundant information!

Each of these answer choices says essentially the same thing, and all are grammatically correct. In situations such as this, pick the shortest and simplest answer. This answer can also be derived from the *redundancy* of information provided. The prior sentence stated it was in Portugal already, so any answer choice which mentions Portugal is redundant.

Tip: *the ACT hates redundancy!*

30. Answer: G.

Concept: *E208 Moving sentences.*

"Who" was doing the pickups is unknown and so is "what" the pickups were. The previous sentence must clearly provide that information. "Pollack" was picking up the "corks."

31. Answer: C.

Concept: *E204 Short and Simple*

Each of these answer choices is grammatically correct. In situations such as this, pick the shortest and simplest answer *that is correct.*

Answer choice **D** is actually the shortest, but leaves an incomplete comparison: "one as translucent white as" needs a noun to complete it. Furthermore, **A** is redundant (it repeats New Mexico), and so is **B** ("translucent *white...* as the *white* sands").

32. Answer: J.

Concept: *E102 Commas*

Big 3 Comma Rules
1. No commas between subject and verb
2. No commas before or after prepositions
3. No commas between describing words and the things they describe

Answer choice **F** is wrong because there is a comma before "and," but the "and" isn't separating two independent clauses, so there shouldn't be a comma. There should be no comma between "sand" and "heated" because "heated" is an adjective describing "sand." Answer choice **J** corrects this error, which is why it's correct. Answer choice **G** is wrong because the parentheses are not setting off a nonessential clause.

33. Answer: C.

Concept: *E201 Relevancy: Adding, Deleting, and Replacing Information*

The keywords in this sentence are "dramatic nature." "Burns" is the most dramatic answer because it is the most explicit and defined.

34. Answer: G.

Concept: *E104 nonessential Information: Commas, Dashes, Parentheses*

A pair of commas means that there is a nonessential clause that can be removed. Only answer choice **G** leaves an independent clause whenever the nonessential information is removed along with the two commas. Answer choice **J** has only one comma which would render both the first and second clause dependent.

35. Answer: A.

Concept: *E201 Relevancy: Adding, Deleting, and Replacing Information*

For questions such as this, look for the key word in the sentences immediately before and after the sentence to be inserted. The sentence before says "experts are rarely able to locate a fully intact fulgurite" and the sentence after says "occasionally . . . an unbroken." So, the correct answer is **A**, "breaks easily."

36. Answer: J.

Concept: *E202 Word Choice: Correct Word*

Each conjunction word (e.g. "while," "however," "so") turns the entire sentence into a dependent clause. Only by deleting the underlined portion is there actually an independent clause.

37. Answer: C.

Concept: *E201 Relevancy: Adding, Deleting, and Replacing Information*

This question is asking which answer connects to *both* the sentence before and the sentence after. The sentence before says "strong, sustained winds" can reveal fulgurites, and the sentence after indicates the narrator is "hopeful" that they would see a fulgurite, so the answer that connects those two ideas is **C**.

38. Answer: F.

Concept: *E204 Short and Simple*

Each of these answer choices is grammatically correct. In situations such as this, pick the shortest and simplest answer. Notice that each wrong answer, while mechanically correct, is wordier than necessary, as well as redundant.

39. Answer: D.

Concept: *E201 Relevancy: Adding, Deleting, and Replacing Information*

This question is asking which answer connects to *both* the underlined clause and the sentence after. This is tricky because the sentence after is on the next page. Don't be lazy. The next sentence "Their interiors, *though*" indicates that there is a contrast. The contrast is between their interiors and their exteriors.

40. Answer: H.

Concept: *E201 Relevancy: Adding, Deleting, and Replacing Information*

The keywords in this question are "light, sporadic arrangement," which means that the correct answer will be similar to "light and sporadic." Given the options, that can only be "speckled."

41. Answer: B.

Concept: *E206 Modification: Moving Modifiers*

Since the underlined portion ("formed by air and moisture") is acting as an adjective, the question is *who* or *what* was formed by air in moisture. Answer: the bubbles were.

42. Answer: F.

Concept: *E211 Parallel Structure*

When a verb is underlined, look for other verbs in the same sentence, in the sentences immediately before, or immediately after. Make sure all of the verbs are in the same form. Here, "to unearth" has to match with "to stop."

43. Answer: C.

Concept: *E201 Relevancy: Adding, Deleting, and Replacing Information*

For questions such as this, the keyword is in the sentence itself. "Anna laughed" matches with "light moment. . . good-natured joke."

44. Answer: G.

Concept: *E105 Pronouns: Agreement/Case*

Whenever a pronoun is underlined, immediately look for its antecedent (the noun it replaces). The pronoun and its antecedent must agree in number, gender, and/or case. It may seem like this is a case of "our," but immediately after the underlined portion it reads "she wanted to keep searching," indicating that "she" is the subject of the sentence.

45. Answer: A.

Concept: *E201 Relevancy: Adding, Deleting, and Replacing Information*

For questions such as this, the answer is in the question itself: "new information." Scan back through the passage, and it is clear that only answer choice **A** provides new information in the form of which states she had been to.

46. Answer: F.

Concept: *E105 Pronouns: Agreement/Case*

Always define what proper noun is being replaced by a pronoun. In this case, it is the "facility." Answer choice **J** can be eliminated because "it's" means "it is," which isn't appropriate. "Their" can be eliminated because it is a place, not a person. "These" can be eliminated because "facility" is singular.

47. Answer: B.

Concept: *E101 Verbs: Agreement/Tense*

Always remove nonessential clauses when they are crowding around the answer ("which . . . New Hampshire"). With that removed, it's easier to see that the subject is "weather conditions," so the verb must be "have earned."

48. Answer: G.

Concept: *E104 Nonessential Information: Commas, Dashes, Parentheses*

A nonessential clause within a nonessential clause! Parentheticals always refer to the information *prior* to it, so commas always come after parentheses, not before. That means that the first comma after "mountains" must be removed. The second comma in the underlined portion must remain because it is offsetting the nonessential clause "for example."

49. Answer: D.

Concept: *E201 Relevancy: Adding, Deleting, and Replacing Information*

There are two keywords here: "extreme" and "comparison." Only answer choice **D** uses both a comparison *and* indicates that the weather is extreme by comparing the weather at the peak to Antarctica.

50. Answer: F.

Concept: *E103 Independent Clauses: Period, Semicolon, Comma and FANBOYS*

> **Separating Independent Clauses**
>
> 1. Period
> 2. Semicolon
> 3. Comma FANBOYS

Answer choices **G**, **H**, and **J** would change this clause into a dangling modifier (or an unresolved dependent clause). Answer choice **F** is a standard "comma-FANBOYS" situation which correctly conjoins two independent clauses.

51. Answer: B.

Concept: *E102 Commas*

Parentheses and two commas indicate nonessential information, which this is not, so **A** and **D** can be eliminated. A semicolon separates two independent clauses, but "one of the fastest ever recorded" is a dependent clause. The hyphen is appropriate because hyphens can introduce an explanation.

52. Answer: F.

Concept: *E204 Short and Simple*

Remember: *check for redundancies!*

Each of these answer choices says essentially the same thing. In situations such as this, pick the shortest and simplest answer. In this case, the sentence already contains the word "also," so the incorrect answer choices would be redundant as they all mean "also."

53. Answer: D.

Concept: *E204 Short and Simple*

Each of these answer choices says essentially the same thing. In situations such as this, pick the shortest and simplest answer. (Also, for the sake of parallelism, the preposition "of" has to work with each noun, which it does.)

54. Answer: H.

Concept: *E202 Word Choice: Correct Word*

This one can be tough to see. The correct answer choice will result in an independent clause. Only answer choice **H** provides an independent clause. The incorrect answer choices would make the entire sentence dependent.

55. Answer: D.

Concept: *E205 Transition Words/Phrases*

Answer choice **A** would suggest that the information is contradictory to what has been said before, which it is not. The same is true for **C**. Answer choice **B** would suggest that the information in the sentence is an obvious extension of the previous sentence, which it is not. Answer choice **D** simply removes the transition and provides new information.

Tip: "However" and "though" are interchangeable on the ACT.

56. Answer: H.

Concept: *E202 Word Choice: Correct Word*

This can be a very difficult question if it is unclear what is wrong. The question that needs to be answered is: *who* or *what* is doing the gripping? It is the "vehicle that grips."

57. Answer: A.

Concept: *E103 Independent Clauses: Period, Semicolon, Comma and FANBOYS*

Separating Independent Clauses
1. Period
2. Semicolon
3. Comma FANBOYS

When there are two independent clauses, there are only three options to separate them: a period, a semicolon, or comma with FANBOYS. Therefore, **A** is the only option.

58. Answer: G.

Concept: *E201 Relevancy: Adding, Deleting, and Replacing Information*

The keyword for this question is "contrasts." What's the opposite of venturing up to a windy summit? A "warm recliner."

59. Answer: C.

Concept: *E208 Moving Sentences*

There is a clue in this sentence. "This information" must connect to the sentence before. The information in question is the "data" that is sent to the National Weather Service.

60. Answer: J.

Concept: *E210 Writer's Goal*

Remember that for big picture questions (including "main point" and "main purpose" questions in the reading section) the wrong answers are typically wrong because the *scope* is wrong. That is, the wrong answers are typically too broad or too specific. If the main purpose had been to "describe how mountain ranges affect weather patterns,"

this passage would fall short. This passage does not discuss mountain ranges generally but one specific observatory on one specific mountain.

61. Answer: C.

Concept: *E106 Apostrophes: Possessive, Plural, Contractions*

That's = that is
It's = it is

There is no such thing as " *its'* ", so **A** is incorrect by default, but all answer choices **A**, **B**, and **D** also have the problem of using a pronoun without a known antecedent noun it is replacing. Answer choice **C** says "that *something* is the genuine article," which provides all the necessary information to make the sentence complete.

62. Answer: G.

Concept: *E102 Commas*

Remember: *commas separate clauses! They aren't for pauses!*

"Named" is a verb that needs an object: "Elijah McCoy." Therefore, **F** and **H** are incorrect. (The other comma in answer choice **H** is also wrong.) Answer choice **J** does the same thing, but puts the comma in the middle of the noun. **G** removes all of the commas, which is correct.

63. Answer: D.

Concept: *E204 Short and Simple*

Remember: *double-check for redundancies!*

Each of these answer choices says essentially the same thing. In situations such as this, pick the shortest and simplest answer. Read each wrong answer and it will be apparent that each one repeats information already given.

64. Answer: J.

Concept: *E206 Modification: Dangling Modifiers*

Remember to look for -ing words at the beginning or close to the beginning of a sentence. The one in this sentence is "working." The question this asks (which must be answered by the noun after the comma) is: *who* or *what* is doing the working? The answer is "McCoy."

65. Answer: B.

Concept: *E201 Relevancy: Adding, Deleting, and Replacing Information*

First, read around the place where the sentence would be inserted, and assess if the information in this sentence is absolutely relevant. It appears to be relevant, so look at the reasons given for choice **A** and **B**. Choice **A** reads that it should be added because it "describes the procedures" McCoy followed. "Procedure" means step-by-step and "responsible for oiling" does not indicate that any steps were taken.

66. Answer: F.

Concept: *E202 Word Choice: Correct Word*

There are several words in these answer choices that indicate an amount: "lessening the frequency," "subtracting the amount," and "lowering the amount." "Stops" are countable in whole numbers, so it is not an "amount" but a "number" that must be counted. Answer choice **G** is too lengthy, so **F** is correct.

67. Answer: B.

Concept: *E211 Parallel Structure*

The "device that released oil" is responsible for "reducing the number of maintenance stops *and* making travel more efficient" somehow. The other options suggest that "reducing the number" is what affected those changes in travel, rather than the device.

68. Answer: F.

Concept: *E205 Transition Words/Phrases*

"For example" must be correct because this sentence includes an example of something in the preceding sentence. "Factories . . . relied on steam engines" is an example of how McCoy applied his innovation to "other engineering challenges."

69. Answer: D.

Concept: *E202 Word Choice: Correct Word*

"Therefore" implies that the information being provided is an effect of the information prior to it, which it is not. Answer choice **B** would create another introductory clause when the sentence already has one. "In that" would have nothing to refer to.

70. Answer: F.

Concept: *E104 Nonessential Information: Commas, Dashes, Parentheses*

Notice the pair of commas setting off nonessential information. If the nonessential information is taken out then it is easy to see that McCoy is already doing the action of a verb in the past tense: "designed."

71. Answer: C.

Concept: *E201 Relevancy: Adding, Deleting, and Replacing Information*

The clue is in the question: "clearest and most precise information about how the operation . . . changed." The *how* is important here. Answer choice **C** states that the machines could be run "continuously": that's *how*.

72. Answer: H.

Concept: *E201 Relevancy: Adding, Deleting, and Replacing Information*

This question is asking if the phrase is relevant. Since it is relevant, the answer is *no*, don't delete it. It shouldn't be deleted because "profits" is a "positive effect."

73. Answer: D.

Concept: *E204 Short and Simple*

"Do it" is short, but it's too short. Another way to test answer choice **A** is to remember that "it" is a pronoun that must clearly replace a specific noun, and there's no noun that "it" clearly replaces. Answer choices **B** and **C** are too long. **D** is clear and concise.

74. Answer: F.

Concept: *E201 Relevancy: Adding, Deleting, and Replacing Information*

The main idea of this passage is that McCoy's *name* became shorthand for a legitimate, quality product (i.e. the opposite of a knock-off). Answer choice **F** reiterates the main idea in a very explicit form. Answer choices **G**, **H**, and **J** may be true, but do not reiterate anything about McCoy's name.

75. Answer: D.

Concept: *E208 Moving Sentences*

"The imitators expected" indicates that the sentence before must make clear who the imitators are. "Other innovators inundated the market" - those "other innovators" are the "imitators."

Math 1874

1. Answer: C.

Concept: *M109 Rate & Proportion*

$$\frac{6 \; Servings}{3 \; eggs} = \frac{x \; servings}{5 \; eggs}$$

Solve for x by multiplying both sides by 5.

$$\frac{6 \times 5}{3} = 10$$

C. 10

2. Answer: K.

Concept: *M503 Probability*

35 - 3 officers = 32 to pick from

K. $\dfrac{1}{32}$

3. Answer: B.

Concept: *M205 Exponents & Roots*

$$2^{2x+7} = 2^{15}$$

When the bases are the same, the exponents must be equal (because the equation says so).

$2x + 7 = 15$
  -7   -7

$2x = 8$

$$\frac{2 \times}{2} = \frac{8}{2}$$

$x = 4$

B. 4

4. Answer: J.

Concept: *M214 Functions f(x)*

$$f(x) = 5x^2 - 7(4x + 3)$$

$$f(3) = 5(3)^2 - 7(4 \times 3 + 3)$$
$$5 \times 9 - 7(12 + 3)$$
$$45 - 7(15)$$
$$45 - 105$$

$$f(3) = \; -60$$

J. – 60

5. Answer: D.

Concept: *M503 Probability*

5 $5 *bills,* 7 $10 *bills,* 8 $20 *bills*

$Total = 5 + 7 + 8 = 20$ total bills

$\dfrac{8}{20}$ reduces to $\dfrac{2}{5}$

D. $\dfrac{2}{5}$

6. Answer: H.

Concept: *M211 System Word Problems*

ABC $40 + $2/*book*

$Easy$ $35 + $3/*book*

$40 + 2x = 35 + 3x$
    -2x   -2x

$40 = 35 + x$
-35   -35

$5 = x$

H. 5

7. Answer: D.

Concept: *M303 Quadrilateral; M605 Last Digit Math*

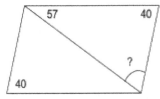

The opposite angles of a parallelogram are congruent. Now form a triangle (180):

$$57 + 40 + x = 180$$

$$97 + x = 180$$
-97   -97

$$x = 83$$

D. 83

8. Answer: G.

Concept: *M202 Solving Equations*

$$x = \frac{1}{2}$$

$$\frac{8\left(\frac{1}{2}\right) - 3}{\frac{1}{2}}$$

$$\frac{4 - 3}{\left(\frac{1}{2}\right)}$$

$$\frac{1}{\left(\frac{1}{2}\right)} = 1 \times 2 = 2$$

G. 2

9. Answer: D.

Concept: *M208 Coordinate Geometry & XY-Plane*

$$(3, 8) \quad (1, -4)$$

$$\text{Midpoint} = \left(\frac{3 + 1}{2}, \frac{8 + (-4)}{2}\right)$$

$$= \left(\frac{4}{2}, \frac{4}{2}\right)$$

$$= (2, 2)$$

D. $(2, 2)$

10. Answer: G.

Concept: *M208 Coordinate Geometry & XY-Plane*

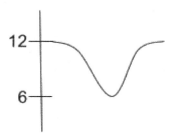

Max $= 12$, Min $= 6$
Difference $=$ Max - Min $= 12 - 6 = 6$

G. 6

11. Answer: D.

Concept: *M207 Linear Functions: y = mx + b*

$$\frac{y_2 - y_1}{x_2 - x_1} = \frac{-5 - 1}{2 - (-2)} = \frac{-6}{4} = \frac{-3}{2}$$

D. $\frac{-3}{2}$

12. Answer: H.

Concept: *M207 Linear Functions: y = mx + b*

$$\frac{221}{17} = 13$$

But remember: he is 13 miles OVER the speed limit of 30, which means ADD to 30 .

$30 + 13 = 43$

H. 43

13. Answer: B.

Concept: *M210 Systems of Equations*

Solve for x and y:

$8x = 12$

$$\frac{8 \times}{8} = \frac{12}{8}$$
$$x = \frac{3}{2}$$

$2y + 10 = 22$
-10   -10

$2y = 12$

$$\frac{2y}{2} = \frac{12}{2}$$

$y = 6$

Now add the solutions:

$$\frac{3}{2} + 6 = 7\frac{1}{2}$$

B. $7\frac{1}{2}$

14. Answer: H.

Concept: *M501 Mean, Average; M502 Median, Mode*

Average = $\dfrac{420}{5}$ = 84

84 is the mean *and* the median, which means we know one of the numbers!

$420 - 84 = 336$

H. 336

15. Answer: D.

Concept: *M204 Absolute Value*

Do the equations before you apply the absolute value! (Order of Operations)

$||-8+4| - |3-9||$

$||-4| - |-6||$

$|4-6|$

$|-2|$

D. 2

16. Answer: K.

Concept: *M205 Exponents & Roots; M601 Plug In a Number*

Note: *The denominator of an exponent is the radical/root.*

$x^{\frac{2}{3}}$

When there is a 3 in the denominator of a fractional exponent plug in 8 for x. Plug in a number, then put x= 8 in for all the answers.

$8^{\frac{2}{3}} = 4$ *because* $\sqrt[3]{8^2} = 4$

K. $\sqrt[3]{x^2}$

17. Answer: B.

Concept: *M207 Linear Functions: y = mx + b*

Put into slope-intercept form (solve for y).

$4x = 7y + 5$

$y = \frac{4}{7}x + \frac{5}{7}$

B. $\frac{4}{7}$

18. Answer: K.

Concept: *M103 Properties of Integers; M601 Plug In a Number*

Plug in 2 and 3 for m & n to eliminate wrong answers.

F. *m* = 3, *n* = 3, 3 + 3 = 6 *wrong*
G. *m* = 3, *n* = 3, 3 + 3 = 6 *wrong*
H. *m* = 3, *n* = 3, 3 + 3 = 6 *wrong*
J. *m* = 2, *n* = 2, 2 + 2 = 4 *wrong*
K. *m* = 3, *n* = 2, 3 + 2 = 5 *RIGHT*!

K. m is an odd integer and n is an even integer

19. Answer: B.

Concept: *M302 Triangles*

Pythagorean proves the hypotenuse is 40.

Tip: This is a 3-4-5 triangle!

(3 × 8, 4 × 8, 5 × 8)

The midpoint of 40 is 20.

B. 20

20. Answer: K.

Concept: *M302 Triangles*

Given only two sides and no angles, the third side cannot be determined.

K. *Cannot be determined from the given information.*

Tip: *"Cannot be determined" is only a correct answer on easy problems. It is ALMOST NEVER correct after question 30 and NEVER after 40. Do not pick it on a hard problem, 41+.*

21. Answer: B.

Concept: *M303 Quadrilaterals*

$(2 \cdot 8 \cdot 10) + (2 \cdot 8 \cdot 15) =$
    $160 + \quad\quad 240 = 400$

$400 - 60 = 340$

B. 340

22. Answer: F.

Concept: *M303 Quadrilaterals*

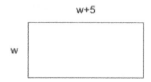

$p = 40$

$w + w + (w + 5) + (w + 5) = 40$

$4w + 10 = 40$
    $-10 \quad\quad -10$

$4w \quad\quad = 30$
$\div 4 \quad\quad\quad \div 4$

$w \quad\quad = 7.5$

A. 7.5

23. Answer: C.

Concept: *M110 Percent; M104 Fractions*

$(.08)(60) = \dfrac{1}{5}(x)$

$4.8 = \dfrac{x}{5}$

$(4.8)(5) = \dfrac{x}{5}(5)$

$24 = x$

C. 24

24. Answer: J.

Concept: *M212 Linear Function: Rate*

How many games must he attend?

$\dfrac{\$175}{\$14} = 12.5$

J. 13

25. Answer: A.

Concept: *M205 Exponents & Roots*

$\dfrac{4.8 \times 10^{-7}}{1.6 \times 10^{-11}}$

$\dfrac{4.8}{1.6} = 3 \times 10^{-7-(-11)} = 10^4$

A. 3×10^4

26. Answer: H.

Concept: *M208 Coordinate Geometry &*
XY-Plane; M305 Circles

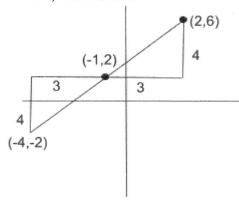

Make a triangle! Find the distance from center
x-coordinate to the *x*-coordinate on the circle.
Do the same for *y* and then work backwards.

H. $(-4, -2)$

27. Answer: A.

Concept: *M218 Polynomials*

$x^3 - 64$

The difference of the cubes
$a^3 - b^3 = (a - b)(a^2 + ab + b^2)$

The sum of the cubes
$a^3 + b^3 = (a + b)(a^2 - ab + b^2)$

$x^3 - 64 = (x - 4)(x^2 - 4x + 16)$

A. $x - 4$

Trick: **Backsolve**! *A "factor," when put into a polynomial, solves for a "zero" or "root." A zero, when put back into the equation, makes the entire equation equal to zero. You can backsolve this question by setting each answer choice equal to zero and plugging in. A: x = 4 is the only one that works!*

28. Answer: H.

Concept: *M501 Mean, Average*

First list, solve for a + b+ c:

$$\frac{a + b + c + 80}{4} = 90$$
_{x4}   _{x4}

$a + b + c + 80 = 360$
      -80   -80

$a + b + c = 280$

$$\frac{(280 + 96)}{4} = 94$$

H. 94

29. Answer: E.

Concept: *M105 Number Line; M205 Exponents & Roots*

$a = -2.5$

$a^2 = (-2.5)(-2.5)$

$a^2 = 6.25$

E. 6.25

Note: *The square of a negative number is ALWAYS positive. Be sure to enter it into your calculator using parentheses. Example:*
$(-2)^2 = 4$ *whereas* $-2^2 = -4$

30. Answer: J.

Concept: *M104 Fractions*

$$Whole - \frac{2}{9} = \frac{7}{9}$$

$$\frac{7}{9} \div 3 = \frac{7}{9} \times \frac{1}{3} = \frac{7}{27}$$

J. $\dfrac{7}{27}$

31. Answer: E.

Concept: *M103 Properties of Integers*

$1001 = 7 \cdot 11 \cdot 13$

$$\frac{30030}{1001} = 30$$

Factor 30:

$30 = 2 \times 3 \times 5$

Therefore $30030 = 2 \times 3 \times 5 \times 7 \times 11 \times 13$

E. $2 \cdot 3 \cdot 5 \cdot 7 \cdot 11 \cdot 13$

Note: **Backsolve**! *Answers A, B, & D contain numbers that are NOT prime! C does not multiply to 30,030!*

32. Answer: G.

Concept: *M303 Quadrilaterals*

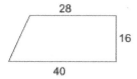

$$Area = \frac{28 + 40}{2} \times 16$$

$Area = 544$

G. 544

Note: *Know the area of a trapezoid: Average of bases times the height.*

33. Answer: E.

Concept: *M303 Quadrilaterals*

1 in = 1.5 ft

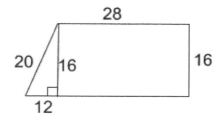

$Perimeter = 20 + 28 + 16 + 40 = 104\ inches$

$104 \times 1.5 = 156\ ft$

E. $156\ ft$

34. Answer: H.

Concept: *M110 Percent*

North = 28 in   South = 40 in

$$\frac{40}{28} \times 100\% = 142.857$$

H. $142\frac{6}{7}\%$

35. Answer: C.

Concept: *M308 Multiple Figures*

BIG rectangle -   small rectangle

$(36 \times 30) - (30 \times 24) = 360$

C. 360

36. Answer: J.

Concept: *M212 Linear Function: Rate*

3 rooms, 3 fans

3 small windows, 1 large window

$3(52) + 3(39.50) + 2(39.50) = 353.50$

J. 354

37. Answer: A.

Concept: *M503 Probability*
$(.2)(.2) = .04$

Probability Decision Square:

	Rain	Not Rain
Rain	$(.2)(.2)=$ .04	$(.2)(.8)=$ .16
Not Rain	$(.8)(.2)=$ .16	$(.8)(.8)=$ .64

Sum of all the possible outcomes = 100%

A. 0.04

38. Answer: K.

Concept: *M205 Exponents & Roots*

Evaluate each answer choice

A. $\dfrac{\sqrt{2}}{\sqrt{8}} = \dfrac{\sqrt{2}}{\sqrt{2} \, x\sqrt{4}} = \dfrac{1}{2}$ rational

B. $\dfrac{\sqrt{8}}{\sqrt{2}} = \dfrac{\sqrt{2} \times \sqrt{4}}{\sqrt{2}} = 2$ rational

C. $(\sqrt{8})^2 = \sqrt{8} \cdot \sqrt{8} = 8$ rational

D. $\sqrt{2} \cdot \sqrt{8} = \sqrt{2} \cdot \sqrt{2} \cdot \sqrt{4} = 4$ rational

E. $\sqrt{2} + \sqrt{8} = \sqrt{2} + 2\sqrt{2} = 3\sqrt{2}$ irrational

39. Answer: D.

Concept: *M401 Trigonometry*

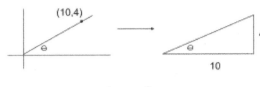

$\tan = \dfrac{opp}{adj} = \dfrac{4}{10} = \dfrac{2}{5}$

D. $\dfrac{2}{5}$

40. Answer: K.

Concept: *M204 Absolute Value*

$|2x - 8| + 3 = 5$
   $-3 \quad -3$
$|2x - 8| = 2$

$2x - 8 = 2$ or $2x - 8 = -2$

K. $2x - 8 = 2$ or $-(2x - 8) = 2$

Tip: *To solve for absolute value, find both the positive and negative values. A little tricky here because the negative sign is moved to the left, whereas all teachers put it on the right.*

41. Answer: A.

Concept: *M506 Tables*

The keyword here is *cumulative.*

65-80 has 13 total students
65-70 has 12 total students

$13 - 12 = 1$

A. 1

42. Answer: G.

Concept: *M206 Logarithm*

$d = 10log(\frac{I}{k})$

$d = 10log(\frac{1000k}{k})$

$d = 10log(1000);$ $\qquad log(1000) = 3$

$d = 10 \cdot 3 = 30$

G. 30

43. Answer: C.

Concept: *M110 Percent; M506 Tables*

$(1\,pt)(80)(.75) + (2\,pt)(60)(.90) + (3\,pt)(60)(.25)$

$60 + 108 + 45 = 213$

C. 213

44. Answer: F.

Concept: *M214 Functions f(x); M204 Absolute Value*

$y = |x|$ transforms$\rightarrow y = |x - 6|$

F. Translation right 6 units

45. Answer: A.

Concept: *M300 Geometry*

Volume $= l \cdot w \cdot h$

To find the volume of an irregularly-shaped object, submerge it and multiply length x width x <u>change</u> in height.

$8 \times 6 \times (6.6 - 4) = 124.8$

A. 125

46. Answer: J.

Concept: *M307 Solids*

Volume of cube $= 18^3$

Volume of cylinder $= \pi(6)^2(12)$

J. $18^3 - \pi(6)^2(12)$

47. Answer: B.

Concept: *M303 Quadrilateral*
Area $= 15\,ft \times 21\,ft$

Convert to yards by dividing by 3

$\frac{15}{3} \times \frac{21}{3} = 5 \times 7 = 35$

B. 35

48. Answer: G.

Concept: *M505 Charts & Graphs*

To solve, find 5 miles on x-axis and value from y-axis

ABC 5 mi = $12

Tary 5 mi = $9

G. $9

49. Answer: B.

Concept: *M208 Coordinate Geometry & XY Plane; M308 Multiple Figures*

To solve, break into triangles and a quadrilateral.

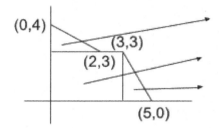

$\frac{1}{2}bh = \frac{1}{2}(2)(1) = 1$

$3 \times 3 = 9$

$\frac{1}{2}bh = \frac{1}{2}(2)(3) = 3$

B. 13

50. Answer: J.

Concept: *M210 Systems of Equations; M216 Quadratics & Parabolas*

$x + y = 151$

$x = 19 + \sqrt{y}$

Substitute
$19 + \sqrt{y} + y = 151$

Rearrange
$y + \sqrt{y} - 132 = 0$

Factor
$(\sqrt{y} + 12)(\sqrt{y} - 11) = 0$

$\sqrt{y} = 11$

$y = 121$

Solve for x

$x + 121 = 151$
$-121 \quad -121$

$x = 30$

$121 - 30 = 91$

J. 91

51. Answer: C.

Concept: *M501 Mean, Average; M502 Median, Mode*

Put numbers in order:

15, x=15, y, 30, 35, 41

y <u>must</u> be less than 30 because the median is 25:

$\frac{y + 30}{2} = 25$
$y + 30 = 50$
$y = 20$

$\frac{15 + 15 + 20 + 30 + 35 + 41}{6} = 26$

C. 26

52. Answer: F.

Concept: *M210 Systems of Equations*

$y = x^2$
$rx + sy = t$

Substitute, then put into quadratic form:

$s(x)^2 + rx - t = 0$

Use the <u>discriminant</u> $b^2 - 4ac$ to find two real solutions

$r^2 - 4(s)(-t) = r^2 + 4st$

If the discriminant is greater than zero, there are <u>two</u> real solutions.

53. Answer: A.

Concept: *M106 Sequence*

___ ___ <u>13</u> <u>18</u>

The common difference is 18-13=5
$13 - 5 = 8$
$8 - 5 = 3$

3 is the first number in the sequence.

To find the nth term, use the formula:
$A_n = A_1 + (n - 1)d$
$A_{50} = 3 + (50 - 1)(5)$
$\quad\quad = 3 + 245$
$\quad\quad = 248$

A. 248

54. Answer: H.

Concept: *M403 Trig Functions*

$sin^2 + cos^2 = 1$

H.

55. Answer: E.

Concept: *M403 Trig Functions*

<u>Period</u> of function $f(x) = csc(4x)$

Period of $f(x) = AsinB(x + h) + k$ is $\dfrac{2\pi}{B}$

$B = 4$

$\dfrac{2\pi}{4} = \dfrac{\pi}{2}$

E. $\dfrac{\pi}{2}$

56. Answer: H.

Concept: *M503 Probability*

Multiply probability of heads (½) by 3 pt
$= \dfrac{3}{2}$
Add 3 coins' value
$\dfrac{3}{2} + \dfrac{3}{2} + \dfrac{3}{2} = \dfrac{9}{2}$

H. $\dfrac{9}{2}$

57. Answer: B.

Concept: *M220 Matrix; M216 Quadratics & Parabolas*

$$\begin{bmatrix} K & 4 \\ 3 & K \end{bmatrix}$$

Determinant is $k^2 - 12$

$k^2 - 12 = k$

Rearrange into quadratic form
$ax^2 + bx + c = 0$
$k^2 - k - 12 = 0$

Factor
$(k - 4)(k + 3) = 0$

$k = -3 \text{ and } 4$

B. 4

58. Answer: F.

Concept: *M219 Complex Numbers*

$i^n = 1$

Remember:
$i = \sqrt{-1}, \; i^2 = -1, \; i^3 = -\sqrt{-1}, \; i^4 = 1$

So n <u>must</u> be a multiple of 4

F. When n is divided by 4, the remainder is 0.

59. Answer: A.

Concept: *M402 Unit Circle*

$|sin\theta| \geq 1$

On the unit circle $sin\theta = 1$ when
$\emptyset = \dfrac{\pi}{2}(90°)$

$sin\theta = -1$ when $\emptyset = -\dfrac{\pi}{2}(270°)$

A. $\left\{ -\dfrac{\pi}{2}, \dfrac{\pi}{2} \right\}$

60. Answer: K.

Concept: *M301 Lines & Angles*

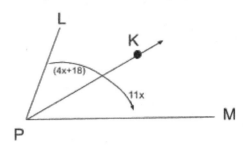

$4x + 18 = \dfrac{1}{2}(11x)$

$\div \dfrac{1}{2} \qquad \div \dfrac{1}{2}$

$8x + 36 = 11x$
$-8x \qquad -8x$
$36 = 3x$
$\div 3 = \div 3$
$12 = x$

To solve for KPM, substitute x = 12
$KPM = (4 \times 12 + 18) = 48 + 18 = 66$

K. 66

Reading 1874

1. Answer: A.

Concept: *R104 Big Picture*

Although this question is phrased as one about the narrator, it's actually asking about the main idea of the passage. Read the answer choices: **C** and **D** are clearly incorrect and can be eliminated. **B** is incorrect because it focuses on the events preceding the trial, whereas **A** more accurately emphasizes the swim itself and the many factors (not strictly events) involved.

2. Answer: G.

Concept: *R303 Chronology*

Remember, "chronologically" refers to the order of events in time, *not* in the narrative structure. In these questions, the answer will almost always be something that was recalled or reminisced about rather than a standard plot point. Although this text is in past tense, there are still distinct anecdotes within it. Which of these answers fits these guidelines? **G**, recalled in paragraphs 4-5.

3. Answer: A.

Concept: *R203 Inference/Assumption*

This question is a bit more difficult. The reason **A** is correct is that it highlights the significance of the empty room: the narrator had detailed the "energetic" meet he had hoped for, so the empty natatorium *contrasts* with that expectation. Answer choice **B** incorrectly states that the meet actually *was* energetic, but it wasn't. Answer choices **C** and **D** could be eliminated early on, because they are self-disproving (both say there is an explanation here, but neither of the events are explained by the empty room).

4. Answer: J.

Concept: *R201 Detail*

Go back to the text! Skim for the section of the passage in which he swims the 1,000-yard freestyle, and then read closely for the detail. The narrator explicitly states "Sometimes a moment comes along when the world slows down... we're afforded the opportunity to reflect in real-time." Thus, answer choice **J** is clearly correct.

5. Answer: C.

Concept: *R201 Detail*

Although multiple answer choices here resemble ideas in the text, note that the question asks specifically for something he understood "for the first time." It is this detail that makes **C** the only correct answer. The text indicates that he "understood - not later, but right then, in the water" that swimming was important to him "alone."

6. Answer: G.

Concept: *R101 Line Number; R301 Main Idea/Function: Passage*

Answers **H** and **J** are easily eliminated: there is no memory mentioned here at all and he is swimming alone. Between the remaining answers, which one makes more sense for the passage? Given the importance the narrator placed upon Junior Nationals in the first few paragraphs, it is a natural conclusion that the *end* in question is referring to his last chance to qualify, not "fitness."

7. Answer: D.

Concept: *R201 Detail*

The description of the time trial is in the first paragraph. It reads that the event was an "informal, unadvertised event thrown together at the last minute." That correlates exactly to answer choice **D**.

8. Answer: H.

Concept: *R101 Line Number; R201 Detail*

This is not a direct quotation by the boy, rather it is what the narrator attributes to the boy.

9. Answer: C.

Concept: *R203 Inference/Assumption*

When describing the indoor pool, the narrator juxtaposes the "open sky" with the "dank and moldy indoor pool" to emphasize how much less pleasant it was. The other answer choices here are not related to the descriptions given of the indoor pool.

10. Answer: F.

Concept: *R203 Inference/Assumption*

Although the text does not directly state where the exclamation comes from, the structure of the sentence strongly indicates it is from "that day" when the author jumped for the flags. Note that the question indicates he was "remembering" something.

11. Answer: D.

Concept: *R203 Inference/Assumption*

Don't overthink this question. Note that these descriptions are of the apple orchards. It only stands to reason that the descriptions are emphasizing "the magnitude of wild apples in Kazakhstan."

12. Answer: G.

Concept: *R203 Inference/Assumption*

Answer choice **F** is incorrect because it falsely attributes all domestic apples to one locale. Similarly, answer choices **H** and **J** suggest that the apples in Tian Shan are those that would be produced for consumption. In reality, the Tian Shan mountains' apples resemble those in grocery stores because they are undomesticated ancestors of the domesticated apple crop, or answer choice **G**.

13. Answer: D.

Concept: *R201 Detail*

Don't try and answer this question without double-checking the text. These answers are confusingly similar for a reason. The detail in question is explicitly stated in the passage in lines 32-36.

14. Answer: J.

Concept: *R201 Detail*

The passage states quite clearly that witnessing the starvation of Russian families "motivated [Vavilov] to become an agricultural scientist." Thus, it can be inferred that the passage is suggesting Vavilov was interested in helping to feed others (**J**).

15. Answer: A.

Concept: *R202 Vocabulary in Context*

This is a case where the incorrect answers are too *specific* in their blame. Answer choices **B** and **C** both suggest that it was scientists that did the whittling, but the passage does not say that the scientists have done so. Answer choice **D** is clearly incorrect because in 1904 the varieties were at their highest. At the end of the passage, it states that some thousands of apple varieties "have been lost from nursery catalogs, farmers' markets, *and* from the American table."

16. Answer: G.

Concept: *R202 Vocabulary in Context*

The point of this question is to find synonyms for "named and nurtured." The passage is saying that sixteen thousand varieties have been found and grown. In this context, it is clear that "identified and cultivated" are the obvious choices.

17. Answer: B.

Concept: *R203 Inference/Assumption*

Nothing in Passage B has indicated that consumers' interests stretch to crop diversity; therefore, **C** is incorrect. Answer choice **D** is a trick based on an incorrect reading of the passage and could not be reasonably inferred. It may be inferred that plant breeders are interested in plant species in Asia, but that is clearly not the "crucially important" point that could be inferred. It is more clear that experts are required whenever there is a crisis in crop diversity, making **B** the clear choice.

18. Answer: H.

Concept: *R104 Big Picture; R304 Both Passages*

The answer can be discovered using only the first passage! Only answer choice **H** correctly characterizes the first passage as "celebratory." Passage A could not be reasonably said to be "defensive," "solemn," or "accusatory." Do not be fooled by the comparison questions. If any aspect of the answer is incorrect, then the whole answer is incorrect.

19. Answer: A.

Concept: *R304 Both Passages*

This question is a little bit of a trick. It is essentially asking what the author of Passage B is *doing*? The question makes it seem like they are both doing the same things, but they are not. Vavilov is barely mentioned in Passage B and the entirety of Passage A is about him, so answer choice **B** is easily removed. Neither passage talks about apple varieties in Kazakhstan *today*, nor does either passage talk about determining which regions have the most diversity, so both **C** and **D** are wrong. Answer choice **A** is correct because the author of Passage B talks about the "reduction in the number of apple varieties in North America over the past four centuries" and the author of Passage A does not.

20. Answer: H.

Concept: *R201 Detail*

Be careful! This is not *quoted* in Passage B; it is *paraphrased*. This is a strong indicator to the correct answer. Fortunately, this paraphrase comes up at the very beginning of Passage B, so it should not take long to find.

21. Answer: C.

Concept: *R201 Detail*

Much of the passage addresses this subject, most notably in paragraph 5. He was not a gregarious, outgoing, or difficult personality. He was reserved and "easygoing," as in answer choice **C**.

22. Answer: G.

Concept: *R203 Inference/Assumption*

Don't overthink this question! Answer choice **H** and **J** should immediately sound ridiculous. The question is whether or not the solo proves Berry's little-known stature in the world of music or his musical excellence. Simple logic should suggest that the solo isn't an example of *why* Berry isn't well-known. Although **G** is the most rhetorically simple, it is correct.

23. Answer: D.

Concept: *R203 Inference/Assumption*

Consider the rhetoric behind each answer, and evaluate how well it fits with the piece. Does the author criticize jazz scholarship, or claim to be more knowledgeable than the scholars? No. But answer **D** is a natural fit for an essay introducing a little-known figure: explaining why and how they are so little-known.

24. Answer: H.

Concept: *R201 Detail*

Answer choice **F** is ridiculous and there's nothing in the passage to suggest that he ever played many solos at all (answer choice **J**). Although he did play ensemble passages, the entire point of the passage is that he didn't draw attention! Only answer choice **H** correctly states why his solos were short.

25. Answer: D.

Concept: *R201 Detail*

This is a specific answer that is found almost verbatim in the passage. It states explicitly that "swing was fodder for dance parties, not music worthy of study," as in **D**. Answer choices **A** and **B** could be reasonably inferred

based on what swing music is, but the answer must be in the passage to be correct. (**C** is absurd!)

26. Answer: F.

Concept: *R202 Vocabulary in Context*

Always refer to the vocabulary in context, as sometimes these are tricky. There are multiple valid definitions here, but only *one* that makes sense in context. There is no suggestion of "romance" with history, dangerous history, or passing judgment. Answer choice **F** is clearly correct.

27. Answer: C.

Concept: *R204 Main Idea/Function: Paragraph*

What does this comparison show? What is its purpose in the text? Look at the context: the similarity given is that both salesman and sidemen are relying on using "the best style they could manage" to market "someone else's wares." Answer choices **A** and **B** are not relevant. The comparison is made primarily to illustrate that the sidemen work to support major frontmen like Duke Ellington, not that they were hard workers.

28. Answer: J.

Concept: *R201 Detail*; R202 *Vocabulary in Context*

Quickly scan the passage for titles - they are in capital letters. It says quite clearly that "Blues in C Sharp Minor" is "odd, haunting, and ultimately relaxing," which is remarkably similar to answer choice **J**!

29. Answer: A.

Concept: *R201 Detail*

Quickly scan for the title! It states specifically what is necessary to answer the question: "the sole recording in Berry's career to feature him from start to finish."

30. Answer: F.

Concept: *E203 Inference/Assumption*

This metaphor should be somewhat obvious if the reader is aware of what a cathedral is. The passage clearly indicates that solo was "indulgent" with "flourishes, angles, [and] ornamentations." These all align with answer choice **F**.

31. Answer: D.

Concept: *R301 Main Idea/Function: Passage*

There are several true statements in the answer choices, but only one could be considered as the *main idea*. Answer choice **A** is correct, but is clearly only setting the stage for the main idea. **B** is correct, and several paragraphs were spent talking about this, but all in service of explaining what was introduced in the beginning of the passage. **C** can easily be disregarded. Check the last sentence and see that the author returned to the main idea at the end: the warp possibly being created by the Sagittarius Dwarf, which is answer choice **D**.

32. Answer: H.

Concept: *R101 Line Number*

Refer to the line number and read the context to grasp the question. It is clearly referring to the line prior, which indicates that the problem is "physical processes [that] caused the warp in the Milky Way."

33. Answer: B.

Concept: *R203 Inference/Assumption; R101 Line Number*

Refer to the lines to understand the context. Immediately after the reference given, a new paragraph begins with an introduction of the Sagittarius Dwarf. While this could technically be a bizarre transition, it can be "reasonably inferred" that this is the same galaxy.

34. Answer: J.

Concept: *R104 Big Picture*

His study was testing an existing theory, so **F** can be ruled out. Answer choice **G** is not supported by the text and **H** would suggest that Bailin's discoveries discarded previous support for the problem, but this isn't so. Answer choice **J** correctly describes that Bailin's discoveries simply provide further evidence for an ongoing theory.

35. Answer: C.

Concept: *R201 Detail*

"Angular momentum" is a good phrase to scan for. It comes up several times, but the last time it is mentioned it reads "that the two angular momenta are identical in both quantity and direction."

36. Answer: G.

Concept: *R201 Detail*

Don't be tricked by the answer choices! All of these things were mentioned in the passage, but scan for the "central bulge" and it will be apparent that it is comprised of "older stars and a black hole."

37. Answer: A.

Concept: *R103 Keyword*

Skim the text for the word "hurricane." The author calls upon the hurricane image to provide a more accurate analogy than the one used just before: "the pizza is not accurate; really it's more of a hurricane." This helps the reader to understand the flaws of the former description.

38. Answer: G.

Concept: *R201 Detail*

Be careful! These are all examples from the text, but only one is describing the phenomenon in question. The question is asking about the "disk as it is affected by its warp." Answer choice **F** is describing the dwarf galaxy as it is affected by the Milky Way. **H** is describing the shape of the Milky Way itself. **J** is tricky because it seems to be describing how the two galaxies are affecting each other; however, the question is not interested in how the two galaxies are interacting, but how the Milky Way's warp has affected its structure.

39. Answer: A.

Concept: *R201 Detail*

The passage is very explicit about this point. The Sagittarius Dwarf's orbit is described early on in the introduction of the dwarf galaxy: "it appears to be in a roughly polar orbit around the Milky Way."

40. Answer: J.

Concept: *R201 Detail*

Again, scan quickly for the first instance of the term "angular momentum," that is where the definition states "a measure of how much a system is spinning or rotating."

Remember: *the answers are in the passage!*

Science 1874

1. Answer: C.

Concept: *S202 Reading a Graph*

The question refers to Figure 1, which is the bar graph on the left, and asks for the mass of cheese remaining at 4 hours. At the 4 hour mark (x-axis), the top of the white bar reaches just between the 180 and 190 mg lines (y-axis), which makes the best answer 185 mg.

2. Answer: J.

Concept: *S207 Infer from Data*

The question asks which food would best attract the species in the experiment. According to the bar graph, there was the smallest amount of peanuts remaining. From this, we can infer that the cockroaches preferred the peanuts and that peanuts would make the best bait.

3. Answer: B.

Concept: *S204 Trends*

The question requires looking at the protein column on Table 1 and noticing that the amount of protein increases as we go down the table from cat food to peanuts. On Figure 1, at 28 hours, the amount remaining decreases as we go from cat food to peanuts. Thus, as protein increases, the amount remaining in the experiment decreases.

4. Answer: J.

Concept: *S202 Reading a Graph*

The question is asking whether the quantity of each food decreased between each interval in the experiment. On Figure 1, the bar representing each food is shorter in each subsequent time interval, implying that the cockroaches ate some of each of the 4 foods during each time interval.

5. Answer: A.

Concept: *S202 Reading a Graph*

The question is asking whether the cockroaches ate more cat food or ham during the experiment. According to Figure 1, at the end of the experiment, there was about 168 mg of cat food and about 113 mg of ham remaining, a difference of about 55 mg. Thus, the cockroaches ate approximately 55 mg more ham than cat food, which supports the student's prediction.

6. Answer: G.

Concept: *S201 Reading a Table; S302 Science Math*

The question asks which food has more than 100 mg of water in 200 mg of the food. 100 mg/200 mg = 0.5, or 50%. According to Table 1, cat food and ham have greater than 50% water.

7. Answer: C.

Concept: *S202 Reading a Graph; S101 Find in Text*

The question asks which two samples would be the same according to Student 1, who stated that two samples need to have all five properties the same in order to be the same substance. In Table 1, Samples C and D have the same values for all five properties, as do E and F (which is not an answer choice).

8. Answer: J.

Concept: *S202 Reading a Graph; S101 Find in Text*

Student 3 states that two samples are the same if they have the same mass, volume, and density. There are four couples that could be matched together (A and B, C and D, E and F, G and H). The only option that is an answer choice is J: samples G and H.

9. Answer: C.

Concept: *S201 Reading a Table; S304 Chemistry*

According to Table 1, Sample A has a melting point of 126°C and boiling point of 747°C. Below 126°C, the sample would be solid. Between 126°C and 747°C, the sample would be liquid. The correct answer states that the sample would be liquid at 250°C because its melting point is 126°C.

10. Answer: J.

Concept: *S106 Conflicting Viewpoints*

Each of the students states the belief that *multiple* properties must be the same in order for the substances to be the same. Therefore, two substances having only one property in common would not be enough to convince any of the students. Thus, none of the students would agree with the given statement.

11. Answer: A.

Concept: *S201 Reading a Table; S101 Find in Text*

According to Table 1, Samples A and B have the same mass, volume, and density, but different melting and boiling points. This fits Student 2's and Student 3's criteria for identical substances.

12. Answer: F.

Concept: *S106 Conflicting Viewpoints*

Student 2 states that two substances are the same if they have 3 or more properties in common, which fits the statement. Student 4 states if they have different melting points they can not be the same substance, which does not fit.

13. Answer: A.

Concept: *S304 Chemistry*

According to Table 1, Sample D has a boiling point of 885°C, so it will be a gas at 890°C. For this question, it is imperative to understand that gases have lower density than liquids or solids.

14. Answer: H.

Concept: *S202 Reading a Graph*

In Figure 2, Ni at 30°C created 128 mL gas. In Figure 1, the Ni line passes 120 mL at 0.30 g. Remember to check units!

15. Answer: B.

Concept: *S202 Reading a Graph; S102 Experimental Design/Parameters*

The description of Experiment 1 states that all metals were tested at the same temperature. In Experiment 2, different temperatures were used, and the XY Graph shows data points at 5 different temperatures.

16. Answer: J.

Concept: *S102 Experimental Design/Parameters; S202 Reading a Graph*

The descriptions of the experiments state that Experiment 1 is done with multiple masses but Experiment 2 is done with the same mass.

17. Answer: A.

Concept: *S301 Inquiry Process; S102 Experimental Design/Parameters*

The description of the experiments states that the atmospheric pressure was kept the same (758 mmHg) throughout the entire experiment.

18. Answer: H.

Concept: *S205 Extrapolation*

In Figure 2, the volume of gas collected increases as temperature increases, and decreases as temperature decreases. At 10°C, the Zn line is at 107 mL, so at a lower temperature, the volume would be less than 107 mL.

19. Answer: A.

Concept: *S304 Chemistry*

In the balanced equation, the coefficient of HCl is 2 and the coefficient of H_2 is 1 (no coefficient = 1), so for every 2 moles of HCl consumed there is 1 mole of H_2 produced. Thus, for every 10 moles of HCl consumed, 5 moles of H_2 are produced.

20. Answer: G.

Concept: *S207 Infer from Data; S102 Experimental Design/Parameters*

According to Table 1, at 0.25 g, the Zn line is at 95 mL. One test tube will hold 60 mL, which would leave 35 mL of gas remaining to fill part of the second test tube. Thus, two test tubes are required.

21. Answer: C.

Concept: *S202 Reading a Graph*

In Figure 2, the VS line (dashed line) is highest at 250 V.

22. Answer: H.

Concept: *S202 Reading a Graph; S305 Physics*

In Figure 3, the VL line (dashed line) completes one cycle and returns to voltage where it started after 20 msec. One cycle is represented here by starting at the maximum, going to the minimum, and returning to the maximum, or a complete wave.

23. Answer: C.

Concept: *S204 Trends*

The voltage with the least variation is represented by the line with the smallest range, which is VL (dashed line) in Figure 3.

24. Answer: H.

Concept: *S202 Reading a Graph*

In Figure 3, the VL line (dashed line) is always positive when the VC line (dotted line) is negative, and vice versa.

25. Answer: D.

Concept: *S202 Reading a Graph; S101 Find in Text*

The text states that when the current flows counterclockwise, the current is negative. In Figure 2, the current (I, solid line) is negative after 10 msec and before 20 msec, including at 15 msec.

26. Answer: J.

Concept: *S206 Correlation*

In the table, charge increases then decreases from 7 to 13 msec, with a peak at 10 msec. In Figure 2, I only decreases in this interval, but in Figure 3, VS (dashed line) increases and decreases, with a peak at 10 msec, just like charge in the table.

27. Answer: C.

Concept: *S101 Find in Text; S201 Reading a Table*

According to the first paragraph, His+ revertants are bacteria that regain the ability to synthesize histidine, and therefore survive on the dish. The greatest number of His+ revertants would be on the dish with the most colonies, which is Dish 4. According to Table 1, Dish 4 is Substance N.

28. Answer: F.

Concept: *S101 Find in Text; S201 Reading a Table*

According to the third paragraph, Dishes 2-5 were treated with suspected mutagens, but Dish 1 was not.

29. Answer: B.

Concept: *S101 Find in Text; S201 Reading a Table*

The second paragraph states that the number of His+ revertants shows how mutagenic the substance is. The number of colonies growing on each substance, from least to most, is Dish 5 (P), Dish 2 (L), Dish 3 (M), and Dish 4 (N).

30. Answer: F.

Concept: *S102 Experimental Design/Parameters*

The table shows concentration increasing from 10 to 50, and 50 to 100, as the number of colonies also increases. Therefore, as the concentration of Substance P increases, the potential to cause mutations also increases.

31. Answer: D.

Concept: *S102 Experimental Design/Parameters*

The control dish is the dish that didn't contain any treatment (suspected mutagen). All of the dishes contained no histidine to test whether bacteria mutated the ability to make their own histidine. All dishes had nutrient agar. Thus, the control dish had no mutagen or histidine.

32. Answer: F.

Concept: *S201 Reading a Table*

According to Table 1, Dish 2 had substance L and Dish 3 had substance M. On table 2, Dish 3 has 25 colonies, which is about 2 times the number of colonies on Dish 2 (14).

33. Answer: D.

Concept: *S104 Inference*

The passage states that the scientists were testing substances to see whether they caused genetic mutations in bacteria. From this information, we can infer that the scientists didn't want to use bacteria that would repair the genetic mutations.

34. Answer: G.

Concept: *S306 Earth/Space Science*

It is necessary to know what "porous" and "permeable" mean to answer this question. "Porous" means containing holes and "permeable" means allowing substances to pass into it. If researchers want all the water to flow from the box rather than into the box's walls, the box would have to be made of a material that is nonporous and impermeable.

35. Answer: A.

Concept: *S306 Earth/Space Science*

The freezing point of water is 0°C, so -1°C would be below the freezing point, and the water would not have melted. Therefore, the runoff would have been "near or at zero."

36. Answer: J.

Concept: *S202 Reading a Graph*

In Figure 1, the 2.5 line (diamonds) and the 1.0 line (circles) reach 0 at 400 min and 450 min, respectively. Therefore, the wind speeds of 2.5 and 1.0 decrease to zero before 500 min.

37. Answer: D.

Concept: *S202 Reading a Graph*

In Figure 2, the greater maximum value was achieved by the layer without sand (white circles). The layer without sand also decreased to zero first.

38. Answer: J.

Concept: *S208 Conversion*

At 200 min on Figure 1, the 2.5 line (diamonds) is the lowest, the 0 line is next

(squares), and the 0.5 and 1.0 lines (star and circle) are at the same highest point.

39. Answer: B.

Concept: *S102 Experimental Design/Parameters*

In Study 1, the 4 trials differed by wind speed, which is described both in Table 1 and the text. In Study 1, the wind speed was the same, but the presence of sand changed.

40. Answer: G.

Concept: *S203 Reading a Figure*

According to the description of the experiment, the box was filled with 30 cm of sand, which corresponds to the height dimension. The width of the sand layer would be the width of the box, 60 cm, and the length would correspond to the length of the box, 120 cm. Since the volume of a rectangular solid is length x width x height, the volume of sand would be calculated as 30 cm x 60 cm x 120 cm.

ACT 1572 (2015)

English

1. Answer: A.

Content: *E102 Commas*

Tip: *find the independent clause!*

The only necessary comma in the underlined portion is the one already there, which serves to separate the leading independent clause from the dependent clause that follows it.

2. Answer: J.

Content: *E205 Transition Words/Phrases*

Regardless of where they are placed in a sentence, transition words are used to indicate the flow of information from sentence to sentence. The previous sentence states that snowflakes are normally six-sided. The correct transition word will indicate that a triangular snowflake is contrary to the previous information. "Similarly," "for example," and "additionally" both indicate that the next sentence is introducing similar information, which it is not. Answer choice **D**, "however" clearly indicates that new and differing information is being introduced.

Note*: a studious test-taker will notice that "similarly," "for example," and "additionally" are all the same. The outlier ("however") is the obvious answer.*

3. Answer: D.

Concept: *E101 Verbs: Agreement/Tense*

The verb "suggests" needs an object in this case. Notice, as it stands now, that the subject ("shape of those snowflakes") has not *done* anything yet. Answer choices **A**, **B**, and **C** would not finish the sentence. Answer choice **D** provides an object for the verb "suggests" as well as a subject for the verb "to form."

4. Answer: H.

Concept:*E206 Modification: Dangling Modifiers*

The opening clause is a modifier for the subject "the scientists," and the subject should be immediately following the comma. The only answer choice that begins with the scientists is **H**.

5. Answer: B.

Concept: *E103 Independent Clauses: Period, Semicolon, Comma and FANBOYS; E102 Commas*

Separating Independent Clauses
1. Period
2. Semicolon
3. Comma FANBOYS

As the sentence stands, there is a run-on sentence: two independent clauses without any punctuation. Answer choices **C** and **D** both create a second independent clause after the comma without using a period, semicolon or a conjunction (FANBOYS). That is a comma splice and is *always incorrect*. Answer choice **B** turns the second independent clause into a dependent clause by removing the subject and placing a participle. The dependent clause can be appended to the independent clause with only a comma, so answer choice **B** is correct.

6. Answer: J.

Concept: *E101 Verbs: Agreement/Tense*

There must be a plural verb to match the plural "molecules," as well as a present-tense verb to match the rest of the passage. Answer choice **J** provides a plural, present-tense form of "bump."

7. Answer: B.

Concept: *E201 Relevancy: Adding, Deleting, and Replacing Information*

Answer choices **C** and **D** are not relevant to the underlined portion: there is no visual description or explanation of a reaction. **A** is incorrect because the underlined portion is not actually an explanation, but merely the mention of a step. Answer choice **B** correctly states that it is a "detail" and a "step."

8. Answer: J.

Concept: *E101 Verbs: Agreement/Tense*

The subject for the underlined verb is "snowflakes," so the verb must agree in tense and number ("form"). There is no need for the wordiness in answer choice **G**, so **J** is correct.

9. Answer: C.

Concept: *E107 Colons and Dashes*

As the sentence stands, it should be clear that "dust" needs to be disconnected from the initial independent clause. "Dust" is a further explanation of the "one significant addition to the process." Answer choice **A** is a run on sentence. Answer choice **D** is incorrect because semicolons only separate two complete sentences. Answer choice **B** incorrectly assumes that "the process" is a

new subject, but it is not. Only answer choice **C** correctly utilizes a colon to introduce a further explanation of information that was given in the initial independent clause.

10. Answer: J.

Concept: *E103 Independent Clauses: Period, Semicolon, Comma and FANBOYS*

This one appears tricky because the answer choice will actually create a subject doing the action of the sentence. As it stands in answer choice **F**, the sentence has no subject. Answer choices **G** and **H** have no independent clause anywhere. The subject is "The greater pressure from the wind" which "causes bonds to form." That makes answer choice **J** correct.

11. Answer: B.

Concept: *E108 Adjectives and Adverbs*

Tip*: adverbs usually end in -ly.*

The word "than" indicates that there is a comparison happening. Answer choices **C** and **D** are superlatives which would require nothing to compare to. "Quick" is an adverb describing how the "forming" is happening. It "forms quickly," not "quick."

12. Answer: G.

Concept: *E104 Nonessential Information: Commas, Dashes, Parentheses*

Only a comma is necessary. The "although" at the start creates a dependent clause, ruling out all options other than the comma, which correctly conjoins the dependent to the independent clause.

13. Answer: A.

Concept: *E201 Relevancy: Adding, Deleting, and Replacing Information*

Note that the question asks for the most effective way to "conclude the sentence *and the essay.*" Answer choice **B** is too broad, speaking about all of science in relation to the snowflakes. Atmospheric conditions were not in question in the passage so answer choice **C** is not correct. Answer choice **D** focuses too specifically on the shapes of snowflakes, which does not end the essay well. **A** maintains the greater focus of the essay and concludes it effectively.

14. Answer: H.

Concept: *E208 Moving Sentences*

"This growth" is the subject of the sentence, meaning that the growth has already been indicated in the previous sentence. Answer choice **H** is preceded by a sentence which states that "the flake grows."

15. Answer: D.

Concept: *E210 Writer's Goal*

Notice that what is important here is not the yes/no answer, but the *reasoning*. The only answer with supporting evidence that is both *relevant* to the text and *true* is answer choice **D**.

16. Answer: H.

Concept: *E104 Nonessential Information: Commas, Dashes, Parentheses*

The first clause is a dependent introductory clause, it does not need the conjunction "and" with the comma. Therefore, **F** is incorrect. Answer choice **G** would extend the dependent clause and never create a complete sentence. Answer choice **J** does the same thing. Answer

choice **H** correctly uses a comma to offset an introductory dependent clause with nothing else.

17. Answer: B.

Concept: *E101 Verbs: Agreement/Tense*

It's necessary to have the appropriate form of the verb "need" in this sentence. "Will need" is improperly future tense. "Would have needed" implies that they did not in fact need them. "Need" is present tense and does not fit with the telling of a story that has already happened. The past tense and appropriate option is "would need," which shows that although the story is taking place in the past tense, the travelers would need something in the near future.

18. Answer: J.

Concept: *E204 Short and Simple*

This is a classic example of a short and simple. Answer choice **F** is extremely redundant. Answer choices **G** and **H** are also redundant to a lesser degree. Answer choice **J** ends the sentence without repeating any information.

19. Answer: C.

Concept: *E101 Verbs: Agreement/Tense*

The past tense of the story immediately eliminates options **B** and **D** for their present-tense verbs. The difference between **A** and **C** is the preposition. "With" is appropriate, because "on" would imply the roof was literally atop the fallen rocks.

20. Answer: H.

Concept: *E102 Commas*

Answer choice **F** is incorrect for a variety of reasons, but is easily recognized as a run-on sentence. Answer choice **G** is quickly ruled out because it creates a new independent clause without a conjunction. While **J** is dependent, it does not have a comma. Only answer choice **H** provides a dependent clause properly punctuated with a comma.

21. Answer: A.

Concept: *E202 Word Choice: Correct Word*

"The route," as it is being used in this sentence, is akin to "the trek," or the entire hike, not a physical trail. Answer choice **B** is improper because "most" is comparative and "part" is not in this case. Answer choice **C** lacks the proper article "the" to make it correct, because "majority" needs to be specified as "the majority" as there is only one possible majority. Answer choice **D** is incorrect because "more" is directly comparative, but there is no other option to which it is compared. Simply, the hikers were spread out "for most of the route."

22. Answer: F.

Concept: *E101 Verbs: Agreement/Tense*

Don't be thrown off by the clause between the hyphens. It does not impact the rest of the sentence. Because there is a comma and no conjunction, the second clause must be dependent. Only "forming," which does not add a pronoun to create a new subject, is correct.

23. Answer: B.

Concept: *E202 Word Choice: Correct Word*

The keyword of this question is "slowness." Answer choices **A**, **C**, and **D** do not emphasize slowness in any way. Only answer choice **B** shows how slowly they went.

24. Answer: H.

Concept: *E102 Commas*

The sentence is a simple dependent clause introducing an independent clause. As always in these situations, a simple comma is the best way to punctuate. The other options provided all require beginning with an independent clause, regardless of what follows.

25. Answer: C.

Concept: *E106 Apostrophes: Possessive, Plural, Contractions*

"The cliffs" are not possessing anything; they are simply "*at* the crater's edge." Therefore, they do not require an apostrophe. However, the cliffs are a part of the edge of the crater. This means that the crater does receive an apostrophe to indicate its possession of the cliffs. Therefore, **C** is correct.

26. Answer: F.

Concept: *E201 Relevancy: Adding, Deleting, and Replacing Information*

A number of these answers can be eliminated right away. Answer choice **G** is incorrect because the idea of waiting was *already* introduced. Eliminate answer choice **H** because, necessary or not, it does not contradict anything. Eliminate **J** because it is not an image at all. **F** is correct because it is a restatement of waiting or "anticipation" as mentioned in the sentence prior.

27. Answer: D.

Concept: *E205 Transition Words/Phrases*

The word which is most appropriate here is "finally," because the author has just described that the group was waiting. The other options do not appropriately connect the idea of waiting with the sudden appearance of sunlight.

28. Answer: G.

Concept: *E202 Word Choice: Correct Word*

If "ruggedness" is being emphasized, it is necessary to find words that are most similar to the definition of "rugged." "Smothered" and "squelched" would not be included in any list of synonyms with "rugged." "Went over" does not dramatically emphasize anything at all, so it is also incorrect. Only answer choice **G**, "shattered over," matches.

29. Answer: A.

Concept: *E209 Moving Paragraphs*

Answer choice **A** mentions "the other hikers" just as the proposed addition does. It also fits into the chronology of the narrative, as they use flashlights once it is dark.

30. Answer: F.

Concept: *E210 Writer's Goal*

This question is just as easy to answer using elimination as it is finding the correct answer. Answer choices **G**, **H**, and **J** are incorrect because the passage does not *focus* on their tools, the rewarding nature, or the beauty—it just mentions them. They are all part of the story which, overall, describes the challenges involved in their journey.

31. Answer: B.

Concept: *E102 Commas*

Remember: *commas separate clauses! They are not for pauses!*

The underlined portion does not separate clauses, list articles, or anything else. The modifier "named Juan Quezada" can

immediately follow the modified "boy" and similarly lead directly into the predicate.

32. Answer: H.

Concept: *E104 Nonessential Information: Commas, Dashes, Parentheses*

Remember*: parentheses, two dashes, and two commas do the same thing - they offset nonessential information.*

In this case, there are three answer choices which are functionally identical. In this case, the extra comma after "pots"in answer choice **H** makes it incorrect because it is redundant.

33. Answer: B.

Concept: *E103 Independent Clauses: Period, Semicolon, Comma and FANBOYS*

This question is a trick. Just because "Quezada wondered" doesn't mean that a question mark would be grammatically correct. This is because the sentence is not actually a question, the sentence is a statement about Quezada wondering. The comma in answer choice **C** is also incorrect because nothing is being separated.

34. Answer: H.

Concept: *E205 Transition Words/Phrases*

To form a good transition, the sentence will include an idea from the last paragraph and the upcoming paragraph. Answer choice **H** is the only answer that combines Quezada's desire to emulate the pots with his experimenting with the clay.

35. Answer: A.

Concept: *E101 Verbs: Agreement/Tense*

Answer choices **B** and **C** imply Quezada was selling a dedication to teaching and a teacher, which he was not. Answer choices **A** and **D** correctly introduce a new verb ("taught"), but "has taught" is incorrectly present-tense. Thus, answer choice **A** is correctly past-tense.

36. Answer: F.

Concept: *E201 Relevancy: Adding, Deleting, and Replacing Information*

There is no reason to infer from the passage that Quezada wasn't a good potter. Answer choices **G** and **J** are pejorative, criticizing Quezada's work. The passage states that he "thought they were prehistoric," suggesting that he was tricked into thinking they were not contemporary. Thus, answer choices **F** and **H** are the likely choices. The entire passage is about Quezada being inspired by the Paquime tradition, so it would make sense that the correct answer reinforces that fact.

37. Answer: A.

Concept: *E101 Verbs: Agreement/Tense; E105 Pronouns: Agreement/Case*

Remember: *"led" is the past-tense of "to lead."*

The verb in this sentence must match the subject, "his search." "Himself" is a reflexive pronoun, which means the subject was both "doing" the action and receiving it. As "his search" did the acting, it cannot receive a reflexive pronoun. "Led him" is past-tense and agrees with the subject and the antecedent.

38. Answer: F.

Concept: *E202 Word Choice: Correct Word*

The only option which implies delay is "eventual." The others have different meanings, none of which respond to the question accurately.

39. Answer: C.

Concept: *E105 Pronouns: Agreement/Case*

Although omission is often correct, here it is not as it would create a new independent clause. The fact that answer choice **C** is much shorter and simpler is a good hint that it's a better option. "Where" is also necessary to create a dependent clause, as there is no conjunction.

40. Answer: J.

Concept: *E204: Short and Simple.*

The shortest answer is often correct. Answer choice **A** incorrectly uses the conjunction "so." Answer choice **G** incorrectly uses "then" instead of "than." The strange pronoun "them" in option **H** is incorrectly applied to "the money he earned." Answer choice **J** correctly indicates that Quezada wanted to "do more [to help his village]."

41. Answer: C.

Concept: *E201 Relevancy: Adding, Deleting, and Replacing Information*

The problem here is that any answer other than answer choice **C** is structurally *too vague*. Answer choice **A** has the problem of using a preposition which requires an object ("around"). Answer choice **B** indicates that there are only four hundred people making art now *anywhere*. Answer choice **D** would create a dependent clause followed by two more dependent clauses.

42. Answer: G.

Concept: *E105 Pronouns: Agreement/Case*

"Which" is not used for people. "Them" would create an independent clause, which is incorrect as there is no conjunction. "Who" does not follow the preposition "of." The correct pronoun here is "whom" as it is the object of the clause.

Tip: *the preposition "of" means "who" cannot be used - it must be "whom."*

43. Answer: D.

Concept: *E105 Pronouns: Agreement/Case*

"They're" is a contraction of "they are" and clearly incorrect. Answer choice **B** incorrectly uses a reflexive pronoun, when the people described are acting upon a separate entity. The word "each" means "her" is correct, not "hers," because it refers to multiple singular people instead of a group. Thus, answer choice **D**, "his or her," is the correct way to use possessive pronouns in this sentence.

44. Answer: J.

Concept: *E208 Moving Sentences*

The reference to "each artist" should point us in the direction of a sentence discussing the artists. The only option that does this is answer choice **J**.

45. Answer: C.

Concept: *E210 Writer's Goal*

This piece is not one of historical information, but a biographical story of *one* artist in particular, which eliminates both "yes" answers (**A** and **B**). Since the essay does not focus on the Casas Grandes culture (**D**), the correct answer is **C** by default, but it does

accurately state that this essay is about one artist.

46. Answer: J.

Concept: *E106 Apostrophes: Possessive, Plural, Contractions*

Its = possessive

Don't be tricked by a possessive apostrophe! The noun "it" is replacing is the Lyceum Theatre. Therefore, "they're" and "their" are incorrect by default because they are pronouns for people. "It's" is a contraction, not a possessive. The possessive form of the pronoun "it" is "its." Therefore, answer choice **J** is correct.

47. Answer: D.

Concept: *E102 Commas*

> # Big 3 Comma Rules
> 1. No commas between subject and verb
> 2. No commas before or after prepositions
> 3. No commas between describing words and the things they describe

No comma is necessary here. The group of nouns acting as the subject of this sentence is "Tourists and New Yorkers alike." They are performing the action of the sentence. They "regularly fill" the theater. There is no comma necessary between the subject and the verb being performed. Thus, answer choice **D** is correct.

48. Answer: H.

Concept: *E205 Transition Words/Phrases*

The information being presented after the transition word is contrasting the information before it. Therefore, "however" is the correct word. The others do not imply this contrast, but rather causation or reinforcement.

49. Answer: B.

Concept: *E206 Modification: Moving Modifiers*

Another pronoun agreement question!
Answer choices **A** and **D** immediately create a
new independent clause without resolving
the first sentence created with "a few" as the
subject. Answer choice **C** would mean that the
subject is the object of some action, which it is
not. Rather, the "few" are "there to admire"
the buildings (**B**).

50. Answer: F.

Concept: *E103 Independent Clauses: Period,
Semicolon, Comma and FANBOYS*

Separating Independent Clauses
1. Period 2. Semicolon 3. Comma FANBOYS

On the ACT a semicolon is functionally the
same as a period. If a semicolon is ever an
option, substitute a period and see if it is
correct. Here are two independent clauses,
separated correctly by a semicolon.

51. Answer: D.

Concept: *E201 Relevancy: Adding, Deleting,
and Replacing Information*

Answer choices **A** and **C** are easily eliminated
because they have such weak reasoning, but **B**
is a tempting choice. The evidence is true,
because it does provide this context; however,
this answer is incorrect because this detail is
not relevant to the focus of the essay, as
option **D** points out. By reading through all
the answers, it should be apparent by answer
choice **D**.

52. Answer: J.

Concept: *E201 Relevancy: Adding, Deleting,
and Replacing Information*

Remember: *check for redundancies!*

This question is actually testing redundancy.
In the immediately preceding sentence it
states that the structure is made of "gray
limestone." Any mention of those words
would be a redundancy because it is only
descriptive information and does not need to
be repeated. Therefore, the correct answer is
J.

53. Answer: A.

Concept: *E104 Nonessential Information:
Commas, Dashes, Parentheses*

This is an explanatory dependent clause at
the end of the sentence. This could be
punctuated with either a comma, a colon, or a
hyphen. In this case, the only grammatically
correct option is **A**: a comma.

54. Answer: F.

Concept: *E101 Verbs: Agreement/Tense; E108
Adjectives and Adverbs*

First, *find the sentence*. There is only one
option that would create a cohesive sentence
with a subject performing a verb in the
correct tense. "Elegant chandeliers illuminate
rose-colored walls." Now it is clear that
elegant is an adjective describing the
chandeliers that are illuminating the walls.

55. Answer: B.

Concept: *E203 Word Choice: Tone*

This is the rare case where the longest answer is the best! This is because it directly answers the question's request for a "positive" and "elaborate" phrase. Answer choices **A** and **D** are not positive in any way. Answer choice **C** is negative, using words "marred" and "gaudy." Answer choice **B** is both positive and elaborate.

56. Answer: G.

Concept: *E201 Relevancy: Adding, Deleting, and Replacing Information*

Answer choice **F** is simply false; **H** misidentifies the essay's claim, and **J** incorrectly assumes the purpose of the sentence. Answer choice **G** correctly states that the information is a contribution to the rest of the passage.

57. Answer: C.

Concept: *E209 Moving Paragraphs*

The first sentence of the paragraph is describing the windows between the columns. Even if it were not clear that these are exterior elements, the following sentence (answer choice **A**) explicitly says "exterior." The next sentence continues to talk about the exterior balcony, so answer choice **B** would still be inappropriate. Answer choice **C** is followed with "ornate interior," which indicates a change from the exterior to the interior. Therefore, **C** is correct.

58. Answer: F.

Concept: *E205 Transition Words/Phrases*

Transitions words aren't placed for no reason! This paragraph begins a new topic

("patrons"), so none of these transitions are appropriate.

59. Answer: D.

Concept: *E204 Short and Simple*

Except for answer choice **D**, each of these answer choices are redundant.

60. Answer: G.

Concept: *E210 Writer's Goal*

Answer choices **F** and **J** incorrectly claim the passage focuses on a number of buildings and styles, despite the clear focus on the Lyceum Theatre. Answer choice **H** is easily ruled out as it doesn't focus on the sets.

61. Answer: C.

Concept: *E202 Word Choice: Correct Word; E108 Adjectives and Adverbs*

The preposition "with" signals that a noun is necessary. "Inaccuracies" is the noun while "inaccurate" is the adjective form. As such it must be modified by the adjective form "factual", not the adverb "factually." Thus, the correct form will read "riddled with factual inaccuracies" (**C**).

62. Answer: G.

Concept: *E107 Colons and Dashes*

Although it is unlikely that an explanation after a colon will be an independent clause, it does happen. Also, by process of elimination, notice that answer choices **F**, **H**, and **J** are grammatically incorrect. The colon is appropriate here because it introduces an explanation or extrapolation of the information in the independent clause prior to the colon.

63. Answer: D.

Concept: *E101 Verbs: Agreement/Tense*

Remember to remove the nonessential information between the hyphens to discover the sentence. "These untruths" require a verb that agrees in number and tense. "Matter" is the correct plural, present-tense option, so answer choice **D** is correct.

64. Answer: F.

Concept: *E103 Independent Clauses: Period, Semicolon, Comma and FANBOYS*

> **Separating Independent Clauses**
>
> 1. Period
> 2. Semicolon
> 3. Comma FANBOYS

"For" is a conjunction which, with a comma, combines two independent clauses. This is correct as is. Do not be tempted to pick the period or semicolon - the conjunction "for" makes the clause dependent! Also note that if two options use a period and semicolon in the same way, *they must both be wrong* because they are functionally the same on the ACT and there can't be two right answers.

65. Answer: C.

Concept: *E205 Transition Words/Phrases*

The words "rather" and "instead" should indicate good transition words. Between answer choices **C** and **D**, only one leads into the thesis of the essay as a whole. Consider reading ahead and coming back to this to determine just what that topic is.

66. Answer: H.

Concept: *E106 Apostrophes: Possessive, Plural, Contractions*

Jones was "an advocate *of* the movement," which means that "movement" requires a possessive apostrophe. It also says that Jones was "one" of many advocates, so advocate is plural and not possessive.

67. Answer: D.

Concept: *E102 Commas*

Note: *reflexive pronouns are often used for emphasis and do not require comma separation.*

There is no need for a comma here, as "she herself" is not a clause, but only the subject of this sentence.

68. Answer: G.

Concept: *E201 Relevancy: Adding, Deleting, and Replacing Information*

Remember, the only important part of the answer is the *evidence*. In this case, the incorrect answers disregard the importance of this information in creating character, while **G** supports why the detail is important.

69. Answer: D.

Concept: *E103 Independent Clauses: Period, Semicolon, Comma and FANBOYS*

> **Separating Independent Clauses**
>
> 1. Period
> 2. Semicolon
> 3. Comma FANBOYS

Don't know how to use a semicolon? Use a period! Both separate independent clauses, and are functionally the same on this test. In this case, a semicolon is correct.

70. Answer: J.

Concept: *E201 Relevancy: Adding, Deleting, and Replacing Information*

The first word or phrase of each answer will indicate how correct the answer is. The answer will either "question," "reinforce," "reiterate," or "provide support." Answer choice **F** should strike the reader as unfounded. Answer choices **G** and **H** align with the verb "travel" in the sentence, but are not supported by the text. The only answer which is relevant to the text is **J**. It is important to read the passage well, and if necessary go back into the text. Without the context, questions like this are very difficult.

71. Answer: A.

Concept: *E201 Relevancy: Adding, Deleting, and Replacing Information*

It's important to read the answers carefully, because some are designed to trick the reader. Obviously the comparison is not unrelated, nor is it repeated, so answer choices **C** and **D** are incorrect. Answer choice **B** suggests that she cared most about "relatives" which is not backed up by the passage. Answer choice **A** is the best answer because the metaphor is central to the text.

72. Answer: F.

Concept: *E107 Colons and Dashes*

The clause after the colon is an example or explanation, so it is used appropriately. Answer choice **D** would require something after the preposition "by." Answer choices **B** and **C** are lengthy and unnecessary.

73. Answer: B.

Concept: *E205 Transition Words/Phrases*

The only transition word here which implies causation, as the text would imply, is "because." The others would imply she was contrary to the workers or a similarly incorrect relationship.

74. Answer: H.

Concept: *E106 Apostrophes: Possessive, Plural, Contractions*

"Their" is the form which refers to possession by a plural. "Behalf" does not need to be transformed in any way, and the strange apostrophe in **J** should be reason enough to ignore it.

75. Answer: D.

Concept: *E210 Writer's Goal*

Keep in mind that many of the "writer's goal" answers are incorrect because the *scope* is too broad or too specific. This passage is specific to Mother Jones and so would be inappropriate for the summary of all women's contributions to labor movements. Therefore, answer choice **D** is correct.

Math 1572

1. Answer: D.

Concept: *M503 Probability*

Add the number of two types and divide by total participants.

$67 + 6 = 73$

D. $\dfrac{73}{150}$

2. Answer: H.

Concept: *M501 Mean, Average*

$$\dfrac{370 + 310 + 380 + 340 + 310}{5} = 342$$

H. 342

3. Answer: E.

Concept: *M109 Rate & Proportion*

Set up a proportion.

$\dfrac{1}{2} in = 18\ miles$

Cross multiply:

$\dfrac{.5}{18} = \dfrac{2.5}{x}$

Solve for x.

$.5x = 45$
$\div 0.5 \quad \div 0.5$

$x = 90$

E. 90

4. Answer: F.

Concept: *M202 Solving Equations*

$450 = c(10)^3$

$450 = 1000c$
$\div 1000 \quad \div 1000$

$c = 0.45$

F. 0.45

5. Answer: E.

Concept: *M214 Functions f(x)*

$f(x) = (3x + 7)^2$

$f(1) = (3 \times 1 + 7)^2$

$f(1) = 10^2$

$f(1) = 100$

E. 100

6. Answer: H.

Concept: *M110 Percent*

6% increase

$(12)(1.06) = 12.72$

H. $12.72

7. Answer: E.

Concept: *M106 Sequence*

1, -3, 9, -27, ___ ___ ___

Geometric means *multiply* by a common ratio (r). In this problem r = -3.

Multiply by -3.

$(-27)(-3) = 81$ 5th

$(8)(-3) = -243$ 6th

$(-243)(-3) = 729$ 7th term

E. 729

> Tip: *You should be familiar with the first twelve squares and first 5 cubes.*
> *Squares: 1, 4, 9, 16, 25, 36, 49, 64, 81, 100, 121, 144*
> *Cubes: 1, 8, 27, 64, 125*

8. Answer: H.

Concept: *M109 Rate & Proportion*

1 box = 15 lbs

Fee + Price per pound

$\$10 + (.65)(15) = \$19.75$

H. $19.75

9. Answer: A.

Concept: *M307 Solids*

First, subtract the top and bottom layers (.03) from the total thickness. Then, divide by inner thickness to get the number of layers.

$$\frac{.32 - 2(.03)}{.02} = 13$$

A. 13

10. Answer: K.

Concept: *M502 Median, Mode*

To find the median, they must be *in order*, smallest to largest.

$13, 15, 16, 19, 19, 22, \ 25, \ 25, \ 26, \ 27, \ 28, \ 29$

Since there is an even number of elements, the middle numbers (22 and 25) must be averaged.

$$\frac{22 + 25}{2} = 23.5$$

K. 23.5

11. Answer: C.

Concept: *M207 Linear Functions: y=mx+b*

1. Plug in $t = 0$, $d = 14$
   A. $14 = (\ 0\ ) + 14$
   C. $14 = (6)*(0) + 14$
   Eliminate B, D, E

2. Plug in $t = 1$, $d = 20$
   A. $20 = 1 + 14$ NO
   C. $20 = 6 + 14$ YES

C. $d = 6t + 14$

12. Answer: K.

Concept: *M303 Quadrilaterals*

$l \times w = 54$

$\underset{\div 9}{9} \times \underset{\div 9}{w} = 54$

$w = 6$

$2(9) + 2(6) = 30$

K. 30

13. Answer: B.

Concept: *M301 Lines & Angles; M302 Triangles*

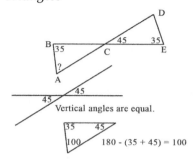

B. 100°

14. Answer: H.

Concept: *M306 Sectors & Arcs; M505 Charts & Graphs*

$$\frac{4\ core}{9\ total} = \frac{\varnothing(angle)}{360°}$$

Solve for θ by cross-multiplying:

$$\varnothing = \frac{4(360)}{90}$$
$$\theta = 160°$$

H. 160°

Tip: *The ACT loves this problem: the angle of a sector of a pie chart. Know it!*

15. Answer: B.

Concept: *M211 System Word Problems*

$S + L = 70$

$\$12L = \$8S$

Solve for small figurines:

$S = 70 - L$

Substitute the equation of S into the equation for L.

$12L = 8(70 - L)$

$12L = 560 - 8L$
$+\ 8L \qquad\qquad +\ 8L$

$20L = 560$
$\div\ 20 \qquad \div\ 20$

$L = 28$

B. 28

16. Answer: H.

Concept: *M207 Linear Functions: y = mx + b*

$$\frac{220 - 88}{3} = 44$$

H. 44

17. Answer: D.

Concept: *M301 Lines & Angles*

Draw a picture!

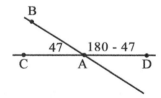

$<BAD = 133$

D. 133°

18. Answer: F.

Concept: *M104 Fractions; use your calculator*

$$\frac{1}{2} \quad \frac{5}{6} \quad \frac{5}{8}$$

LCD = 24

$$\frac{12}{24} \quad \frac{20}{24} \quad \frac{15}{24}$$

"Ascending" means smallest to largest.

$$\frac{12}{24} < \frac{15}{24} < \frac{20}{24}$$

F. $\quad \dfrac{1}{2} < \dfrac{5}{8} < \dfrac{5}{6}$

19. Answer: D.

Concept: *M205 Exponents & Roots*

$$670,000,000$$
$$6.7 \times 10^8$$

$$700,000,000$$
$$7.0 \times 10^8$$

Add 13.7×10^8

Moving the decimal point over by one will increase the exponent by one.

D. 1.37×10^9

20. Answer: F.

Concept: *M303 Quadrilaterals; 302 Lines & Angles*

Notice if you extend the lines of a trapezoid, it is two parallel lines cut by a transversal!

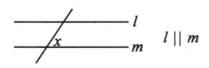

$l \parallel m$

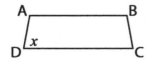

F. $(180 - x)$

21. Answer: B.

Concept: *M110 Percent*

$$(1,000)\left(\frac{80}{100}\right)\left(\frac{60}{100}\right)$$
$$(1,000)(.8)(.6) = 480$$

B. 480

22. Answer: H.

Concept: *M205 Exponents & Roots*

$$a^b = x \quad c^b = y$$

$$x \times y = \;?$$

Substitute:

$$a^b \times c^b = (ac)^b$$

H. $(ac)^b$

23. Answer: A.

Concept: *M201 Algebraic Operations*

$$\frac{1}{2}y^2(6x + 2y + 12x - 2y)$$

Combine like terms:

$$\frac{1}{2}y^2(18x) = 9xy^2$$

Multiply.

A. $9xy^2$

24. Answer: H.

Concept: *M217 Factoring & FOIL*

$$500p - p^2 = 60,000$$
$$_{+p^2} _{+p^2}$$
$$500p = p^2 + 60,000$$
$$_{-500p} _{-500p}$$
$$0 = p^2 - 500p + 60,000$$

$$0 = (p - 200)(p - 300)$$

H. 200

Tip: *When there is a factoring problem, let the answers give you a clue.*

---

25. Answer: B.

Concept: *M505 Charts & Graphs*

$$\frac{254}{900} = 0.282$$

B. 28%

26. Answer: G.

Concept: *M301 Lines & Angles*

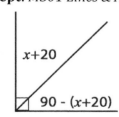

$$90 - (x + 20)$$

$$90 - x - 20$$

$$70 - x$$

G. $(70 - x)°$

27. Answer: E.

Concept: *M302 Triangles*

E. $16 + 8\sqrt{2}$

28. Answer: H.

Concept: *M216 Quadratics & Parabolas*

Solution is where *y*=0 or *x* intercept.

H. 1 positive, 1 negative real solutions

Tip: *"Real solution" means the parabola crosses the x-axis. If the solution is not real it is imaginary.*

---

29. Answer: C.

Concept: *M219 Complex Numbers*

$(-3i + 4)(3i + 4)$ - FOIL!

$$-3i \times 3i - 4 \times 3i + 4 \times 3i + 16$$

$$-9i^2 + 16; \; [where \; i^2 = -1]$$

$$-9(-1) + 16 = 25$$

C. 25

30. Answer: G.

Concept: *M401 SOHCAHTOA*

$$S\frac{O}{H} \quad C\frac{A}{H} \quad T\frac{O}{A}$$

G. $\tan \dfrac{7}{5}$

31. Answer: D.

Concept: *M503 Probability*

$750 + 5 \ extra = 755$

$$\frac{5 \ extra}{755 \ total} = \frac{5}{755}$$

D. $\dfrac{5}{755}$

32. Answer: K.

Concept: *M104 Fractions*

Halfway is simply the average.

$$\left(\frac{2}{3} + \frac{3}{4}\right) \div 2$$

Find LCD:

$$\left(\frac{8}{12} + \frac{9}{12}\right) \div 2$$

$$\frac{17}{12} \div 2$$

$$\frac{17}{24}$$

K. $\dfrac{17}{24}$

Note: *questions 33 – 35 are three of the most missed questions!*

33. Answer: B.

Concept: *M109 Rate & Proportion*

.25 inch = 2 ft

Cross-multiply:

$$\frac{x}{0.25} = \frac{15}{2}$$

$2x = 3.75$
$\div 2 \quad \div 2$
$x = 1.875$

B. 1.875

34. Answer: H.

Concept: *M308 Multiple Figures*

Not covered = whole − cabinet

Whole = 12 × 15 = 180

Cabinets:

4		2
16	4	24	12

$180 - (16 + 24) = 140$

H. 140

35. Answer: D.

Concept: *M207 Linear Functions: y = mx + b*

$2,150 = 650 + (10)(x)$

There are 10 cabinets.

Price per cabinet = $\dfrac{2150 - 650}{10} = 150$

Twice as many: $10 * 2 = 20$

$650 + 20 * 150 = 3650$

D. 3650

36. Answer: J.

Concept: *M210 Systems of Equations; 203 Inequalities*

$1 < x + y < 2$

Break a compound inequality into two inequalities:

$1 < x + y$
$\quad x + y < 2$

Graph line in standard form, using intercepts:

$1 < 0 + y \quad (0, 1)$
$1 < x + 0 \quad (1, 0)$

Plot

$x + y < 2$
$0 + y < 2 \quad (0,2)$
$x + 0 < 2 \quad (2,0)$

Plot

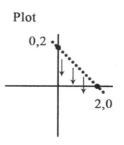

combined:

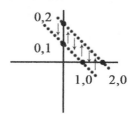

Note: *90+% of students miss this one!*

J. *See the graph*

37. Answer: A.

Concept: *M501 Mean, Median; M502 Median, Mode*

$\dfrac{3 + 8 + 10 + 15}{4} = 9$

3, 8, __, 10,15

Median = 9

Difference:

$9 - 9 = 0$

A. 0

38. Answer: F.

Concept: *M216 Quadratics & Parabolas; M210 Systems of Equations*

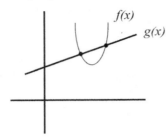

Where do they intersect?

That is where the functions are equal.

F. $f(x) = g(x)$ *for exactly 2 values of x*

39. Answer: B.

Concept: *M208 Coordinate Geometry & XY-plane*

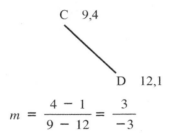

$$m = \frac{4 - 1}{9 - 12} = \frac{3}{-3}$$

B. -1

40. Answer: F.

Concept: *M208 Coordinate Geometry & XY-Plane*

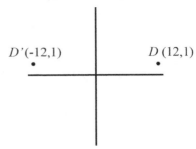

F. $-12, 1$

41. Answer: E.

Concept: *M303 Quadrilaterals*

Top: $\frac{(3 + 9)}{2} = 6$ Bottom: $\frac{(2 + 12)}{2} = 7$

$$\frac{(6 + 7)}{2} = 6.5$$

Midpoint means average!

"Cut a trapezoid into two equal areas" means the midpoint of the midpoints of the bases, *b1* and *b2*.

E. 6.5

42. Answer: K.

Concept: *M214 Functions f(x)*

$$f(x) = x - \frac{1}{x}$$

$$g(x) = \frac{1}{x}$$

$$f\left(g\left(\frac{1}{2}\right)\right) = f\left(\frac{1}{\frac{1}{2}}\right)$$

$$f\left(g\left(\frac{1}{2}\right)\right) = f(2)$$

$$f(2) = 2 - \frac{1}{2} = \frac{3}{2}$$

K. $\frac{3}{2}$

43. Answer: D.

Concept: *M201 Algebraic Operations*

$$p = \frac{\frac{1}{2}ary + a}{12y}$$

Factor out *a*

$$p = \left(\frac{\frac{1}{2}ry + 1}{12y}\right)a$$

"Multiply *a* by 2" means balance equation by 2.

D. *p is multiplied by 2*

44. Answer: G.

Concept: *M208 Coordinate Geometry & XY-Plane*

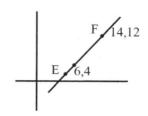

$$EF = 4 \times (ED)$$

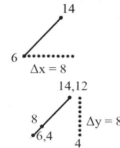

$8 \ is \ 4 \times 2$

$6 + 2 = 8$

$4 + 2 = 6$

G. $(8, 6)$

45. Answer: D.

Concept: *M220 Matrix*

A matrix can have a coefficient.

Distribute the *a*:

$$\begin{bmatrix} 2a & 6a \\ a & 4a \end{bmatrix} = \begin{bmatrix} x & 27 \\ y & z \end{bmatrix}$$

$x + z \ is \ the \ same \ as \ 2a + 4a = 6a$

$6a = 27$

D. 27

46. Answer: J.

Concept: *M104 Fractions*

$\dfrac{1}{8}$ *of the whole*

$x = whole$

Solve for x.

$$\dfrac{1}{8}x + 10 = \dfrac{3}{4}x$$

$$-\dfrac{1}{8}x \qquad\qquad -\dfrac{1}{8}x$$

$$10 = \dfrac{5}{8}x$$

$$\div \dfrac{5}{8} \quad \div \dfrac{5}{8}$$

$x = 16$

J. 16

47. Answer: B.

Concept: *M108 Ratio*

Tenth grade ratio: $86 : 255$

Eleventh grade ratio: $18 : 51$

These are the same *whole* (the high school).

$51x = 255$

$x = 5$

$18 \times 5 = 90$

10th	11th	12th
86	90	79

Most likely = 11th $\dfrac{90}{255}$

B. 11th

48. Answer: G.

Concept: *M104 Fractions; M205 Exponents & Roots*

$$\dfrac{4}{\sqrt{2}} + \dfrac{2}{\sqrt{3}} = ?$$

Find LCM.

$$\dfrac{4\sqrt{3}}{\sqrt{2}\sqrt{3}} + \dfrac{2\sqrt{2}}{\sqrt{3}\sqrt{2}}$$

G. $\dfrac{4\sqrt{3} + 2\sqrt{2}}{\sqrt{6}}$

49. Answer: A.

Concept: *M210 Systems of Equations; M215 Equation of a Circle; M207 Linear Functions: y=mx+b*

First find the linear inequality.

 $y<-x+2$

Second, the circle is shaded inside. Solutions must be less than radius.

$$(x-1)^2 + (y-2)^2 < 9$$

A. $y < -x + 2$
$(x-1)^2 + (y-2)^2 < 9$

50. Answer: F.

Concept: *M307 Solids*

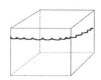

Volume of water:
$$40 \times 30 \times 20 = 24,000$$

It increases by .25:
$$40 \times 30 \times 20.25 = 24,300$$

Displacement = Difference
$$24,300 - 24,000$$

F. 300

51. Answer: E.

Concept: *M108 Ratio*

$x : y = 5 : 2 \qquad y : z = 3 : 2$

$(5 : 2)3 = 15 : 16$

$(3 : 2)2 = 6 : 4$

$x : z = 15 : 4$

E. 15 : 4

52. Answer: H.

Concept: *M203 Inequalities*

$-5 < 1 - 3x < 10$

Break into parts:

$$-5 < 1 - 3x$$
$${}_{-1} \phantom{<} {}_{-1}$$
$$-6 = -3x$$
$${}_{\div -3} {}_{\div -3}$$

Switch the sign.
$2 > x$

$$1 - 3x < 10$$
$${}_{-1} \phantom{-3x <} {}_{-1}$$
$$-3x < 9$$
$${}_{\div -3} \phantom{<} {}_{\div -3}$$

Switch the sign.
$x > -3$

H. $-3 < x < 2$

53. Answer: B.

Concept: *M307 Solids*

A = $2lw + 2lh + 2wh$

Double each dimension (*l, w, h*).

$2(2l)(2w) + 2(2l)(2h) + 2(2w)(2h)$

$8lw + 8lh + 8wh$

Increase by factor of 4.

B. 4

54. Answer: K.

Concept: *M212 Linear Function: Rate*

$$\frac{(7 \ cans)}{(3 \ days)}$$

$$3 + d = ?$$

$$3\left(\frac{7}{3}\right) + d\left(\frac{7}{3}\right)$$

K. $7 + \dfrac{7d}{3}$

55. Answer: E.

Concept: *M504 Counting, Permutations, & Combinations*

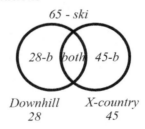

65 - ski

28-b both 45-b

Downhill X-country
28   45

$$28 + 45 - 65 = 8$$

E. 8

56. Answer: K.

Concept: *M308 Multiple Figures; M104 Fractions*

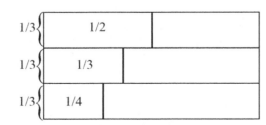

$$\frac{1}{3} \times \frac{1}{2} + \frac{1}{3} \times \frac{1}{3} + \frac{1}{3} \times \frac{1}{4}$$

$$\frac{1}{6} + \frac{1}{9} + \frac{1}{12} = \frac{6}{36} + \frac{4}{36} + \frac{3}{36} = \frac{13}{36}$$

Use your calculator

K. $\dfrac{13}{36}$

57. Answer: A.

Concept: *M403 Trig Function*

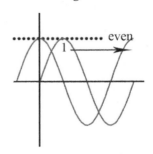

1. function translation
   $f(x) + b$ moves function ↑
   since these two are EVEN
   $b = 0$

2. This function moves left
   $f(x-a)$ $a<0$

   $a < 0$ and $b = 0$

A. $a < 0$ *and* $b = 0$

58. Answer: K.

Concept: *M204 Absolute Value*

$$|x - 5| < -1$$

The smallest value for $|x - 5|$ is 0!

There CANNOT be a negative absolute value.

K. *Empty Set*

59. Answer: E.

Concept: *M503 Probability*

$$\frac{1}{3} \times \frac{1}{3} \times \frac{1}{3} \times \frac{1}{3} = \frac{1}{81}$$

E. $\dfrac{1}{81}$

60. Answer: J.

Concept: *M404 Trigonometry: Law of Sines and Cosines*

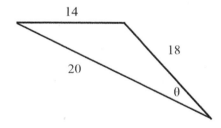

Note: *The smallest angle is opposite the smallest side.*

J. $14^2 = 18^2 + 20^2 - 2\,(18)\,(20)\,cos\theta$

Reading 1572

1. Answer: A.

Concept: *R301 Main Idea/Function: Passage*

Look at the first word of each answer: "explanation," "description," "argument," and "concerns." Note that the question is asking what role the *narrator* is playing. From this, it is likely that the choices can be narrowed down to just **A** and **B**, from which point it should be clear that **B** is not the purpose of the passage.

2. Answer: J.

Concept: *R201 Detail*

Note: *this is a frequently missed question - be careful!*

Immediately scan for Bombay's "first great photographer" and it will be apparent that they had a negative influence on the narrator. However, it is necessary to distinguish that the narrator was not turned away from photography itself, but from the particular *style* of those photographers. Further reading will make it clear that it influenced the narrator's style in a different direction, which is reflected in answer choice **J**.

3. Answer: C.

Concept: *R204 Main Idea/Function: Paragraph*

Tip*: do "narrow scope" questions first! They include line numbers, quotations, etc., that indicate where to find the answer!*

The answer will be inside the lines specified in the question. It is clear when reading the lines that the narrator is "musing over," or *thinking about*, the possibility of the building being built for his arrival at birth, but then

rejects the idea as too "solipsistic," essentially meaning *conceited* or *narcissistic* in this context. Therefore, only answer choice **C** makes sense.

4. Answer: H.

Concept: *R402 Vocabulary in Context; R101 Line Number*

In the lines specified, the narrator claims that he was forced to share his parents' love with the city of Bombay. He refers to Bombay with the pronoun "her." This would be an example of *personification*. Therefore, answer choice **H** is correct.

5. Answer: B.

Concept: *R104 Big Picture*

A significant amount of the third paragraph is structured around the way the narrator's parents alternated in taking care of their child. Some of these answers address *one* parent's work habits somewhat reliably, but only answer choice **B** shows how *both* parents participated by taking turns.

6. Answer: J.

Concept: *R202 Vocabulary in Context; R101 Line Number*

As used in line 9, the "sweep" is describing a *physical location*. This should be enough to determine that the appropriate answer choice is **J**: a broad area.

7. Answer: A.

Concept: *R203 Inference/Assumption; R101 Line Number*

This question is quite literal. What do these four lines do? They compare landmarks. It is not important *why* they do this, or what they are trying to accomplish, only that this is the "primary function" of these lines as stated in the question.

8. Answer: H.

Concept: *R103 Keyword*

If it is not immediately apparent, a couple of answer choices are quite obviously wrong. Despite some of the flowery language, the narrator *never* mentions living an extravagant lifestyle, so **F** is removed. The narrator's exhaustion after their hard work is not mentioned in connection with a lack of safety, so answer choice **G** is incorrect. It might be tempting to pick answer choice **J** because the narrator clearly admires his parents. However, the third paragraph begins with a statement that the narrator was "insanely jealous of the city," which suggests answer choice **H** is correct. Given the answer choices, always choose the option that is *explicitly* stated in the correct context.

9. Answer: B.

Concept: *R202 Vocabulary in Context; R101 Line Number*

The passage states that the narrator's parents "drew up that weekly rota (list) of shared responsibilities." Now, it is a decision of which verb most directly means "drew up." In this case it is safe to assume that "drew up" means "wrote" a list. Only answer choice **B** would be appropriate in this sense.

10. Answer: J.

Concept: *R204 Main Idea/Function: Paragraph; R203 Inference/Assumption*

Look at the first word of each answer and determine whether it is the father's purpose to "teach," "convince," "clarify," or "illustrate." While he may be teaching, the rest of answer choice **F** rules it out because it is clearly *not* related to what he is saying. The quotes in the

last passage should catch the reader's attention; they are the father's own words, so they are the best indicator of his intentions. The answer most aligned with what he says is **J**.

11. Answer: A.

Concept: *R104 Big Picture*

The vivid descriptions in the passage often refer to the size, majesty, and seemingly impossible features of the topic. Through these many descriptions, it is clear that the author is in "awe and fascination." However, one could easily come to this conclusion by recognizing that answer choices **B**, **C**, and **D** are all clearly incorrect given the tone of the passage. Although the author of this passage comes off as mostly objective, do not mistake this objectivity for "indifference" as is suggested in answer choice **D**.

12. Answer: J.

Concept: *R201 Detail*

Answer choice **F** should appear incorrect immediately, since the passage is about an underwater land feature. Answer choices **G** and **H** both refer to specific words in the passage that are used as "assumptions" that people made about the underwater mountain range. Answer choice **J** correctly identifies the feature.

13. Answer: C.

Concept: *R204 Main Idea/Function: Paragraph; R102 Paragraph Number*

The last sentence of the first paragraph mentioned in the question states "the unperturbed surface offers no hint of the grand and sweeping energies below." This matches very well with answer choice **C**. The wind is only mentioned to enhance the stillness in relation to the sea floor, no islands are mentioned at all, nor is the *Cramer*'s wake.

14. Answer: J.

Concept: *R201 Detail*

This question is entirely answered in the text. If it was not apparent on the first skim, scan for the Grand Canyon and it will be obvious that the passage is comparing the length of the Grand Canyon to that of the canyon in the Atlantic mountain range.

15. Answer: B.

Concept: *R203 Inference/Assumption; R101 Line Number*

Look at the first word or phrase in each answer choice to quickly rule them out. Answer choices **C** and **D** say "provide statistics" and "list the names," which are both incorrect. Answer choice **A** seems to fit, but the passage says nothing about a "first trip." The lines in question state that the scientists named the "hills in this otherworldly setting after distant, lifeless planets." Thus, answer choice **B** is clearly correct.

16. Answer: H.

Concept: *R204 Main Idea/Function: Paragraph*

The best practice with questions like these is to read the answers and return to the passage in question. Remember, the question does not ask for details from that paragraph; it asks for a *purpose*. Only one answer here is both supported by the text *and* an appropriate answer to the question: **H**.

17. Answer: B.

Concept: *R201 Detail; R203 Inference/Assumption*

This question most notably looks for what is "most strongly implied" because it is never stated outright. Line 11 states "contrary to what one might guess, Atlantic's deepest waters...are along her edges." The reader can imply the opposite of this: that people commonly assume the deepest waters are "at the middle of the ocean," making answer choice **B** correct.

18. Answer: F.

Concept: *R202 Vocabulary in Context; R101 Line Number*

Always read for context! Often these questions will choose words and phrases with multiple meanings. The context is: "one naval officer paid out eight miles of hemp rope." Insert the synonyms into the sentence and it will be clear that it isn't possible to "suggest" rope or "compensate" rope. More context would indicate that the sailor is "releasing" the rope or "dispensing it." So, answer choice **F** is correct.

19. Answer: D.

Concept: *R201 Detail*

Quickly scan for those specific words (i.e. Mount St. Helens, Himalayas, Pacific Ocean, and dry land of continents) and check their context. It should only take a couple of seconds to find that although the Himalayas are mentioned, the passage specifically states that "it covers almost as much of earth's surface as the dry land of continents." Therefore, answer choice **D** is correct.

20. Answer: F.

Concept: *R201 Detail*

Tip: *Practice looking for the keywords from the question rather than rereading altogether.*

Similar to the last question, check the passage for keywords from the answers, then compare their context to the question. Lines 55-58 indicate that the black mountains are covered in white patchy "skeletal remains of tiny microscopic animals." Therefore, answer choice **F** is correct.

21. Answer: A.

Concept: *R104 Big Picture; R101 Line Number*

Actually, despite the mention of a specific line number, this question can be answered without referring back to the line. Answer choices, **B**, **C**, and **D** are all simply not true to the essay: Bradbury never talks about walking with old friends in person, writing about the present, and nowhere is there even a suggestion of other writers teaching him new methods. However, to be clear, the entire first passage is about word-association.

22. Answer: G.

Concept: *R301 Main Idea/Function: Passage*

The text answers this question indirectly: Bradbury writes that "like every beginner" he thought he could "beat, pummel, and thrash an idea into existence." Therefore, answer choice **B** is correct.

23. Answer: D.

Concept: *R203 Inference/Assumption; R101 Line Number*

The question here is which answer is most synonymous with "take arms against the word." The answer choices offer "attempt to find," "often reject," "deliberately choose" and "struggling to find a word." Of these options, answer choice **D**, "struggle," is most clearly synonymous with "take arms."

24. Answer: J.

Concept: *R204 Main Idea/Function: Paragraph; R101 Line Number*

Bradbury states he "strolled" through "*recollections*," indicating that the process was a *mental* one. He does not have physical objects to remind him of the past. The three incorrect answers here all suggest some sort of physical interaction on his part, when in reality he is only using memory and imagination. Thus, answer choice **J** is correct.

25. Answer: C.

Concept: *R201 Detail*

Note: *This is a frequently missed question!*

Passage A only mentions John Huff in lines 39-42. Answer choices **A** and **B** are obviously incorrect, but are frequently chosen. The passage says clearly that he moved John Huff from Arizona (where he was really from) to Green Town (an assumed fictional story place). Therefore, answer choices **A** and **B** are incorrect. Answer choice **D** has the term "borrowed" in quotes which is also in the passage, but this is a trick. Answer choice **C** correctly states that he moved John to a town other than where he had actually grown up.

26. Answer: G.

Concept: *R203 Inference/Assumption; R102 Paragraph Number*

This is another question in which the answer choices' key words will help identify a correct answer. Looking back at the paragraph in question, Bradbury's descriptions begin in earnest childlike praise but eventually grow to impossible scale, even calling John a god. This over-the-top description is the key to identifying the correct answer, which says he is "exaggerating" (**G**).

27. Answer: C.

Concept: *R302 Organization of the Passage; R101 Line Number*

If time allows, always read the lines *in context*; that is, the lines before and after. The image of the cloud is an example of the literary technique *foreshadowing*. That isn't because it's about a shadow, but because it suggests what is about to happen. In this case, the sudden change in weather from sunny to dark *foreshadows* the upcoming shift from carefree friendship to sadness at the news of John Huff's departure. Therefore, answer choice **C** is correct.

28. Answer: J.

Concept: *R304 Both Passages; R203 Inference/Assumption*

For each answer choice, it must fit *both* passages. The narrator is easily checked, and is not consistent. There is nothing to suggest satire in these writings, and his sense of humor only shows in Passage A. Even if there is an allegory to be found here, there is no hint at a philosophical question, especially not in *both*. What remains is answer choice **J**. This is abundantly clear in Passage B, and looking back at Passage A, examples can be found, such as lines 43-45.

29. Answer: C.

Concept: *R304 Both Passages; R301 Main Idea/Function: Passage*

Answering this question requires a good understanding of the method described in Passage A. His method began with a word or phrase, and led to a story written around it by association. If the story in Passage B is one such story, it is very possible the words that led to it were "train ticket," and that **C** is a viable answer. Don't be thrown off by the hypothetical realm of this question: use what is known for sure about each passage to determine a logical conclusion.

30. Answer: G.

Concept: *R304 Both Passages; R104 Big Picture*

This question asks how the new lines provided apply to Passages A and B. "Surprise" is not Bradbury's main focus in either passage, so answer choice **F** is incorrect. Answer choice **H** says that the new lines are proof of something that is never mentioned in either passage. Answer choice **J** is in direct conflict with what Bradbury spent most of Passage A describing. Answer choice **G** correctly states that the lines "reinforce" Bradbury's use of his own life, but also that fiction allows those facts to be altered.

31. Answer: A.

Concept: *R301 Main Idea/Function: Passage*

Remember: *do main purpose questions last!*

The key word of the correct answer here is "overview," while other answer choices relate to *one* part of the passage or a detail.

32. Answer: G.

Concept: *R302 Organization of the Passage; R101 Line Number*

Dismiss answer choices **H** and **J** quickly, because the tone is not combative and the author does not bring up personal anecdotes. The remaining choices can be difficult to discern, as they involve similar topics (sarcasm often indicates humor). The key is the second part of the answer, describing the passage as either "mostly casual and playful" or "primarily technical." It should be clear that the passage is a technical one, given the scientific language and factual evidence.

33. Answer: A.

Concept: *R202 Vocabulary in Context; R101 Line Number*

The context of the question is that the ants developed their jaws "to *penetrate* the well-defended prey." The only answer choice which offers something that can be penetrated is **A**, prey with "hard outer shells."

34. Answer: J.

Concept: *R201 Detail*

Check for main phrases in the answers, but the answer is in line 22 where it states that the jaws' speed "comes from stored energy produced by the strong but slow muscles of the jaw." Thus, answer choice **J** is correct.

35. Answer: D.

Concept: *R203 Inference/Assumption*

Always scan for the out-of-place word. In this case, scan for popcorn to discover in what context the analogy is made. It describes the difficulty of scientists grabbing at the ants as they "bounced around," which is reflected in answer choice **D**. Answer choice **A** seems to emphasize the heat of the ant's bite, which is mentioned in the passage, but this is a trick. However, the question asks about the analogy of "trying to grab popcorn as it pops."

36. Answer: H.

Concept: *R204 Main Idea/Function: Paragraph; R201 Detail*

Look back at the last paragraph. Line 86 says the jumping in question "must have arisen from a different, perhaps accidental kind of behavior," which indicates answer choice **H** is correct.

37. Answer: B.

Concept: *R202 Vocabulary in Context; R101 Line Number*

Look at the context! More than one answer choice is a correct definition of "domain," but only one is relevant to the usage in the text. Clearly "domain" in this context is referring to an "area." The introduction of an expert should be a strong clue that the correct answer is **B**.

38. Answer: J.

Concept: *R201 Detail*

Scan for the information! Discussion on how the trap jaws actually work takes up the main bulk of the passage, so it must be done quickly. Lines 49-51 say that the "mandibles started to decelerate before they meet - possibly to avoid self-inflicted damage." Therefore, answer choice **J** is correct.

39. Answer: A.

Concept: *R201 Detail*

Scan for "escape jump," or simply recall its location from earlier. The answer will be a "benefit" of the jump. Answer choice **B** indicates that the "sting" is a result of the jump, which it is not. Answer choice **C** would mean that the jump is used as a signal, which it is not. Answer choice **D** is directly contradicted by the information in the passage. Answer choice **A** correctly states what is supported in the passage.

40. Answer: H.

Concept: *R201 Detail*

The bouncer-defense jump is discussed in the lines 65-75. It states specifically that the trap-jaw "propels the interloper in one direction, out of the nest, and the ant in the other." This would indicate that answer choice **H** is correct.

Science 1572

1. Answer: C.

Concept: *S202 Reading a Graph*

On Figure 1, all lines reach zero (x-axis) before 75 days, so answer choices **B** and **D** are incorrect. Answer choice **C** is a trick, there is no 5% SY medium in Study 1. On Figure 2, only the 5% SY medium (line with circles) does not reach zero before 75 days. Therefore, answer choice **A** is correct.

2. Answer: G.

Concept: *S104 Inference; S102 Experimental Design/Parameters*

The second paragraph of the text states that only female flies were used in the experiment. Females alone cannot reproduce, so the birth rate must be 0. Therefore, answer choice **G** is correct.

3. Answer: D.

Concept: *S102 Experimental Design/Parameters*

Both the graph keys and the text state that Study 1 used 15% SY medium and Study 2 used 5% SY medium. The text explains that the percent SY medium refers to the percentage of sugar and yeast. Thus, the two experiments differ because the percentage of yeast used in Study 1 is greater than that of Study 2. Therefore, answer choice **D** is correct.

4. Answer: G.

Concept: *S205 Extrapolation*

12% falls in between 10% and 15%. The Strain X row of the table shows 10% medium has an average lifespan of 58.6 days and 15%

medium has an average lifespan of 55.6 days. Thus, the Strain X flies in 12% medium would have an average life span between 55.6 days and 58.6 days: answer choice **G**.

5. Answer: C.

Concept: *S207 Infer from Data; S102 Experimental Design/Parameters*

The text states that Strain X flies cannot detect odors very well. The prediction states that decreasing odor detection would increase life span. Table 1 shows that Strain X, with less odor detection, has a longer lifespan than Strain N in every trial, which is consistent with the prediction.

6. Answer: F.

Concept: *S102 Experimental Design/Parameters*

Study 1 uses 15% SY medium with normal flies. The question describes the same parameters of Study 1, except for the files that are unable to detect odors (Strain X). This scenario is described in answer choice **F**.

7. Answer: A.

Concept: *S102 Experimental Design/Parameters*

According to the text, Tube 1 and Tube 4 did not have additional odors or live yeast. Therefore, these tubes should be compared and answer choice **A** is correct.

8. Answer: F.

Concept: *S101 Find in Text*

According to the text of Hypothesis 1, butterflies "first store lipids before they begin their migration" and then "must store lipids again" later, which clearly describes two distinct periods. Answer choice **F** is correct.

9. Answer: D.

Concept: *S101 Find in Text*

In Hypotheses 1 and 2, the butterflies use energy from stored lipids during migration, so answer choices **A** and **B** are incorrect. Hypothesis 3 states that butterflies use stored lipids for energy during the overwintering period, so answer choice **C** is incorrect. Therefore, none of the proposed hypotheses are correct, and answer choice **D** is correct.

10. Answer: J.

Concept: *S105 Text to Data*

Hypothesis 3 states that "lipid mass continuously increases from the beginning of migration to the end of migration," so the correct graph must have a line with a steady upwards (positive) slope. This correlates to answer choice **J**.

11. Answer: C.

Concept: *S104 Inference*

The statement in the question implies that the mass of stored lipids decreases during migration, meaning the butterflies are converting stored lipids to energy during migration. Hypotheses 1 and 2 state that butterflies use stored lipids for energy during migration. So, answer choice **C** is correct.

12. Answer: F.

Concept: *S104 Inference*

This questions asks which hypothesis would support the claim that nectar must be present at the overwintering sites if the butterflies are storing lipids during overwintering. Only Hypothesis 1 states that butterflies store lipids during overwintering. Hypotheses 2 and 3 specifically state that the butterflies do

not store more lipids during overwintering. Therefore, answer choice **F** is the only correct option.

13. Answer: B.

Concept: *S101 Find in Text*

Hypotheses 1 and 2 state that lipid mass decreases during migration. Hypothesis 3 states that lipid mass increases during migration. Thus, all three hypotheses state that butterflies' lipid mass *changes* during migration.

14. Answer: F.

Concept: *S303 Biology*

This question requires some science knowledge or a very acute process of elimination. Simply put, cells use energy from the energy-rich molecules called ATP (adenosine triphosphate).

15. Answer: C.

Concept: *S202 Reading a Graph*

Do not be tricked by the information on the axes. In Figure 2, the x-axis indicates thousands of years ago, going from low to high from right to left. Solar radiation intensity is represented by the left-hand axis. The dashed line represents solar radiation. At 8 thousand years before present, the dotted line crosses 500, which is answer choice **C**.

16. Answer: F.

Concept: *S205 Extrapolation*

In Figure 2, if CH_4 (solid line) had matched the solar radiation line (dashed line), it would've decreased to approximately where the solar radiation line hits the right side of the graph, which is less than 550. So, answer choice **F** is correct.

17. Answer: B.

Concept: *S204 Trends*

This question poses that if there is an increase in methane, there is an increase in global temperature and visa versa. In Figure 2, CH_4 (solid line) first decreases then increases from 11 thousand years ago to 0 thousand years ago. The only graph to show a decrease and then an increase is answer choice **B**.

18. Answer: H.

Concept: *S204 Trends*

In Figure 1, all of those numbers are at some point touched by the dashed line that indicates solar radiation. Answer choice **H** is closest to what is the middle of the graph and the middle of the range of the solar radiation line.

19. Answer: B.

Concept: *S202 Reading a Graph*

In Figure 1, the length of time from one maximum (highest point) to the next maximum for solar radiation (dashed line) is slightly more than 2 vertical lines, which is slightly more than 20 thousand years (between 15,000 and 35,000 years).

20. Answer: J.

Concept: *S306 Earth/Space Science*

It is clear from the information provided in the study that an increase in methane results in a corresponding increase in global temperature. Answer choices **F** and **G** are speaking of light, which is not the focus of the study. Answer choice **H** indicates the opposite of the study's results. Answer choice **J** is correct.

21. Answer: D.

Concept: *S305 Physics*

Friction acts in the direction opposite to movement, so if a block is pulled towards the east, friction acts to the west.

22. Answer: F.

Concept: *S202 Reading a Graph*

In Figure 2, the 2.00 kg block reaches 15 first, followed by the 2.50 kg block, and then the 3.00 kg block, which is reflected in answer choice **F**.

23. Answer: B.

Concept: *S305 Physics*

Find the 3.00 kg line on the graph in Figure 2 and find where it crosses the 1 second mark on the x-axis. It crosses the 1 second line at 5 meters per second.

24. Answer: J.

Concept: *S204 Trends; S302 Science Math*

Study 1 states that it is measuring "pulling force," which eliminates answer choices **F** and **G**. The final point on Figure 1 has a pulling force of 20 and a mass of 4. The only equation that fits these numbers is **J**.

25. Answer: B.

Concept: *S204 Trends*

For each point in Figure 2, the blocks with greater mass moved with lower speed (more slowly). For example, after 3.00 seconds, the 2.00 kg block was moving at 30.00 m/sec but the 3.00 kg block was moving at 15.00 m/sec. Thus, as block mass increased, block speed decreased, and answer choice **B** is correct.

26. Answer: H.

Concept: *S205 Extrapolation*

In Figure 1, when the pulling force was 10.00 N, the block's mass was 2.00 kg. When the pulling force is doubled to 20.00 N, the block's mass is also doubled to 4.00 kg. Thus, if the pulling force were tripled to 30.00 N, the block's mass would also triple—to 6.00 kg.

27. Answer: A.

Concept: *S102 Experimental Design/Parameters*

The text and Table 2 both state that Experiment 2 was done with solutions that had a known pH, whereas the text states that Experiment 3 was done with solutions of unknown pH. So, answer choice **A** is correct.

28. Answer: J.

Concept: *S102 Experimental Design/Parameters; S104 Inference*

The liquids of all colors would be easiest to see on a white plate.

29. Answer: C.

Concept: *S201 Reading a Table; S101 Find in Text*

In Table 1, curcumin is the yellow for all liquids, so the transition must be at a pH of greater than 7. In Table 2, curcumin is orange at a pH of 8 and red for all other solutions, so the transition is at a pH of around 8 (7.4-8.6).

30. Answer: F.

Concept: *S207 Infer from Data*

In Table 1, indigo carmine is blue at both 1 and 6, so could not be used to distinguish between the two solutions. This is commensurate with answer choice **F**.

31. Answer: B.

Concept: *S206 Correlation*

According to the question, propyl red has a transition around 5. In Table 1, resorcin blue has a transition around 5-6, which indicates answer choice **B**.

32. Answer: G.

Concept: *S207 Infer from Data*

Solution III is red with resorcin blue. In Table 1, resorcin blue is red for a pH of 4 or lower, so Solution III must have a pH of 4 or lower. This is support for answer choice **G**.

33. Answer: D.

Concept: *S201 Reading a Table*

In Table 1, metanil yellow is orange at a pH of 2 and yellow at a pH of 3 or greater. Solution IV is orange in metanil yellow, whereas the others are yellow, so solution IV must have a pH of 2 and the others must have a pH greater than 2.

34. Answer: J.

Concept: *S306 Earth/Space Science*

This is an intuitive answer, which one might discover quickly by recognizing that there is no other information available. At noon, incoming solar radiation is the most intense.

35. Answer: A.

Concept: *S102 Experimental Design/Parameters*

In the study, type of vegetation and density of vegetation cover are both held constant, so the only variable is the amount of DM sprayed.

36. Answer: H.

Concept: *S104 Inference*

In Figure 1, the lines for all three plots take a sharp turn down between July 25 and July 27. This fits the scenario in the question in which there is a measurement taken on July 25, no measurement taken on July 26, and then a lower measurement taken on July 27. Therefore, answer choice **H** is correct.

37. Answer: B.

Concept: *S101 Find in Text*

In the paragraph at the top of the second column, the text states that the sensor records data every 5 seconds. Since there are 60 seconds in a minute, the sensor records data 12 times per minute.

38. Answer: F.

Concept: *S102 Experimental Design/Parameters*

In the last paragraph of the first column, the text states that albedo is calculated for each

cloudless day. Figure 1 has no data points on July 20, so it must not have been a cloudless day.

39. Answer: D.

Concept: *S204 Trends*

Plot 1 (line with circles) had no DM and Plot 3 (line with triangles) had the most DM. In Figure 1, Plot 1 always has higher albedo than Plot 3, so albedo decreases with DM. In Figure 2, Plot 1 is always lower than Plot 3, so temperature increases with DM.

40. Answer: J.

Concept: *S202 Reading a Graph; S302 Science Math*

In Figure 1, the albedo on August 3 at Plot 2 (line with squares) was around 0.20. According to the text, albedo is the proportion of radiation reflected, so 20% of radiation was reflected. This leaves 80% of radiation NOT reflected.

ACT 67C (2012)

English

1. Answer: B.

Concept: *E102 Commas*

> ## Big 3 Comma Rules
> 1. No commas between subject and verb
> 2. No commas before or after prepositions
> 3. No commas between describing words and the things they describe

This question requires good knowledge of comma rules! The phrase "curving and bending" does not need any commas as there are only two participles and therefore do not need to be separated. Answer choice **A** is incorrect for this reason, so is answer choice **D**. Remember: commas can be used to separate independent clauses from dependent clauses. Answer choice **C** would make the independent clause *dependent*. Answer choice **B** correctly separates the dependent clause from the independent clause.

2. Answer: J.

Concept: *E103 Independent Clauses: Period, Semicolon, Comma and FANBOYS*

Watch out: this is a *NOT* question! There is only one incorrect option here. Answer choice **J** is a run-on sentence because "The county cleared this path" is an independent clause and *must* have some sort of punctuation after it. All of the other options are complex sentences correctly structured.

3. Answer: D.

Concept: *E105 Pronouns: Agreement/Case*

This is a pronoun agreement question! As it is written, the antecedent to the pronoun "they" would be "the county," which would mean the county was making trails so that the county would have a place to hike. Thus, "people," answer choice **D**, correctly provides a proper receiver of the county's actions.

4. Answer: F.

Concept: *E107 Colons and Dashes*

There is an independent clause and a dependent explanation after it. Answer choice **G** improperly uses a semicolon between an independent clause and a dependent clause; answer choice **J** does the same thing. Answer choice **H** is clearly a run-on sentence. Answer choice **F** correctly uses a dash to offset an explanation of how the narrator rides the trail.

5. Answer: B.

Concept: *E201 Relevancy: Adding, Deleting, and Replacing Information*

A quick check on the next page will show that Luigi is mentioned many more times, which means it isn't irrelevant and answer choice **D** is incorrect. His wheelchair is not an adequate explanation of why the narrator is in the forest and is not supported by the text. The sentence in question *is* lighthearted and therefore does not *contrast* to the rest of the essay. Answer choice **B** is correct because it correctly identifies the information as a detail that is important to the rest of the essay.

6. Answer: J.

Concept: *E103 Independent Clauses: Period, Semicolon, Comma and FANBOYS*

Separating Independent Clauses

1. Period
2. Semicolon
3. Comma FANBOYS

Quickly recognize that the first part of this sentence is an independent clause, so it must be separated with either a period, semicolon, or a comma-conjunction. The only answer choice that does so is answer choice **J**. Answer choice **F** is a comma splice; **G** would mean that the phrase between the commas is nonessential and removing them would create a run-on sentence, and answer choice **H** doesn't have a conjunction.

7. Answer: D.

Concept: *E202 Word Choice: Correct Word*

Remember: *if there is a question, there is a keyword!*

The question asks for the answer that will emphasize both "positive" and "friendly." Answer choices **A**, **B**, and **C** are all more or less synonyms for "moving cautiously." Answer choice **D** says "purrs," which is the "most logical and effective" choice.

8. Answer: F.

Concept: *E105 Pronouns: Agreement/Case*

Notice that the sentences both before and after begin with either "I can hear" or "I hear," which should be a clue as to how this sentence should begin. This essay is written in first person and so answer choice **F** correctly maintains that voice. Answer choices **G** and **H** are grammatically correct, but do not match the voice of the essay.

Answer choice **J** is a dependent clause and grammatically incorrect.

9. Answer: A.

Concept: *E103 Independent Clauses: Period, Semicolon, Comma and FANBOYS; E204 Short and Simple*

While answer choices **B** and **C** are grammatically correct (although they do not have an appropriate pronoun), answer choice **A** is the most clear and concise. Answer choice **D** is a dependent clause.

10. Answer: H.

Concept: *E103 Independent Clauses: Period, Semicolon, Comma and FANBOYS; E108 Adjectives and Adverbs*

Big 3 Comma Rules
1. No commas between subject and verb
2. No commas before or after prepositions
3. No commas between describing words and the things they describe
---

Each of the answer choices suggested break one of the major comma rules. Answer choices **F** and **G** put a comma between an adjective or an adverb and the noun it is describing. (Also, **G** incorrectly uses the adjectival "gentle" instead of the adverbial "gently.") Answer choice **J** would put a comma before a preposition ("in"), which is also incorrect.

11. Answer: A.

Concept: *E201 Relevancy: Adding, Deleting, and Replacing Information*

The quickest way to the answer here is to read the entire sentence and recognize the pronoun "their" in the second clause is referring to whatever the answer is in number 11. "Their" is not underlined, so it is correctly referring to whatever the correct answer is. Thus, answer choices **B** and **C** are incorrect. "Days" and "bicyclists" are both plural, but days don't create dust as they go by. Therefore, answer choice **A** is correct.

12. Answer: H.

Concept: *E103 Independent Clauses: Period, Semicolon, Comma and FANBOYS*

Separating Independent Clauses

1. Period
2. Semicolon
3. Comma FANBOYS

Both the sentence before the underlined portion and the sentence after are complete and therefore must be separated accordingly. Only answer choice **H** correctly separates the two independent clauses with a period.

13. Answer: D.

Concept: *E211 Parallel Structure*

Answer choices **A** and **C** both incorrectly use a semicolon to separate an independent clause and a dependent clause. Answer choice **B** uses a comma incorrectly after looking when there is a conjunction.

14. Answer: G.

Concept: *E106 Apostrophes: Possessive, Plural, Contractions*

"The trail" is singular possessive. The trail has *one* end. Therefore, answer choice **G** is correct.

15. Answer: B.

Concept: *E210 Writer's Goal*

Let's rephrase the question: does this essay illustrate the pleasure that people can take in nature? Even if the reader believed that the essay didn't accomplish this goal, answer choices **C** and **D** give incorrect support: the essay is neither about the city or about the functioning of the wheelchair. Answer choice **A** is incorrect because its support is that the essay focuses on wildflowers, which it does not. Answer choice **B** correctly states that the essay does accomplish that goal *because* the essay "focuses on the narrator's joy at having access to nature."

16. Answer: G.

Concept: *E104 Nonessential Information: Commas, Dashes, Parentheses*

Introductory clauses always receive a comma, but in this case there is also a *date*, and dates also receive a comma between the date and the year. (The nonessential clause commas do not apply here, even though there are two.) This introductory clause ends after "1904," so that is where the comma should go. The semicolons in answer choices **F** and **H** are incorrect because the introductory clause is not an independent clause. Answer choice **J** would incorrectly place a comma before a preposition. Answer choice **G** correctly places a comma between the number and year as well as after the introductory clause.

17. Answer: C.

Concept: *E107 Colons and Dashes*

The colon is used to present a list, example, or explanation. In this case, it correctly introduces *an incredible engineering feat* in answer choice **C**. A semicolon is incorrect because the second clause is not independent, nor punctuation be removed as in answer choice **D** or the sentence would become fused. The preposition *over* in answer choice **B** would give the sentence a new meaning, suggesting that the city was celebrating literally above the completed subway.

18. Answer: G.

Concept: *E201 Relevancy: Adding, Deleting, and Replacing Information*

This question relies on comprehension skills. The phrase to be possibly deleted "clarifies" which part of the subway system had actually been completed, which aligns with answer choice **G**. Answer choices **F** and **J** *should* seem incorrect, as the support in the question is not supported by the passage. Answer choice **H** *could* be inferred, but is not explicitly stated, whereas answer choice **G** is explicitly supported by the passage.

19. Answer: D.

Concept: *E204 Short and Simple*

When deletion is an answer, always give it special attention: it is often correct. In this case it is; however, we still must determine why. The beginning of the sentence already states that the route took 26 minutes, so any answer that repeats this information is redundant and incorrect. Thus, answer choices **A** and **C** are incorrect. Answer choice **B** repeats the phrase "complete the route," so it is also redundant and incorrect.

20. Answer: F.

Concept: *E201 Relevancy: Adding, Deleting, and Replacing Information*

So, the correct answer will "effectively conclude sentence" and "clearly...address the problem" mentioned in the first part of the sentence. The problem mentioned is "traffic jams." Answer choices **G**, **H**, and **J** do not "clearly" states how subways address this

problem. Answer choice **F** indicates explicitly that subway systems allow New Yorkers to travel "underneath the streets."

21. Answer: B.

Concept: *E105 Pronouns: Agreement/Case*

This is a tough question! First, notice that the second clause must be an independent clause with a subject and predicate because the portion that is not underlined contains a comma and a conjunction ("but"). Therefore, the correct choice will become the subject of the second clause. Insert each of the answer choices and see which one makes sense. "That" and "those" would make "the proposals" from the previous sentences capable of resolving "political, financial, and technical challenges." This is not possible! The correct answer ("it") is an idiomatic construction used in English to state how long things "take" to happen. So, **B** is correct.

22. Answer: J.

Concept: *E104 Nonessential Information: Commas, Dashes, Parentheses*

This sentence has a fairly simple subject and predicate. "The engineer William Barclay Parsons" is the subject, and "accepted responsibility for overseeing this project" is the predicate. There are no commas necessary, nor would the dash be correct because there is no explanation.

23. Answer: C.

Concept: *E108 Adjectives and Adverbs*

This question tests whether or not the reader can recognize an adjective and the noun it is modifying. The method is an "engineering method" and "innovative" is the adjectival form of the noun "innovation." The correct phrase will be "an innovative engineering method": answer choice **C**.

24. Answer: F.

Concept: *E204 Short and Simple*

More complicated does not mean more correct! Answer choices **G** and **H** are overly complicated. Note that the omission in answer choice **J** is not correct because in this case the passage would lose an important detail. While the sentence *could* end here, it is not the same as specifying what they were digging. Thus, answer choice **F** correctly states what is being dug without being verbose.

25. Answer: C.

Concept: *E107 Colons and Dashes*

While the start of this sentence ("Tunnel walls were created") is an independent clause, the fact that the word "with" is included in all of the answer choices makes the solution more clear. Answer choice **A** incorrectly uses a colon which would negate the use of the preposition "with." Answer choice **D** actually has the same problem. Answer choice **B** incorrectly places a comma between "created" and "with," and commas never go around prepositions. Simply put, no punctuation is necessary for this sentence to function.

26. Answer: G.

Concept: *E109 Relative Pronouns*

Note: *"whom" will almost always follow the preposition "of."*

"Whom" is an object pronoun of "who." "Them" is incorrect because the antecedent noun it is replacing would be the subject of the sentence: "stations." Answer choice **J** may be tempting, but it would actually create a new independent clause as well as a comma splice. Out of answer choices **G** and **H**, it is necessary to know that the pronoun is replacing the *object* of the antecedent clause.

27. Answer: A.

Concept: *E205 Transition Words/Phrases*

Remember: *transition words require context! Read sentences before and after!*

"Therefore" means the information after the transition word is *caused by the information prior to it.* "For instance" provides an example of the information presented. "That is" introduces a clarification. "However" introduces information that is contrary to what was just presented. If it helps, the transition word could be placed at the beginning of the sentence instead of the end, which should make it clear that the New Yorkers quickly adapting is contrary to their prior skepticism. Thus, answer choice **A** is correct.

Tip: *"however" is the only transition word that presented contrary information, which should have been a clue that it was correct!*

28. Answer: G.

Concept: *E201 Relevancy: Adding, Deleting, and Replacing Information*

The question is: which answer "describes the magnitude and expansiveness" of the subway system today? Answer choice **F** does not refer to scale at all. Answer choice **H** refers more to a feat of management than of magnitude; however, it does not flow from the paragraph. Answer choice **J** has a similar problem in that, while directly speaking to size, is only referencing subway platforms. Answer choice **G** emphasizes "the magnitude and expansiveness of the New York City subway system today," as requested in the question.

29. Answer: C.

Concept: *E209 Moving Paragraphs*

The clue here is the phrase "this technique" in the proposed sentence. Quickly scan to see which answer choice follows a sentence that mentions a technique of some sort. Answer choice **C** follows a sentence which refers to an "innovative engineering method," so **C** is correct.

30. Answer: J.

Concept: *E202 Word Choice: Correct Word*

The correct answer choice will indicate a change *from a decline* following Rivera. Answer choices **F** and **G** are both neutral, and in no way suggest the previous decline. While answer choice **H**, "influenced," is a more vivid word, it also does not reference the decline addressed in the question. Answer choice **J** "revived," implies frescoes had been dying and in need of revival.

31. Answer: B.

Concept: *E101 Verbs: Agreement/Tense*

The verb being used is "to cater," but the preposition or pronoun in the answer choices makes a large difference. If art is being brought *out* of "elite galleries" then it is unlikely that this was done "by catering to the upper class." Instead, what is necessary is a preposition that will alter the sentence to show a change of hands. Answer choice **B** states that frescoes "brought art out of the elite galleries *that catered* to the upper class and literally to the public."

32. Answer: J.

Concept: *E207 Modification: Moving Modifiers*

Note: *there are no commas separating any clauses!*

This is a complicated question. "Rivera" is the subject and needs a predicate or action to take. What makes the most sense is "Rivera attracted." Answer choice **H** can be immediately discarded because Rivera doesn't have a predicate. Answer choice **F** is incorrect because it's inappropriate to say "Rivera attracted for his belief" - "for his belief" is not an object that can be attracted. Answer choice **G** states that Rivera should wield more power, but that is clearly at odds with the rest of the passage. Answer choice **J** states in a grammatically correct way exactly what Rivera attracted.

33. Answer: D.

Concept: *E204 Short and Simple*

As always, when deletion is an option make sure to consider it strongly. Answer choice **A** repeats "art," which is redundant and the ACT hates redundancy. **B** and **C** state that Rivera was "interested in" or "focused on" his "dominant artistic subject," which is also clearly redundant. Therefore, answer choice **D** is correct.

34. Answer: H.

Concept: *E202 Word Choice: Correct Word*

In this context "as" is a comparison word that denotes equality. Notice the construction: "as _____ as." In no circumstances will it be correct to say "as expansive than" because "than" denotes an unequal comparison (e.g. "I'm taller *than* you.") Answer choice **G** is a temporal pronoun ("then") and inappropriate no matter what. Answer choice **J** ("if") is a conjunction that denotes a *condition*, which is also inappropriate here.

35. Answer: B.

Concept: *E101 Verbs: Agreement/Tense*

The action verb "depict" here is the clue to the answer. "Depict" must have a plural subject, while "depicts" would be the singular form (E.g. "the artist *depicts*," "the artists *depict*"). Answer choice **B** correctly corresponds the subject to the predicate, which is plural.

Note: *three of the answer choices all mean "one" or "singular," which should indicate that the outlier is correct.*

36. Answer: H.

Concept: *E104 Nonessential Information: Commas, Dashes, Parentheses*

Tip: *find the independent clause!*

The word "after" changes how this sentence can be constructed. "After" is a preposition of time and indicates that this sentence is not finished at the period as in answer choice **F**. If a period is incorrect, then a semicolon is also incorrect, so **G** is wrong. Because the first clause is not independent the dash also cannot be correct. Answer choice **H** correctly indicates that the second clause is nonessential and requires a second comma.

37. Answer: C.

Concept: *E101 Verbs: Agreement/Tense*

The subject of the sentence is "the empowerment," so the verb must agree in number. The plural "were" immediately rules out leaving the sentence unchanged, so answer choice **A** is incorrect. The addition of "if" in both **B** and **D** actually causes the predicate to become part of the subject by turning it into a descriptor, making the

sentence into a fragment. Answer choice **C** is incorrect and concise.

38. Answer: F.

Concept: *E102 Commas*

Because there are only two adjectives here, not the three required to make a list, there does not need to be any punctuation. If there was one more adjective it would be necessary to punctuate. Therefore, answer choice **F** is correct because it leaves out any unnecessary punctuation.

39. Answer: C.

Concept: *E201 Relevancy: Adding, Deleting, and Replacing Information*

What *detail* is provided in the underlined portion? Is it elsewhere in the sentence? These are the two questions to consider when given an omission question. Because the information is not presented elsewhere, answer choice **A** is incorrect. Answer choice **B** is not true because the sentence is still complete without the knowledge of what is being painted. Answer choice **D** is incorrect because, while one could argue it is unnecessary, it is in no way ambiguous. Answer choice **C** correctly points out that the detail is new and relevant.

40. Answer: J.

Concept: *E103 Independent Clauses: Period, Semicolon, Comma and FANBOYS*

This is an "independent clause" question in disguise! Notice that there are two independent clauses here, each with their own subject-predicate construction. Therefore, the conjunction must correctly separate the two sentences. "And" is the only explicit FANBOYS in the answer choices, but "thus" could technically be a conjunction.

However, "thus" would incorrectly suggest cause and effect in this sentence.

41. Answer: B.

Concept: *E101 Verbs: Agreement/Tense*

Tip*: -ing words aren't verbs!*

There must be a proper verb for this sentence to be complete. Here, "depicting" serves as an adjective, so answer choice **A** is incorrect. Answer choice **C** and **D** similarly fail to create a predicate. Only answer choice **B** creates a predicate, and thus a complete, independent clause.

42. Answer: F.

Concept: *E201 Relevancy: Adding, Deleting, and Replacing Information*

What matters is not whether it should be added, but rather the support used. Answer choices **G** and **H** do not have sufficient support. Answer choice **J** does not provide a true digression, but only examples stated in the primary clause. Answer choice **F** correctly states that the phrase adds "examples" that "specify a broad term."

43. Answer: B.

Concept: *E104 Nonessential Information: Commas, Dashes, Parentheses*

Tip*: remove the nonessential clause!*

It is helpful to read the sentence without the nonessential information which splits the independent clause from the nonrestrictive clause after it. Imagine the sentence now reads: "The fresco is a dynamic work because celebrates all working men and women." This is clearly incorrect. Replace each word in the blank and it will be apparent that only answer choice **B** is appropriate.

44. Answer: J.

Concept: *E205 Transition Words/Phrases*

As is often the case, the deletion is correct. It's important to note that each of the three provided transition words introduce an *exception* or something *contrary* to what was just said. Grammatically, "it" in the primary clause must be referring to the fresco in the sentence before. The sentence before does not indicate that he is unhappy with the fresco and so it wouldn't be correct to use a contrasting transition word. Thus, answer choice **J** is correct.

45. Answer: A.

Concept: *E102 Commas*

The structure of this sentence is: independent clause, independent clause, dependent clause. This means the last clause can't be separated by a period or semicolon as in answer choices **C** and **D**. The addition of "yet" can be deemed redundant because "even though" already serves the purpose of connecting these ideas, so answer choice **B** is incorrect. Answer choice **A** correctly separates the dependent clause from the independent clause with a comma.

46. Answer: J.

Concept: *E103 Independent Clauses: Period, Semicolon, Comma and FANBOYS*

Separating Independent Clauses

1. Period
2. Semicolon
3. Comma FANBOYS

Be careful! This is a *NOT* question. There are two independent clauses here. That means that the correct answer will be the *incorrect* way to conjoin two independent clauses. Answer choice **J** is neither a period, semicolon, or comma and conjunction: it is a run-on sentence.

47. Answer: C.

Concept: *E102 Commas*

This can be a difficult comma question. Answer choices **B** and **D** should be eliminated fairly quickly because they do not offer adverbs, and "enjoyed" is already the active verb. "Though" is a transition word that must be offset by a comma. The first comma is offsetting the dependent introductory clause, and the second comma offsets the transition word. Thus, **C** is correct.

48. Answer: F.

Concept: *E202 Word Choice: Correct Word*

The correct answer will express "fondness" and show a "positive reaction." Answer choices **G** and **H** are very neutral, with almost no expression. Answer choice **J** expresses surprise, which though not exclusive to fondness is nowhere near as direct, positive, and fond as answer choice **F**.

49. Answer: B.

Concept: *E109 Relative Pronouns*

The pronoun here ("who," "whom," "whose," or "which") must refer to the noun or noun-phrase previously used. "Which" cannot be correct because the parents are people. The parents are not receiving any action; in fact, they are taking their own action. Therefore, they cannot use the pronoun "whom." "Whose" is possessive and is, therefore, incorrect. Answer choice **B** correctly uses the simple pronoun "who."

50. Answer: F.

Concept: *E105 Pronouns: Agreement/Case*

Double-check for context, but the narrator hasn't changed and this isn't a quotation of someone else speaking. The narrator is a single person speaking in first-person, so the correct pronoun is "I": answer choice **F**.

51. Answer: B.

Concept: *E208 Moving Sentences*

This one can be a little tricky! Sentence 1 is a good introductory sentence that talks about the narrator going to Fairbanks for work. Sentence 3 also mentions Fairbanks, which serves as an indicator that they are next to each other. Sentence 2 moves on from the location to Joan herself. Thus, **B** is correct.

52. Answer: J.

Concept: *E204 Short and Simple*

In this question, deletion is again correct. The most common reason for deletion is redundancy, and this sentence is no exception. Notice that in the second clause it already states "to keep the battery from freezing," so the final phrase would be redundant.

53. Answer: D.

Concept: *E203 Word Choice: Tone*

All of these are viable past-tense notations for "shine" except "shoned," which is not a word. The hint should be that "shone" is already clearly past-tense as written in the passage; adding a "D" to the end would be superfluous (and incorrect).

54. Answer: H.

Concept: *E201 Relevancy: Adding, Deleting, and Replacing Information*

Be careful: the question refers to the sentence before!

The sentence in question offers a setting and some simple imagery. It does not include a response to the weather, nor does it analyze the plugging. While the detail may seem unnecessary, it does not repeat anything. Thus, answer choice **H** is the most correct option.

55. Answer: A.

Concept: *E202 Word Choice: Correct Word*

All answers here are grammatically correct, but imply very different things. Answer choice **B** implies they found the habits by chance; answer choice **C** that they paid the habits a visit, and **D** that they left without the habits and came back with them. "Slipped into" correctly suggests they unknowingly recommenced their old habits.

56. Answer: H.

Concept: *E207 Modification: Moving Modifiers*

Order here is very important! As is written in the passage, the sentence states Joan's house was on top of the rabbit hutch. Answer choice **G** says the field is on the hutch. Answer choice **J** also places the field atop the hutch. Only answer choice **H** accurately places Joan and the narrator on the hutch.

57. Answer: B.

Concept: *E202 Word Choice: Correct Word*

Be careful, this is a *NOT* question! All of the options except answer choice **B** show Joan being extremely occupied by her work.

Answer choice **B** suggests her work gained possession of her.

58. Answer: H.

Concept: *E202 Word Choice: Correct Word*

Another *NOT* question! The word "along" suggests positioning, which is incorrect. All of the other answer choices show that her decisions were the subject of her firmness.

59. Answer: A.

Concept: *E201 Relevancy: Adding, Deleting, and Replacing Information*

Remember: if any of the information used in the answers is not correct, the whole answer is incorrect. Answer choice **B** suggests that the essay is sad, but it is not. Although the narrator and Joan work creatively, it is certainly not the main idea of the passage as requested by the question. Answer choice **D** would suggest that "remembering Joan" had been an issue, but the narrator indicates that she had never forgotten her.

60. Answer: G.

Concept: *E208 Moving Sentences*

Answer choice **G** is the most logical place to insert the sentence because the suggested sentence is a transition from the description of their bond to their eventual reunion. Words like "yet" and "such" are excellent indicators of where to place sentences in these questions.

61. Answer: A.

Concept: *E204 Short and Simple*

Notice that answer choices **B** and **C** are redundant: they both give another verb synonymous with "attaching" ("connected" and "related") in the second clause.

(Redundancy is always incorrect on the ACT.) Answer choice **D** is incorrect because it would remove the object that is being attached to the stories.

62. Answer: H.

Concept: *E103 Independent Clauses: Period, Semicolon, Comma and FANBOYS*

Separating Independent Clauses

1. Period
2. Semicolon
3. Comma FANBOYS

There are two independent clauses here, so they must be separated accordingly. Only answer choice **H** provides a comma and a conjunction to appropriately separate the two ideas. Answer choices **F** and **J** are technically grammatically correct but would mean that the Sun was setting images somehow, which is nonsensical.

63. Answer: A.

Concept: *E104 Nonessential Information: Commas, Dashes, Parentheses*

In this case, "or constellation" is offering an alternate wording to "the pattern." As it is not a functional part of the subject-predicate relationship, it is best nested between two commas (i.e. it is nonessential). If it is unclear when a phrase is a nonessential detail, see if the sentence makes sense without it. Every other answer choice would incorrectly place a comma between the subject and predicate or improperly use a colon.

64. Answer: H.

Concept: *E201 Relevancy: Adding, Deleting, and Replacing Information*

Read ahead! The question states that Orion "is described later in the essay." It's okay to skip a question like this and come back to it when the context is clear. Near the end, a whole paragraph is devoted to the myth and constellation of Orion. If it is not immediately apparent that Orion is a myth, it is necessary to read further on!

65. Answer: D.

Concept: *E201 Relevancy: Adding, Deleting, and Replacing Information*

The correct answer will have "visual information." The only answer choice with anything resembling a visual representation is answer choice **D** which states that the stars appear in "a straight line." Although somewhat descriptive, the remaining choices are not visual in any way.

66. Answer: G.

Concept: *E202 Word Choice: Correct Word*

The correct answer will not be synonymous with the other three. "Viewers," "observers," "stargazers," and "night-sky watchers" are all synonymous in this context. An "overseer," in answer choice **G**, is more akin to a "manager" or "leader," which is incorrect.

67. Answer: A.

Concept: *E201 Relevancy: Adding, Deleting, and Replacing Information*

The significance comes from the detail of the Karasuki representing a "plow." Since plows are a traditional agricultural tool, it's relevant that the Japanese communities mentioned are agricultural ones. Their distance, population, and historical-ness have no pertinence to the imagery of the plower.

68. Answer: J.

Concept: *E202 Word Choice: Correct Word; E204 Short and Simple*

Answer choices **F** and **G** are not only overly wordy, but also have a very inappropriate tone for the essay. Answer choice **H** is simply verbose. Answer choice **J** clearly states what needs to be stated without adding any unnecessary words.

69. Answer: A.

Concept: *E104 Nonessential Information: Commas, Dashes, Parentheses*

It is simply false to say "In Japan's imagination" in this context, so answer choice **B** can be ruled out. Answer choice **C** is incorrect because it redundantly states "Japan" when it is already clear that these are various interpretations of Japanese astrology. Answer choice **D** would suggest that the stars *only* appear in that symbol, but it is clear from the rest of the paragraph that it is not. Answer choice **A** correctly indicates that it is in *other* parts of Japan that yet *another* interpretation is popular.

70. Answer: G.

Concept: *E101 Verbs: Agreement/Tense*

The subject of the sentence is "stars," which is plural. "Has" is singular and so is "has been" (**F** and **J**). "Could of" is incorrect not only because it doesn't fit, but also because it would be "could have" if it was even an appropriate choice. Only answer choice **G** is appropriately plural and agrees in tense with the subject.

71. Answer: D.

Concept: *E104 Nonessential Information: Commas, Dashes, Parentheses*

"The mythology of the Tswana people of South Africa" is one long subject and requires no comma at all. "In" is a preposition indicating "where" these stars are represented this way. Consider rewriting the sentence this way if it makes more sense: "The mythology of the Tswana people of South Africa represents these same stars as three pigs."

72. Answer: J.

Concept: *E105 Pronouns: Agreement/Case*

This question is difficult! Answer choices **F** and **H** both rely on the word "such" to indicate some prior distance already mentioned for them to be correct; however, that information has not been given so it is incorrect. Answer choice **G** is obviously incorrect because of word order. Answer choice **J** is correct because it is a restrictive clause which requires the necessary conjunction "that" to be correct.

73. Answer: C.

Concept: *E106 Apostrophes: Possessive, Plural, Contractions*

Their = Belonging to them.

They're = They are.

There = That place.

The sentence only makes sense with "there."

74. Answer: G.

Concept: *E103 Independent Clauses: Period, Semicolon, Comma and FANBOYS*

Separating Independent Clauses
1. Period
2. Semicolon
3. Comma FANBOYS

This is a compound sentence with two independent clauses! As with all the others in this test, it can be joined with simply a comma and conjunction. In this case: "and."

75. Answer: D.

Concept: *E201 Relevancy: Adding, Deleting, and Replacing Information*

The important part of the prompt is "free of direct references to a specific culture's view of the three stars." Any sentence that includes "Orion" would indicate a specific culture's view, which does not happen until sentence 7. Therefore, Sentence 7 is the appropriate place to begin a new paragraph.

Math 67C

1. Answer: A.

Concept: *M212 Linear Function: Rate*

$20 per *v*, vehicles; $10 per *p*, persons

A. $20v + 10p$

2. Answer: F.

Concept: *M202 Solving Equations*

$(9 + 5 - (-6))(5 + (-6))$

$(9 + 11)(-1)$

$(20)(-1)$

F. -20

> Tip: *Pay attention to NEGATIVE signs. When substituting and distributing negative numbers ALWAYS use parentheses.*

3. Answer: E.

Concept: *M109 Rate & Proportion*

1st: 60 *per min.* $\rightarrow$ 8 *min* = 480
2nd: 80 *per min.* $\rightarrow$ 6 *min* = 480

Total = 480 + 480 = 960

E. 960

4. Answer: J.

Concept: *M501 Mean, Average*

When asked to keep the average the same, the next value added must simply be *equal to the average*!

$$\frac{(210 + 225 + 254 + 231 + 280)}{5}$$

J. 240

5. Answer: C.

Concept: *M109 Rate & Proportion*

Tip: *The ACT loves to ask about hourly wages (pay per hour).*

She makes $7.50 per hour for 40 hours.

$7.50 \times 40 = 300$

And 1.5 times for more than 40 hours.

$7.50 \times 1.5 \times 2 = 22.50$

$300 + 22.50 = 322.50$

C. $322.50

6. Answer: K.

Concept: *M101 Word Problems - Translation & Vocabulary*

Construct an equation!

"A number squared" is x^2

"is 39 more" is *= 39 +*

"product of 10 and x" is $10x$

K. $x^2 = 39 + 10x$

7. Answer: E.

Concept: *M202 Solving Equations*

$9(x-9) = -11$

$9x - 81 = -11$

+81   +81

$9x = 70$

÷9   ÷9

$x = \dfrac{70}{9}$

E. 70/9

8. Answer: H.

Concept: *M109 Rate & Proportion*

Given: $4.00 is the *discount* price.

Purchased $60 of discount tickets

60/4 = 15 tickets purchased

Discount is $37.50 less

$\dfrac{(\$37.50 + \$60.00)}{15} = \$6.50$

H. $6.50

9. Answer: A.

Concept: *M218 Factoring & FOIL*

FOIL! (If you have to.)

A. $9x^2 - 16y^4$

Tip: *The ACT loves the Difference of the Squares. A skilled test-taker should be able to recognize these backwards and forwards. Memorize these factoring formulas.*

- $(a-b)(a+b) = a^2 - b^2$

- $(a+b)^2 = a^2 + 2ab + b^2$

- $(a-b)^2 = a^2 - 2ab + b^2$

10. Answer: J.

Concept: *M303 Quadrilaterals*

Area $l \times w = 32$

Perimeter $2l + 2w = 24$

Solve for w, by substitution:

$2l + 2w = 24$

-2w   -2w

$2l = 24 - 2w$

÷2   ÷2

$l = 12 - w$

Substitute $12 - w$ for l in $l \times w = 32$

$(12 - w) \times w = 32$

$12w - w^2 = 32$

-32   -32

Rewrite: $w^2 - 12w + 32 = 0$

Factor:

$(w - 8)(w - 4) = 0$
$w = 4\ or\ 8$

J. 4

That's a heck of a lot of algebra. Guess and check is better. Because the area and the perimeter are integers, then the length and the width both have to be integers, since:

Integer x Integer = Integer

Integer + Integer = Integer

So what are the factors of 32?

8 x 4 , 16 x 2.

Guess and check.

> Trap: *K. 8, don't make the mistake of putting the longer side.*

11. Answer: D.

Concept: *M302 Triangles*

The SUM of two angles is $47°$

So, the last angle is simply:

$180° - 47° = 133°$

D. $133°$

12. Answer: K.

Concept: *M504 Counting, Permutations, & Combinations*

To make a lunch you need one of each, so just multiply the number of options together.

$3 \times 3 \times 4 \times 2 = 72$

K. 72

> Traps: *Answer choice F is the average of the numbers and H is the sum. Don't make these mistakes.*

13. Answer: B.

Concept: *M103 Properties of Integers*

Consecutive integers can be represented as $(n,\ n + 1)$

$n + 3(n + 1) = 79$

Solve for n.

$n + 3n + 3 = 79$

$4n + 3 = 79$
   -3   -3

$4n = 76$
÷4   ÷4

$n = 19$

B. 19, 20

> Trap: *Who says the ACT is not tricky? Answer choice E is a trap of two consecutive numbers whose sum is 79.*

14. Answer: F.

Concept: *M214 Functions f(x)*

This is a very basic question that is on every test: evaluate a function for a given value of *x*.

$$f(-3) = -8(-3)^2$$

$$f(-3) = -8(9)$$

$$f(-3) = -72$$

F. -72

Tip: *WATCH OUT FOR NEGATIVE SIGNS! On __every__ ACT, there are simple substitutions and evaluations that include operations with negative numbers. They love subtracting and distributing negative numbers, because you do not.*

---

15. Answer: C.

Concept: *M205 Exponents & Roots*

$$3^x = 54$$

Memorize the powers of 3!
$$3^2 = 9; \quad 3^3 = 27; \quad 3^4 = 81$$

Since 54 is between 27 and 81, *x* MUST be a number between 3 and 4.

C. $3 < x < 4$

Trap: *Answer choice E: a number between 3 and 4 is also less than 5. But a number less than 5, such as 1 or 2 does not HAVE to be between 3 and 4, so while E COULD be true, it isn't always.*

---

16. Answer: J.

Concept: *M103 Properties of Integers*

Break these numbers into factors:

$$70 = 7 \times 10$$
$$60 = 6 \times 10$$
$$50 = 5 \times 10$$

The answer has to have common parts, we only need one 10, because each of them has a 10.

$$(7 \times 6 \times 5) \times 10 = 2100$$

J. 2100

17. Answer: B.

Concept: *M307 Solids*

Volume of a box is $l \times w \times h$

Given volume, and two dimensions, find the third.

$$81,000 = 45 \times 30 \times h$$

B. 60

18. Answer: J.

Concept: *M305 Circles*

DRAW!

Clockwise: move to the right
Counterclockwise: move to the left.

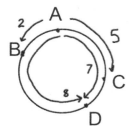

J. *A, C, D, B*

Tip: *When you can draw something for a problem, DRAW! Physically moving your pencil activates a different part of your brain.*

19. Answer: D.

Concept: *M205 Exponents & Roots*

Substitute $t = 5$ into $y = 16(2)^t$

$y = 16(2)^5 = 512$

D. 512

Trick: *NO power of 2 ends in ZERO! 16 is a power of two, therefore the answer MUST be a power of 2. You know that 512 is a power of 2. This could be a 10 second problem – you can solve it faster than most students can pick up and enter the equation in their calculator.*

20. Answer: J.

Concept: *M303 Quadrilaterals*

DRAW!

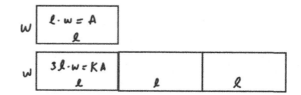

Smaller Rectangle $l \times w = A$

Larger Rectangle: $3l \times w = kA$

$k = 3$

J. 3

21. Answer: E.

Concept: M201: *Algebraic Operations*

$(a + 2b + 3c) - (4a + 6b - 5c)$

Distribute the negative sign:

$(a + 2b + 3c) - 4a - 6b + 5c$

CLT: Combine like terms:

E. $- 3a - 4b + 8c$

Tip: *Be very careful distributing negative signs. This problem does not take long to do, so get it right by being mindful and executing.*

22. Answer: G.

Concept: *M401 Trigonometry*

$$sin \varnothing = \frac{Opp}{Hyp}$$

$$\sin \emptyset = \frac{a}{c}$$

G. $\dfrac{\dfrac{a}{c}}{}$

Tip: *The Trig on the ACT is usually this easy. Practice this problem and gain speed but do it with accuracy.*

23. Answer: B.

Concept: *M504 Counting, Permutations, & Combinations*

Draw a picture:

Label the five players A, B, C, D, E and put them in a circle.
1.   A can only pass to C or D, pick C
2.   C can only pass to E
3.   E can only pass to B
4.   B can only pass to D
5.   D can only pass to A

Thus, it takes five passes for the ball to get back to A.

B. 5th

24. Answer: H.

Concept: *M207 Linear Functions: y=mx+b*

$y = 0.12x + 3000$

The slope of line *p* is 0.12

The slope of line *n* is 0.1 greater than the slope of line *p*.

Add 0.1 to 0.12

H. 0.22

25. Answer: A.

Concept: *M205 Exponents & Roots*

$-8x^3(7x^6 - 3x^5)$

Distribute! (Be careful of the negative signs.)

When multiplying variables with the same base, but different exponents, add them.

$$(-8x^3) \times (7x^6) + (-8x^3) \times (-3x^5)$$

Always use parentheses when manipulating terms in algebraic expressions and equations.

Trick: *Look at the answer choices! The answer must be two terms, first negative, second positive. That leaves only A and C. The answers can be narrowed down to 50/50 just by looking at the signs.*

$(-8 \times 7 \times x^{3+6}) + (-8 \times -3 \times x^{3+5})$

A. $-56x^9 + 24x^8$

26. Answer: G.

Concept: *M204 Absolute Value*

This can be typed directly into a calculator!

$-3 \, |-6 + 8|$

$-3 \, |2|$

G. -6

27. Answer: B.

Concept: *M302 Triangles*

A 3-4-5 right triangle!

Solve for $\overline{BC}$, a 3-4-5 right triangle.

Triangle ACE is a similar triangle.

$\overline{AC} = \overline{BC} * 4$

So, $\overline{AE} = \overline{BD} \times 4 = 3 \times 4 = 12$

B. 12

28. Answer: H.

Concept: *M214 Functions f(x)*

This is a linear function because it says "constant rate."

Substitute $t = 0$ and $y = 14$ into each answer.

That eliminates answer choices **G**, **J**, and **K**.

Then substitute $t = 1$; $y = 19$

$F : (19) = (1) + 14$ *wrong*

$H : (19) = 5(1) + 14$ *correct*

H. $y = 5t + 14$

29. Answer: E.

Concept: *M203 Inequalities*

$6x + 12 > 7x - 35$

Simplify:

$12 + 35 > 7x - 6x$

$47 > x$

E. $x < 47$

30. Answer: K.

Concept: *M208 Coordinate Geometry & XY-plane*

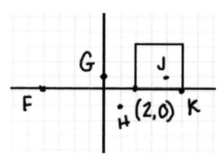

Only K is 3 units away from $(2, 0)$

K. $(5, 0)$

31. Answer: E.

Concept: *M302 Triangles*

It does not get much easier than this:

$A^2 + B^2 = C^2$

$y^2 = x^2 + 4^2$

$y = \sqrt{x^2 + 16}$

E. $\sqrt{x^2 + 16}$

32. Answer: G.

Concept: *M503 Probability*

Change $\dfrac{12}{32}$ to $\dfrac{3}{5}$

Strategy 1: BACKSOLVE

Add answers to both the numerator and denominator and reduce.

The new fraction's denominator is 5, therefore the right combination MUST be a multiple of 5; ending in 5 or 10. Answer choices **J** and **K** can be eliminated.

F: $\dfrac{12 + 13}{32 + 13} = \dfrac{25}{45} = \dfrac{5}{9}$

G: $\dfrac{12 + 18}{32 + 18} = \dfrac{30}{50} = \dfrac{3}{5}$

Strategy 2: Algebraic Solution

$\dfrac{12 + x}{32 + x} = \dfrac{3}{5}$

$5(12 + x) = 3(32 + x)$

$60 + 5x = 96 + 3x$

$2x = 36$

$x = 18$

G. 18

33. Answer: D.

Concept: *M208 Coordinate Geometry & XY-Plane*

$4x - 2y = 8$

The line is in standard form, to plot on *xy*-plane, just find the intercepts (zeros).

$4(0) - 2y = 8$

$-2y = 8$
$\div -2 \qquad \div -2$

$y = -4 \quad \rightarrow \quad (0, -4)$

$4x - 2(0) = 8$

$4x = 8$
$\div 4 \qquad \div 4$

$x = 2 \quad \rightarrow \quad (2, 0)$

Plot:

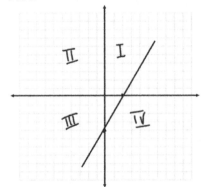

D. I, III, IV only

34. Answer: F.

Concept: *M207 Linear Functions: y=mx+b*

Substitute and solve

$y = -5x^2 + 9$

Substitute $(1, 2a)$

$(2a) = -5(1)^2 + 9$

$2a = -5 + 9$

$2a = 4 \; ; a = 2$

F. 2

35. Answer: D.

Concept: *M108 Ratio*

$$\frac{1}{2}(S) + \frac{1}{3}(S) + x(S) = S$$

$$\div S \qquad\qquad \div S$$

$$\frac{1}{2} + \frac{1}{3} + x = 1$$

$$\frac{5}{6} + x = 1$$

$$-\frac{5}{6} \qquad -\frac{5}{6}$$

$$x = \frac{1}{6}$$

Convert to ratio then multiply the entire thing by 6:

$$\frac{1}{2} : \frac{1}{3} : \frac{1}{6} \text{ is equal to } 3:2:1$$

D. 3 : 2 : 1

36. Answer: F.

Concept: *M215 Equation of Circle*

The equation of a circle in the standard (x, y) plane is:

$$(x - h)^2 + (y - k)^2 = r^2$$

Where (h, k) is the center of the circle and r is the radius.

$$(x - 5)^2 + y^2 = 38$$

$$r^2 = 38 \; ; r = \sqrt{38}$$

$$a = 5, b = 0 \text{ center is } (5, 0)$$

F. *Radius* $= \sqrt{38}$ *Center* $= (5, 0)$

Tip: *Be careful of negative signs for the center of a circle. They move like functions; a negative sign (x-5) moves the circle to the right.*

37. Answer: B.

Concept: *M308 Multiple Figures*

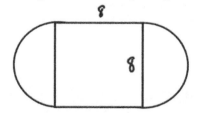

You are asked for the *outside* perimeter the figure. 2 semicircles make one circle; find circumference

$$C = \pi d; C = 8\pi$$

Add only *two* sides of the square.

B. $16 + 8\pi$

38. Answer: G.

Concept: *M308 Multiple Figures*

Two *midpoints* cut a rectangle in half, forming two congruent smaller rectangles.

$$ABEF \cong EFCD$$

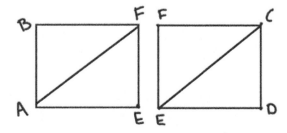

A diagonal of a rectangle cuts the rectangle into equal triangles.

$$\triangle ABF \approx \triangle AEF \; \& \; \triangle EFC \approx \triangle EDC$$

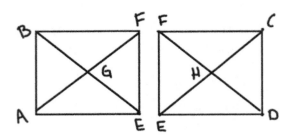

The diagonals of a rectangle intersect at the center of the rectangle and form four congruent triangles.

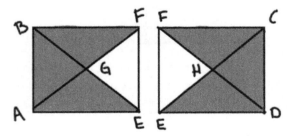

So each half of the rectangle is split into four equal pieces, one non-shaded piece and three shaded pieces, making a ratio of 1:3.

G. 3 : 1

> Tip: *"Midpoints" ALWAYS means cut in half!*

39. Answer: C.

Concept: *M207 Linear Functions: y=mx+b*

Trick: Read the question carefully. It is ONLY asking about x coordinates. The y coordinates are irrelevant.

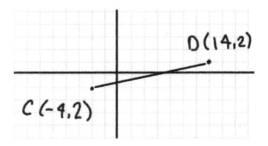

$$\text{Midpoint} = \frac{(14 - (-4))}{2}$$

$$-4 + 9 = 5$$

$$14 - 9 = 5$$

C. 5

40. Answer: G.

Concept: *M307 Solids*

Area of one face of a cube *side* is 8 = $8^2 = 64$

Six sides of a cube $6 \times 64 = 384$

G. 384

41. Answer: B.

Concept: *M210 Systems of Equations*

$$ay + bx = c$$

$$ay - bx = c$$

Put both equations into slope-intercept form:

$$y = -\frac{b}{a} \times + \frac{c}{a} \qquad * \text{slope} = -\frac{b}{a}$$

$$y = \frac{b}{a} \times + \frac{c}{a} \qquad * \text{slope} = \frac{b}{a}$$

I. Parallel Lines – No. Parallel lines have the same slope.

II. Intersecting Lines – Yes. Intersecting lines have different slopes (same y-intercept means that they intersect on the *x-axis*).

III. Single Line – No. Single lines have the same slope and the same y-intercept.

B. II only

42. Answer: F.

Concept: *M401 SOHCAHTOA*

$$S\frac{O}{H} \quad C\frac{A}{H} \quad T\frac{O}{A}$$

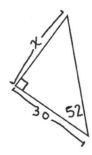

From the angle of 52°, the opposite side is *x* and the adjacent side is 30.

$$\tan\varnothing = \frac{opposite}{adjacent}$$

Solve for x:

$$\tan 52 = \frac{x}{30}$$
$$\scriptstyle \times 30 \qquad\qquad \times 30$$

$x = 30\ tan\ 52°$

F. 30 *tan* 52°

43. Answer: D.

Concept: *M505 Charts & Graphs*

(25 – 35) = 42% (all others) = 58%

42 : 58 = 21 : 29

D. 21 : 29

44. Answer: H.

Concept: *M308 Multiple Figures*

"Lines of symmetry" are lines where, when folded on them, each side is a mirror reflection. There are 8 ways to "fold" this figure.

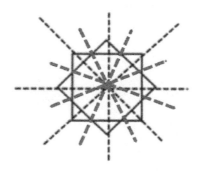

H. 8

45. Answer: A.

Concept: *M305 Circles*

Diameter = 2, so radius = 1

Area = πr^2 = 3.14

A. 3.1

46. Answer: J.

Concept: *M110 Percent*

The window will be 75% longer than 2 feet.

2 × 1.75 = 3.5

J. 3.50

47. Answer: C.

Concept: *M301 Lines & Angles*

BAC & ACD are supplementary (opposite interior and add up to 180.)

BAC = 82

ACD = 180 - 82 = 98

Each are *bisected*

$$\angle EAC = \frac{82}{2} = 41$$
$$\angle ACE = \frac{98}{2} = 49$$
$$\angle AEC = 180 - (41 + 49) = 180 - 90 = 90$$

C. 90

48. Answer: H.

Concept: *M305 Circles*

Arc angle is twice the angle of the two chords (lines).

Find the central angle of $\triangle$PST.

$\angle$TPS = 120.

$\angle$PST is supplementary to $\angle$RPS and therefore is equal to 60.

So, arc length = 60.

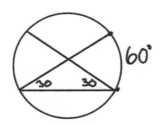

H. 60

49. Answer: B.

Concept: *M210 Systems of Equations*

Infinite solutions means "same line!"

1. Using slope intercept form

$$y = 2x - 8$$
$$y = 2x - \frac{4}{3}a$$

The two lines have the same slope, so now they need to have the same intercept.

Therefore:

$$-\frac{4}{3}a = -8 \qquad Solve\ for\ a$$
$$\div -\frac{4}{3} \qquad \div -\frac{4}{3}$$

$$a = 6$$

B. 6

50. Answer: F.

Concept: *M210 Systems of Equations*

The graph shows a horizontal line at $y = 2$, as the bottom constraint. Because this is a system of inequalities, the shaded area above the line $y = 2$ represents the number of large frames that she can make, whereas the x-axis represents number of small frames.

For example:
At the point (2,3), she *CAN* make 2 small and 3 large. But (3,1) will not be made since it is not shaded.

The *y* axis is the number of large frames. Therefore, she makes a minimum of 2 and a maximum of 8.

F. 2

51. Answer: C.

Concept: *M109 Rate & Proportion; M110 Percent*

For every hour = $3

Find the number of hours worked.

$Large = (3hrs)(4L) = 12hrs$

$Small = (2hrs)(2S) = 4hrs$

$Total = 12 + 4 = 16hrs$

$(\$3/hr)(16hrs) = \$48 \ donated$

Now find profit:
$30(2) + 70(4) = 340$

$Percent \ donated: \ 48/340 = .1411$

C. 14%

52. Answer: J.

Concept: *M210 Systems of Equations*

A maximum comes at the vertex of the polygon formed by the inequalities in linear programming (a system of linear inequalities).

In this case, the maximum profit is when she makes 8 large frames.

$(8 \ frames) \times (\$70) = \$560$

J. $560

53. Answer: E.

Concept: *M220 Matrix*

$ab - cb$

$x \times x - 8x = -16$

Solve for x:

$x^2 - 8x + 16 = 0$

A perfect square! Factor!

$(x - 4)(x - 4) \ or \ (x - 4)^2 = 0$

$x = 4$

E. 4

> Tip: *Don't sweat matrix determinant problems; the ACT is very nice and usually tells you exactly what to do.*

54. Answer: K.

Concept: M201 Algebraic Operations

This is algebra!

$A = P(1 + 0.01i)^n$

Solve for P!

$$\frac{A}{(1 + 0.1i)^n} = \frac{P(1 + 0.01i)^n}{(1 + 0.01i)^n}$$

$$P = \frac{A}{(1 + 0.01i)^n}$$

K. $\dfrac{A}{(1 + 0.01i)^n}$

55. Answer: C.

Concept: *M203 Inequalities*

"Must be true" means that the reader only needs to find one example that proves it wrong. Pick some numbers and get to work!

A. $\dfrac{x}{y} > 1$

Never true: A positive number divided by a negative number is always negative.

B. $|x|^2 > |y|$

This statement *could* be true, but is not always true.

Make $x = 2$ $y = -200$

$4 > 200$

C. $\dfrac{x}{3} - 5 > \dfrac{y}{3} - 5$

Simplify: add 5 to both sides and then multiply by 3

$x > y$

A positive number is always greater than a negative number.

This must be true.

D. $x^2 + 1 > y^2 + 1$

Use the same logic as B.

Make $x = 2$ & $y = -200$.

E. $x^{-2} > y^{-2}$

Use the same logic as B.

Make $x = 2$ & $y = -200$

C. $\dfrac{x}{3} - 5 > \dfrac{y}{3} - 5$

56. Answer: J.

Concept: *M302 Triangles*

Find the *height* of the triangles (also called *altitude*). And then compare triangles.

Set x as the base of both triangles:

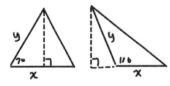

Then the trick is to see that the height is the same. The height, *h*, must be congruent using Angle-Side-Angle.

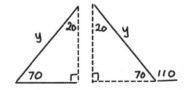

J. 30

57. Answer: E.

Concept: *M404 Laws of Sines/Cosines*

Use the Law of Cosines when there are two sides and an angle between them.

$$\overline{BC}^2 = 12^2 + 18^2 - 2(12)(18)\cos(40°)$$

E. $\overline{BC} = \sqrt{12^2 + 18^2 - 2(12)(18)\cos(40°)}$

Tip: *Memorize the Law of Sines and the Law of Cosines. Look at the examples of when each are used on the ACT. Generally, the ACT only asks you to set up the equation, not solve it.*

---

58. Answer: G.

Concept: *M106 Sequence*

For most sequences, I like to draw a picture of the number blanks.

From 8 to 13 moving 4 spaces is $\frac{(13-8)}{4}$.

Each space is $\frac{5}{4}$.

Find the first 4 terms.

Add them up: $1.75 + 3 + 4.25 + 5.5 = 14.5$

G. 14.5

59. Answer: C.

Concept: *M216 Quadratics & Parabolas*

If the only solution is $x = -3$ then the quadratic is $(x+3)^2 = 0$

Expand: $x^2 + 6x + 9 = 0; m = 6$

C. 6

Tip: *When a quadratic equation is equal to zero, you are solving for the "roots" – otherwise known as "factoring." When there is only one solution or root the quadratic is a "perfect square" with its vertex on the x axis.*

---

60. Answer: F.

Concept: *M204 Absolute Value*

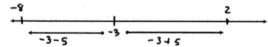

The solution set is (-8,2).

Either put the solution into the equations or solve the equations:

$|x + 3| = 5$

$(x + 3) = -5 \ or \ (x + 3) = 5$

$x = -8 \ or \ x = 2$

F. $|x + 3| = 5$

Tip: *Let the answer choices guide you. Absolute value is used to measure distance from zero. "5 units from -3" means numbers that are a distance of 5 units away from -3. 5 units to the left is -8, 5 units to the right is 2. Simple. .*

Reading 67C

1. Answer: D.

Concept: *R104 Big Picture*

It should be apparent that the narrator's point of view is that of an *adult* who is reflecting on their young-adulthood. As with most "broad scope" or big picture questions, there is support all over the passage, but reading the passage takes lots of time, so do narrow scope questions before returning to this one. Lines 30-60 offer a variety of support for this answer.

2. Answer: H.

Concept: *R201 Detail; R501 Least/Not/Except*

Remember that the reader is looking for an incorrect answer here. The narrator takes a train there and back, so answer choice **J** can be ruled out. Similarly with answer choice **F**, the narrator mentions dreams both on the way to and from her hometown. "Reunions" are not mentioned specifically, but the narrator is reunited with her family and the cosmonaut is reunited with the world upon landing, ruling out answer choice **G**. Photographs are not mentioned at all.

3. Answer: B.

Concept: *R201 Detail; R501 Least/Not/Except*

Read through quickly and see what is mentioned, but do *not* read past the paragraphs cited. The passage states that the train went past Chicago, not that she was from there.

4. Answer: G.

Concept: *R203 Inference/Assumption*

There is no concrete answer in the text, which is why the question asks for an *inference*. The author makes many observations about the changes in her town and her general nostalgia, but none of it is positive. She certainly indicates that it *has* changed, but not for the worse, so answer choices **H** and **J** are incorrect. Her tone indicates that she questions the progress that has been made (**G**), which does not suggest she thinks her hometown has improved.

5. Answer: B.

Concept: *R201 Detail; R501 Least/Not/Except*

Be wary of all the catches in this question! This is an *except* question, and asks specifically about what happened in the *past*. Read the answer choices and scan for the relevant words: "four-digit phone numbers," "football field," "ice cream," and "the depot.". It should be clear that the football field's fence is a new addition.

6. Answer: F.

Concept: *R201 Detail*

This may be intuitive for some readers. The tanning salon is clearly an outlier in terms of a "new business" versus an "old business." Otherwise, read the answer choices and scan the text for them, checking the context to see if they are new or old fixtures in the town.

7. Answer: C.

Concept: *R201 Detail; R101 Line Number*

Look at the context of the line. Having just discussed the dissolution of the Soviet Union, it should be clear that that is an important part of the answer. **D** is not really relevant to the question as it simply states a fact and heroism is never mentioned, so **B** is incorrect. Between answer choices **A** and **C** the correct answer is the one supported by facts from the text. There is no indication of the cosmonaut feeling like a "citizen of space," but there was a very clear political transformation that took place while he was in orbit.

8. Answer: F.

Concept: *R201 Detail; R203 Inference/Assumption*

Note: *this is a frequently missed question!*

Don't overthink this! There is only one person *stated* as meeting her at the train station (the porter), but the conversation suggests that she is speaking to a family member who had been playing cribbage against her father (probably her mother). However, based on the answer choices, it is clear that "her father" is included in who is meeting her at the station.

9. Answer: D.

Concept: *R201 Detail*

This question is quite straightforward. It may have struck the reader that the narrator was most worried about the gambling springing up at the edge of town when she said the other changes in town "pale in comparison" to "Las Vegas-style gambling."

10. Answer: H.

Concept: *R201 Detail*

Be careful to answer based on what the *news reports* said, not the narrator's own thoughts, which were different. The news reports stated that the cosmonaut's knees buckled due to "a lack of exercise," which is answer choice **H**.

11. Answer: C.

Concept: *R104 Big Picture*

It is not asking for the author's claims, but rather asking what the reader would first need to accept in order to appreciate the claims (regardless of what those claims are). However, the correct choice will still be supported by the text. The only relevant answer choice is **C** because it is supported by the passage's emphasis on innovation by small-scale producers, OELA in particular.

12. Answer: F.

Concept: *R101 Line Number*

As long as the basic premise of the passage is understood, answer choices **G** and **H** can be ruled out right away, and answer choice **J** (although it seems to answer the question) is contradictory to the actual process described.

13. Answer: C.

Concept: *R203 Inference/Assumption; R104 Big Picture*

It should be clear that the author is in favor of sustainably harvested wood for stringed instruments, which is also what the OELA is in favor of. Between the positive answers (**C** and **D**), the best answer is the one supported entirely by the text: the passage does not go into the details for the possibility of replicating this project, so it is incorrect.

14. Answer: G.

Concept: *R204 Main Idea/Function: Paragraph; R102 Paragraph Number*

Stick to the lines mentioned in the question; however, consider that this paragraph is introducing a problem. The next paragraph introduces the solution to that problem: Gomes' school. Answer choice **G** correctly states that the passage "explains the necessity" of Gomes' school. Answer choice **F** states the problem, which is important to the paragraph, but not the point. Answer choice **H** is incorrect because the Ford Foundation is only mentioned in a quote. Answer choice **J** is not relevant at all.

15. Answer: D.

Concept: *R204 Main Idea/Function: Paragraph; R102 Paragraph Number*

This question is much like the last one. Remember, the correct answer will be the purpose of the whole paragraph, *not* just a detail in it. Answer choices **A**, **B**, and **C** are *mentioned*, but are not the *purpose* of the paragraph. It should be clear that the paragraph is focused on how Gomes experimented with many different types of woods.

16. Answer: H.

Concept: *R201 Detail; R501 Least/Not/Except*

Tip: *the questions are often in chronological order!*

This question could be answered intuitively: the extinction of woods is the problem that Gomes is trying to solve, not an obstacle that he is facing currently. Thus, only answer choice **H** is correct. However, it can also be understood that the sixth, seventh, and eighth paragraphs introduce obstacles faced by Gomes and his project. These paragraphs mention the information in answer choices **F**, **G**, and **J**, indicating that answer choice **H** is *not* a problem now faced by the "fledgling Amazon guitar industry."

17. Answer: B.

Concept: *R201 Detail*

Read carefully! The question specifically pertains to what "most" students will go on to do, *not* simply what "some" will do. If this isn't apparent, one might incorrectly choose answer choice **D**. While only some go into politics, "virtually all of them return to their hometowns."

18. Answer: J.

Concept: *R201 Detail*

This question is as much basic math as it is reading. Scan quickly for the detail in question (lines 25-28), and do the math: 20 million out of 30 million is two-thirds.

19. Answer: A.

Concept: *R201 Detail; R501 Least/Not/Except*

All of these types of wood are mentioned in the paragraph, but Aniba canellila is "substituted" for ebony. This means that Aniba canellila is one of the new woods that can replace one of the traditional (endangered) woods.

20. Answer: F.

Concept: *R201 Detail*

Note that the question asks what the *student* receives, not the donor. The passage states explicitly that an environmentalist can "'adopt' a student by paying his or her tuition"; thus, answer choice **F** is correct.

21. Answer: C.

Concept: *R104 Big Picture*

Ask whether or not the narrator has *done* any of these things in the passage. He does not "discuss metaphysical questions," "present...key events in his thirty-year career," or "advise educators." He *does* reflect on how he "developed interest in philosophy." Therefore, answer choice **C** is correct.

22. Answer: J.

Concept: *R303 Chronology; R201 Detail*

Because his passion has always been there for him, the correct answer will be whatever topic he first mentions from a chronological perspective. In the text, this is the interest in lizards and butterflies, which he says predates his interest in chemistry.

23. Answer: A.

Concept: *R204 Main Idea/Function: Paragraph; R102 Paragraph Number*

Most of the answer choices are obviously incorrect: there is no indication of doubting Mr. Marsh, nor is there a biographical element beyond an introduction. There is no mention at all of his class. The best answer is **A**, as simple as it is, because it is the only one supported by the text.

24. Answer: J.

Concept: *R201 Detail*

Go back to the text and find the portion regarding the book cover. It states explicitly that the picture "is based on a story...about sitting on a bench...aged 18, pondering the metaphysical question." Therefore, answer choice **J** is correct.

25. Answer: C.

Concept: *R201 Detail; R101 Line Number*

Consider why the author discusses his hobby of drumming. Most of this text is spent discussing his "scholarship," and his lifelong scholarly energy. He provides a number of examples of how he expressed that scholarship, one of which was his interest in music and study of drumming technique. Though he is not a professional musician today, there was a time when he spent his energy on music. Thus, the answer is **C**.

26. Answer: F.

Concept: *R201 Detail; R102 Paragraph Number*

This is a very tough question! Answer choice **G** may seem correct as he states "swashing mental energy" can be "sometimes destructive"; however, that is *not* the same thing as "typically destructive" as stated in the answer. Answer choice **H** baits a similar trap. Answer choice **J** should appear clearly incorrect as it is not supported by the passage at all. This means that the energy is not easily used in a constructive way; thus, answer choice **F** is correct.

27. Answer: C.

Concept: *R104 Big Picture; R101 Line Number*

Look at the statement in question. Does the author seem to be saying that this is a problem for the students to solve, or the educators? Given how the passage goes on to describe Mr. Marsh's success in this regard, the latter is a reasonable inference. As such, the answer is either **A** or **C**. Nowhere does the author indicate that the answer is philosophy; in fact, his point seems more that philosophy just happened to be *his solution*. Answer choice **C** is correct because it is supported by the narrator's explanation of how an educator "tapped into his formless and fizzing mental energy."

28. Answer: J.

Concept: *R203 Inference/Assumption; R101 Line Number*

The question asks for part of the author's argument, so the answer must be one he argues for! Answer choices **F** and **G** are simply not related to the text, because he does not make these arguments anywhere. Answer choice **H** is perhaps even more outlandish an answer, as physical pain is not even alluded to in the text. The narrator states that with pen and paper one can "perform miracles," which indicates that answer choice **J** is correct.

29. Answer: A.

Concept: *R204 Main Idea/Function: Paragraph; R101 Line Number*

The lines in question refer to the descriptions of the cover. Several adjectives are used to describe the scene: "grey and listless," "bleak and melancholy," "pensive...frozen in thought." None of these descriptions suggest "anger" or "frustration," which eliminate answer choices **B** and **D**. Between answer choices **A** and **C**, it is simply a matter of which "best describes" those images. Answer choice **C** suggests a calm environment instead of a tense or grim one, so **A** is correct.

30. Answer: F.

Concept: *R101 Line Number; R501 Least/Not/Except*

This is a tough question! What transition is being described in those lines? The text states writing turns "an invisible thought into a concrete mark," "the ethereal interior into the public external, refining it into something precious." Thus, answer choices **H** and **J** should be immediately ruled out as they are

explicitly stated. (Remember this is a *NOT* question!) Answer choice **G** can be reasonably inferred because writing a thought down is turning something "fleeting" to something "permanent." The word "precious" is mentioned in the passage, but not from "precious to commonplace." Therefore, answer choice **F** does "NOT reasonably describe the transition" and is correct.

31. Answer: B.

Concept: *R301 Main Idea/Function: Passage*

Remember: *do "main idea" questions last!*

Answers **A** and **C** can be ruled out quickly because the text does nothing to support them. Between the remaining answers, which is the best choice as a *main idea*? Because **D** is just a factual detail, and not an idea being presented by the passage as a whole, it cannot be the answer.

32. Answer: H.

Concept: *R104 Big Picture*

Which of these is a significant development as presented in the text? Although **H** is not the only fact that is specifically mentioned, it is the choice which most correctly answers the question. As all of the information stated in the passage relies on Schmidt's discovery of the eel larvae in the Sargasso Sea, it can be reasonably inferred that it had the largest impact.

33. Answer: D.

Concept: *R204 Main Idea/Function: Paragraph; R102 Paragraph Number*

The incorrect answer choices describe *parts* of the correct answer. Answer choice **A** is only partially correct as the eels *also* go from the ocean to the freshwater; answer choice **B** is mentioned, but is not the main purpose; and answer choice **C** is not mentioned at all. Answer choice **D** correctly states the "main purpose" of the paragraph.

34. Answer: J.

Concept: *R201 Detail*

This detail is explicitly stated in lines 11-12: "The sea is...set off from the surrounding waters...by strong currents." Don't be tricked by all of the other geographical information mentioned in the paragraph!

35. Answer: B.

Concept: *R201 Detail*

This question is also just asking for a specific detail explicitly stated in the passage (lines 13-14). Scan quickly for the answer choices and double-check the context.

36. Answer: G.

Concept: *R202 Vocabulary in Context; R101 Line Number*

Always check the context! Often these questions give multiple valid definitions with only one correctly applicable to the passage. In this case, the correct answer is **G** because it refers to *popular* in the sense of pop-culture: "commonly known."

37. Answer: B.

Concept: *R202 Vocabulary in Context; R101 Line Number*

As in the above question, go back and look at the context! They are "reading" the rings of the eel's skull: which answer makes the most sense if substituted for the word "read?" The answer is **B**, because they are "observing" the structure.

38. Answer: F.

Concept: *R201 Detail*

The information about the pupil change is presented *before* the explanation of why. It states that their pupils changed *because* "they will need a new kind of sight adapted to the depths of the sea." Answer choice **G** is a trap because it is later mentioned and it may be assumed that they need a change in chemistry for this change to occur.

39. Answer: A.

Concept: *R201 Detail*

Scan the text for the word "osmosis." Look at the context and read it closely: it states they will use osmosis "to prepare for the tremendous change in water pressure."

40. Answer: F.

Concept: *R201 Detail*

Don't go too far back: this is the last question and the information is likely found near the end of the passage. In this case, it is stated in lines 80-81, that the larvae "were so small that it was certain they had been born recently, and nearby." Thus, it was "size" which provided the best evidence.

Science 67C

1. Answer: D.

Concept: *S202 Reading a Graph*

Study 1 is described in Figure 2. The highest percentage of beaks is represented by the tallest bar. On Island B (second bar chart), the tallest bar is at 10 mm. On Island C (third bar chart), the tallest bar is also at 10 mm.

2. Answer: J.

Concept: *S101 Find in Text; S202 Reading a Graph*

The text states "small seeds are abundant during wet years." The only bar marked "wet" on Figure 3 is 1984, so 1984 must have had many small seeds.

3. Answer: B.

Concept: *S102 Experimental Design/Parameters*

Study 1 mentions using both *G. fortis* and *G. fulginosa* finches. Study 2 only mentions *G. fortis* finches. Therefore, *G. fuliginosa* were not caught in Study 2.

4. Answer: J.

Concept: *S104 Inference; S301 Inquiry Process*

The only mention of the tags includes the information that the birds were tagged, measured, and released. It can be inferred from this information that the finches were tagged to ensure each bird was only measured once.

5. Answer: C.

Concept: *S101 Find in Text*

Figure 3 describes 1977 as a dry year. On the second page, the text states that during dry years, seeds are larger. In the second paragraph of the passage, the text states that birds with shallower beaks can only eat small seeds, and birds with deeper beaks can eat both large and small seeds. Thus, it can be inferred that the larger beak (9.9 mm) allows birds to eat larger seeds.

6. Answer: F.

Concept: *S103 Argumentation and Evidence; S202 Reading a Graph*

According to Figure 2, Island A has *G. fortis* competing with another species, whereas Island B does not. The range of beak sizes is larger on Island A than Island B.

7. Answer: D.

Concept: *S202 Reading a Graph*

Neither of the graphs in Figure 2 has a maximum in February (F). In Figure 3, SO_4^{2-} has a maximum in February (F) and a minimum in July (third J).

8. Answer: G.

Concept: *S205 Extrapolation*

In Figure 2, the average wet deposition for Cu^{2+}, which can be estimated as the middle of many values on the graph, is around 50. Since the maximum is farther away from 50 than the minimum, the average is likely just above 50 (between 50 and 75).

9. Answer: A.

Concept: *S207 Infer from Data*

In Figure 3, the Cl⁻ wet deposition is highest in November, January, February, March, and April, which is most of the winter and early spring.

10. Answer: H.

Concept: *S102 Experimental Design/Parameters*

The second and third paragraphs of the text states that deposition was calculated using collected precipitation. If there was no precipitation, there could be no wet deposition of any of the four substances.

11. Answer: C.

Concept: *S204 Trends*

Study 3 states that Site 2 is farther than Site 1. For both ions shown in Figure 4, Site 2 has a lower value than Site 1. Thus, as distance from the urban site increases, deposition decreases.

12. Answer: F.

Concept: *S301 Inquiry Process; S102 Experimental Design/Parameters*

The text states that Study 1 is done at a "specific urban site," and Study 2 uses the same sample. Since only one site is used, location is held constant.

13. Answer: B.

Concept: *S202 Reading a Graph*

In Figure 1, cloud cover is represented by a dashed line and the measurement is on the left axis. In January 1987, the dashed line is around 13.5%.

14. Answer: H.

Concept: *S205 Extrapolation*

In Table 1, for every 20,000 increase in cosmic ray flux, the cloud cover increases by 0.3%. At 440,000, which is 20,000 more than 420,000, the cloud cover would be 0.3% more than 29.0%, or 29.3%.

15. Answer: A.

Concept: *S206 Correlation*

Figure 3, which shows low cloud cover and cosmic ray flux, shows two lines that follow each other more closely than the cloud cover (dashed lines) on any of the other two graphs.

16. Answer: G.

Concept: *S208 Conversion*

In January 1992, the low cloud cover was around 28, the middle cloud cover was around 20, and the high cloud cover was around 13.5. The correct bar graph has the bars getting lower from left to right (from high to middle to low).

17. Answer: D.

Concept: *S101 Find in Text; S304 Chemistry*

According to the first paragraph, low clouds are 0 km to 3.2 km and high clouds are 6.0 km to 16.0 km. If high clouds are made of ice crystals but low clouds are not, it must mean the temperature in the high clouds is below the freezing point of water ($0°C$) and the temperature of the low clouds is above the freezing point of water.

18. Answer: F.

Concept: *S202 Reading a Graph*

In Figure 1, yellow is represented by the dotted line (left half of the graph). The only listed value that falls when the line is dotted rather than dashed is 0.80 mL.

19. Answer: B.

Concept: *S304 Chemistry; S101 Find in Text*

The passage states that the indicator is yellow if the pH is less than 6 and blue if the pH is greater than 7. Thus, the solution was neutral (pH of 7) where the solution is green, represented by the solid line and text in Figure 2 from 0.95 to 1.00 mL.

20. Answer: J.

Concept: *S205 Extrapolation*

Figure 2 shows that as the volume of titrant added increases (above about 0.30 mL), the conductivity also increases. The conductivity ast 2.00 mL is almost 3.5 kS/cm, so the conductivity for 2.30 mL would be higher. More specifically, at 1.70 mL, conductivity is roughly 2.5 mL and at 2.00 mL, conductivity is roughly 3.5 mL, so following that same pattern, at 2.30 mL, conductivity would be roughly 4.5 (certainly greater than 3.80).

21. Answer: C.

Concept: *S101 Find in Text*

According to the first paragraph, the titrant is an acid or base solution that is added to the sample solution. Experiment 1 states that NaOH is added to an HCl solution, so NaOH is the titrant and HCl is the sample solution. Experiment 2 states that acetic acid is used instead of HCl, so acetic acid would be the sample solution, although NaOH would still be the titrant.

22. Answer: J.

Concept: *S304 Chemistry; S104 Inference*

Experiment 1 states that the probe measures conductivity, which is how well an electrical current can pass through a substance.

23. Answer: A.

Concept: *S103 Argumentation and Evidence; S202 Reading a Graph*

In Figure 2, the line was dotted at 0.20 mL, so the solution was yellow and had a pH below 6. At 1.8 mL, the line was dashed, so the solution was blue and the pH was above 7. Thus, the evidence does not support the claim, since the solution was yellow at 0.2 mL and blue at 1.8 mL.

24. Answer: H.

Concept: *S305 Physics*

Student B states that Algol B "encountered" the Algol system and became part of the system. When stars and other very massive space objects move near each other, the gravitational force between their giant masses pulls them towards each other.

25. Answer: B.

Concept: *S101 Find in Text*

According to Student 1, when matter flowed from Algol B to Algol A, Algol B was a post-MS star. According to fact 4, a post-MS star produces its energy by fusion in a shell surrounding its center.

26. Answer: G.

Concept: *S106 Conflicting Viewpoints*

Student 2 states that Algol B was from a different system than Algol A and Algol C, and would likely agree with the statement that Algol A and Algol C were most similar.

27. Answer: C.

Concept: *S302 Science Math*

The text states Algol C is a 1.7-solar-mass star and a solar mass = the Sun's mass. Therefore, Algol C has a mass 1.7 times the mass of the sun, which is $1.7 \times 2.0 \times 10^{30} = 3.4 \times 10^{30}$.

28. Answer: G.

Concept: *S304 Chemistry*

Fact 3 describes nuclear fusion of protons, which can only occur at high temperature and pressure because protons are positively charged, and like charges repel each other.

29. Answer: B.

Concept: *S101 Find in Text*

Fact 5 states that larger stars move through stages faster than smaller stars. Student 1 states that Algol B was originally the most massive, which means it would have been the first to progress to MS.

30. Answer: H.

Concept: *S106 Conflicting Viewpoints*

Fact 5 states that larger stars move through stages faster than smaller stars. Student 2 states that Algol B was always less massive than Algol A, so Algol A would have spent less time being an MS star because it is more massive than Algol B.

31. Answer: C.

Concept: *S205 Extrapolation*

In Figure 2, Krypton in the 6L vessel is represented by the line with diamonds. Krypton is at around 250 torr at 7 g and 350 torr at 10 g, so would likely be around 450 torr at 13 g.

32. Answer: G.

Concept: *S305 Extrapolation*

5 L is between 3 L and 6 L, but closer to 6 L. In a 3 L vessel, 7 g of CO_2 is at around 1,000 torr. In a 6 L vessel, 7 g of CO_2 is at around 500 torr. In a 5 L vessel, 7 g of CO_2 would likely be between 500 and 1000 torr.

33. Answer: A.

Concept: *S202 Reading a Graph*

In Figure 1, 4 g of O_2 (line with dots) in a 3 L vessel is around 800 torr. In Figure 2, 4 g of O_2 (line with dots) in a 6 L vessel is around 400 torr. Thus, in the 6 L vessel, O_2 is half as much as in the 3L vessel.

34. Answer: J.

Concept: *S304 Chemistry*

In Figure 1, the CO_2 line (line with squares) is always at a lower pressure than the O_2 line (line with dots). O_2 will have more molecules per gram than CO_2 because it is lighter per molecule, so the pressure exerted by O_2 will be greater.

35. Answer: A.

Concept: *S304 Chemistry*

As temperature increases, pressure increases as well, because pressure is directly proportional to temperature. The experiment was done at 22°C, so at 14°C, the pressure would have been less. (Try it out: a balloon in the refrigerator will get smaller.)

36. Answer: G.

Concept: *S203 Reading a Figure; S302 Science Math*

In the figure, the lowest part of the "threshold of hearing" line ends around 2×10^1 Hz, which is 20 Hz.

37. Answer: A.

Concept: *S105 Text to Data; S203 Reading a Figure*

If hearing loss occurs at high frequencies, the top of the graph would be lower after loss (dotted line). Choice A is the only graph that has the top of the line (highest frequency) lower after loss.

38. Answer: F.

Concept: *S203 Reading a Figure*

In the figure, an S of 100% is always at a higher intensity (more to the right on the graph) than any other value of S. Sound in water (dotted line) always has a higher intensity than sound in air (dashed line) at the same frequency. Thus, the highest intensity would be in water at S=100%.

39. Answer: C.

Concept: *S207 Infer from Data*

All values on the "threshold of hearing" line are below 10^5 Hz, so humans can't hear sounds above that frequency.

40. Answer: J.

Concept: *S203 Reading a Figure*

For each S, the frequency changes as S stays the same. Thus, S does not depend on frequency.

ACT 64E (2009)

English

1. Answer: D.

Concept: *E204 Short and Simple; E211 Parallel Structure*

Each of these answer choices is grammatically correct. In this case, pick the shortest and simplest answer choice. However, notice that the specification of a person isn't necessary for the analogy to operate effectively: "unbricking a kiln… is like uncovering buried treasure."

2. Answer: H.

Concept: *E201 Relevancy: Adding, Deleting, and Replacing Information*

The question specifically wants to suggest a "cautious pace and sense of anticipation." The answer choice that does so without being overly wordy is answer choice **H**.

3. Answer: A.

Concept: *E101 Verbs: Agreement/Tense*

Find the subject of the sentence! The subject here is "an expanding view," which is singular. The verb "reward" must agree in number with the subject. Therefore, "an expanding view rewards" (**A**) is correct.

Tip*: Be careful when the word "of" appears in a sentence about verb agreement - it's an easy way to put distance between the subject and the verb.*

4. Answer: G.

Concept: *E202 Word Choice: Correct Word*

Ellen must be "typical *of* something" because that is how the construction works. The sentence correctly structured is simply stating that Ellen is "like" other potters. Between **F** and **G**, answer choice **F** would change the meaning of the comparison to state that Ellen is like "many more" potters without referencing a standard.

5. Answer: D.

Concept: *E204 Short and Simple*

Each of these answer choices says essentially the same thing as the introductory clause "over many weeks." Answer choices **A**, **B**, and **C** repeat this same idea and are, therefore, redundant. Thus, omitting it makes the most sense.

6. Answer: H.

Concept: *E104 Nonessential Information: Commas, Dashes, Parentheses*

Notice that only two of these *could* be correct without breaking a comma rule. Answer choices **F** and **G** would make the second clause an independent clause, which would then require a conjunction after the comma. Therefore, the only two possible choices are **H** and **J**. Answer choice **J** would make the second clause about "bricks" and the description would be incorrect. Answer choice **H** correctly makes the second clause dependent and the description of the kiln accurate.

7. Answer: B.

Concept: *E201 Relevancy: Adding, Deleting, and Replacing Information*

Remember that the correct answer will have the correct *support*. The "yes or no" portion is not as important as the support. The support will correctly match the quotation the author is removing. Answer choice **B** is correct because "transform glazes to glorious colors" explains "the role of kilns." "The role" is to transform glazes.

8. Answer: F.

Concept: *E204 Short and Simple*

Each of these answer choices says essentially the same thing. In situations such as this, pick the shortest and simplest answer: **F**. The wrong answers are redundant or too wordy.

9. Answer: B.

Concept: *E104 Nonessential Information: Commas, Dashes, Parentheses*

If there is a clause or phrase surrounded by commas, see if it can be removed. If so, it is a *nonessential clause*. The main independent clause reads "The next morning she starts a small blaze…," so the nonessential information "using twigs for kindling" must be set between two commas to offset it correctly. Any other answer choice other than **B** would drastically change the sentence, and **C** incorrectly uses a semicolon instead of a colon.

10. Answer: F.

Concept: *E201 Relevancy: Adding, Deleting, and Replacing Information*

The correct answer will indicate that the "fire is extremely intense." Answer choice **J** says "kind of intense," which is (ironically) *not* as

intense as the other choices. Answer choices **H** doesn't indicate intensity, just that there is more heat. Answer choices **F** and **G** are best, but "a controlled inferno" is simply more descriptive.

11. Answer: D.

Concept: *E202 Word Choice: Correct Word*

This is a *NOT* question, so eliminate the correct answers and choose the one that is incorrect. The incorrect answer, **D**, is wrong because the idiomatic expression is "time and again," not "time or again." Each of the other answer choices are synonymous with the underlined portion.

12. Answer: F.

Concept: *E202 Word Choice: Correct Word*

Three of these answer choices indicate the same thing: sparks are coming out of the chimney and into the sky. Only answer choice **F** indicates that sparks are somehow being shot at the chimney which is in the sky.

13. Answer: C.

Concept: *E201 Relevancy: Adding, Deleting, and Replacing Information*

The question specifies that the correct answer choice will have "the most specific detail." Answer choice **C** gives the most specific detail without being overly verbose as in **D**.

14. Answer: J.

Concept: *E206 Modification: Dangling Modifiers*

There's a lot going on here, so take the answer choices one by one. Both **F** and **H** are dangling modifiers indicating that it is "she" (Ellen) that "dies down" or that "she has a blaze that dies." Answer choice **G** creates a new independent clause and fails to separate it correctly from the following independent clause with a period, semicolon, or comma-FANBOYS. So answer choice **J** is correct as it correctly makes the first phrase a proper prepositional introductory clause.

15. Answer: A.

Concept: *E211 Parallel Structure*

Answer choice **A** is correct because "of her labor" and "of the fire's magic" must be parallel. More specifically, since "labor" and "the fire's magic" are objects of *results*, the prepositions must match. Answer choice **D** is grammatically correct, but is too long. Remember, even here, short and simple wins.

16. Answer: J.

Concept: *E204 Short and Simple*

Each of these answer choices says essentially the same thing. In situations such as this, pick the shortest and simplest answer. Notice also that each answer repeats information that is already explicit or implicit in the phrase "business trip."

17. Answer: C.

Concept: *E205 Transition Words/Phrases*

This is a *NOT* question, so three of the answer choices are essentially synonymous with "soon." "Not long," "a short time," and "shortly" are all synonymous when inserted into this sentence. Answer choice **C** would change the meaning of the sentence and would not correctly end the construction of the phrase begun with "as."

18. Answer: F.

Concept: *E102 Commas*

First, eliminate answer choice **J** because semicolons are for separating two independent clauses. Answer choice **G** places a single comma between the subject and verb, which eliminates it. Answer choice **H** is incorrect would make the subject and verb part of a nonessential construction between the comma placed at the beginning of the sentence.

19. Answer: B.

Concept: *E201 Relevancy: Adding, Deleting, and Replacing Information*

"But" is a transition word, and contradicts what comes before it. Answer choice **A** is wrong because this phrase indicates what *did* happen, not what will *eventually* happen. Answer choice **D** just isn't relevant to the short deleted phrase. Answer choice **C** looks similar to **B**, so it's important to look for the differences. Answer choice **C** is wrong because although she might have been expecting a ring or a bracelet, that doesn't necessarily mean those are the types of gifts she usually receives.

20. Answer: F.

Concept: *E101 Verbs: Agreement/Tense*

Answers choices **H** and **J** are simply incorrect. (The contraction is "could've!") Answer choice **G** is grammatically correct, but it would mean that Rosie had "heard about them talking," not them actually talking.

21. Answer: C.

Concept: *E103 Independent Clauses: Period, Semicolon, Comma and FANBOYS*

> ### Separating Independent Clauses
> 1. Period
> 2. Semicolon
> 3. Comma FANBOYS

This is a *NOT* question, so three of the answer choices are the same. There's a quick trick to discovering which answer choice doesn't fit. Answer choice **C** is composed of two *independent clauses* linked by a comma, not a period, semicolon, or a comma-FANBOYS. Words like "after," "when," and "once" are dependent clause markers; without those words, there are two independent clauses without a proper construction to link them.

22. Answer: F.

Concept: *E208 Moving Sentences*

This sentence has to link *very specifically and concretely* to either the sentence before it or the sentence after it. Look for vagueness, particularly vague pronouns, that need a reference or antecedent. There are *two* in this sentence: "this" and "she." The "she" is the same "she" in Sentence 1 and "this" is the tortoise in Sentence 1. Since Sentence 2 begins with "Rosie," she must have already been introduced.

23. Answer: B.

Concept: *E104 Nonessential Information: Commas, Dashes, Parentheses*

Whenever an answer choice has commas around a word or group of words, see if they can be taken out. "It turns out" can be removed and left with a grammatically correct sentence. So answer choice **B** must be the correct answer.

24. Answer: H.

Concept: *E202 Word Choice: Correct Word*

This is a *NOT* question, so eliminate the *grammatically correct* answers and choose the one that is *incorrect*. Answer choices **F**, **G**, and **J** are grammatically synonymous. Answer choice **H** incorrectly uses the preposition "up," which immediately changes the meaning of the sentence.

25. Answer: B.

Concept: *E101 Verbs: Agreement/Tense*

Each of these answers is *grammatically* correct, so it is likely a question of *tense.* Look for other verbs in the sentence: "agreed" is in the past tense, so answer choice **B** is correct. Answer choice **A** indicates that she was going to check but didn't, and **C** and **D** indicate that she would do it in the future.

26. Answer: G.

Concept: *E201 Relevancy: Adding, Deleting, and Replacing Information*

The question asks which choice is most relevant— "effectively introduces" —what follows in the paragraph. The next few sentences indicate that the paragraph is about tortoise care. Thus, the correct answer is **G**.

27. Answer: D.

Concept: *E204 Short and Simple; E203 Word Choice: Tone*

Answer choice **C** is too informal, so eliminate it. Answer choices **A**, **B**, and **D** essentially say the same thing, so pick the shortest and simplest answer.

28. Answer: F.

Concept: *E201 Relevancy: Adding, Deleting, and Replacing Information*

The clue is in the question: "specific and precise." Answer choices **G**, **H**, and **J** are not as specific as answer choice **F**, which indicates *exactly* what kind of food.

29. Answer: A.

Concept: *E106 Apostrophes: Possessive, Plural, and Contractions*

"Parents" is plural and so is "backyards." Therefore, the correct answer is a plural possessive (*s'*) because there are multiple things being owned by multiple people.

30. Answer: G.

Concept: *E202 Word Choice: Correct Word*

"Family" must be plural because there is one out "of" a group. It is simply incorrect to say "families in reptiles." Think of it as "the tortoise is one *of* many reptile families."

31. Answer: B.

Concept: *E106 Apostrophes: Possessive, Plural, and Contractions*

First, "family" must be singular because there is no indication that he had more than one family. Since the "farm" is owned by his parents, it is possessive, so the correct answer is **B**.

32. Answer: F.

Concept: *E206 Modification: Dangling Modifiers*

This is a *NOT* question, so eliminate the *correct* answers and choose the one that is *incorrect*. The correct choice—the grammatically incorrect choice—is **F**. Answer choice **F** would indicate that Banneker himself limited his education, which is not the case here.

33. Answer: B.

Concept: *E105 Pronouns: Agreement/Case*

People are "who" and "whom"; things are "which" and "that." Since there are commas around "after completing . . . contract," that means they're nonessential information commas. If the information between the commas is deleted, answer choice **D** should sound wrong. Since the pronoun is referring to the subject of the sentence, "Banneker's grandmother," the answer must be "who."

34. Answer: J.

Concept: *E201 Relevancy: Adding, Deleting, and Replacing Information*

Remember: the support must be correct for the answer to be correct! While tangentially related, the sentence shifts the focus from biographical information about Banneker's grandmother to a detailed definition of indentured servitude. Thus, the answer is **J**. Answer choice **F** is technically correct, but the support does not mean the answer "should be added," as requested by the question.

35. Answer: C.

Concept: *E103 Independent Clauses: Period, Semicolon, Comma and FANBOYS*

> **Separating Independent Clauses**
>
> 1. Period
> 2. Semicolon
> 3. Comma FANBOYS

This is a *NOT* question and the portion underlined is the point at which two independent clauses meet. Three of the answer choices will be the correct way to conjoin two independent clauses. Answer choice **C** is incorrect because it is a run-on sentence.

36. Answer: H.

Concept: *E102 Commas*

This is a difficult question. In general, it is best to consider what the active verb is in order to determine how to arrange a complex predicate. In this case, the important action is the "displaying." The additional parts are modifications, telling what and how he displayed. There is also a chronological order to this information: his interest and skills must be there before he can actually construct a clock!

37. Answer: C.

Concept: *E106 Apostrophes: Possessive, Plural, and Contractions*

The possessive form should be used because the "components" are possessed by the pocket watch.

Remember: *"its" is possessive; "it's" is a conjunction that means "it is."*

38. Answer: H.

Concept: *E101 Verbs: Agreement/Tense*

This is a difficult question. Answer choices **F** and **J** should appear incorrect immediately as they are present tense and the passage is written in the past tense. The other two answer choices are grammatically correct and may appear to be the same thing. However, "has kept" would mean that the clock *is still* keeping time, but the passage states that the clock was built in 1753. There's no indication that this passage was written in 1793, so it is safe to assume that "kept" would be the correct verb.

39. Answer: D.

Concept: *E203 Word Choice: Tone*

The additional exclamations and adjectives are not only unnecessary, but inappropriate for the tone of the passage. They are informal and should not be included in this informative piece.

40. Answer: F.

Concept: *E103 Independent Clauses: Period, Semicolon, Comma and FANBOYS; E205 Transition Words/Phrases*

The transition word "therefore" is inappropriate in this context because it indicates cause and effect, but there is no reason to believe that his responsibility of the farm *caused* his interest in scientific studies. Answer choice **H** (which has nested commas) would mean that the transition word and the commas could be taken out without altering the sentence, but there are two independent clauses here that must be separated with either a period, a semicolon, or a comma and a conjunction. Therefore, answer choice **F** is correct.

41. Answer: A.

Concept: *E201 Relevancy: Adding, Deleting, and Replacing Information*

It's easiest to answer this question through elimination. There is no direct link to the previous paragraph about the clock he made, ruling out answer choice **B**. There is neither humor present nor an "extensive" digression. If the reader cannot find where the "love of learning" is mentioned (at the end of the first paragraph), process of elimination would easily remove the other answer choices.

42. Answer: G.

Concept: *E105 Pronouns: Agreement/Case*

The use of a pronoun here is simply too ambiguous as there are multiple nouns in the previous sentence that are plural (studies, calculations, celestial bodies). It is far more appropriate to address the calculations directly.

43. Answer: D.

Concept: *E204 Short and Simple*

It is redundant to use any of the answer choices because the word "annual" is used immediately beforehand, already dictating the yearly nature of the data. Only omitting the underlined portion could possibly be correct.

44. Answer: J.

Concept: *E210 Writer's Goal*

How would one best summarize the entirety of the essay? The answer will be neither too broad nor too specific. Answer choice **J** quickly mentions all of the things that Banneker did and summarizes his personality. The other answer choices focus on information that is too specific, turning details into major themes.

45. Answer: A.

Concept: *E209 Moving Paragraphs*

This is the most logical place for the paragraph to be placed. Banneker has been introduced, his character illustrated, and this development was led into by the preceding information. For further proof, double-check the years mentioned in each paragraph and it will be obvious that the paragraph is in the right spot.

46. Answer: J.

Concept: *E204 Short and Simple*

As is often the case, omission is the correct answer. It's redundant to describe the wilderness as "wild," "remote," or "uncivilized."

47. Answer: C.

Concept: *E105 Pronouns: Agreement/Case*

As the prior sentence refers to "kayaks" as a whole, the plural pronoun "they" is appropriate in answer choice **C**. "Which are" would make the entire sentence dependent.

48. Answer: G.

Concept: *E201 Relevancy: Adding, Deleting, and Replacing Information*

Remember, it is not the "yes or no" portion which is important, but the *support* that is being utilized. (Especially in this question where it could go either way!) As it does not differentiate types of kayaks, nor is it wordy or irrelevant, the best option is **G** because it *does* provide a visual description.

49. Answer: C.

Concept: *E103 Independent Clauses: Period, Semicolon, Comma and FANBOYS*

Do not be confused by this, as it seems to begin a list. "The two principal types of kayaks" is the subject of the sentence. Unless the sentence is simply stating that the kayaks exist (i.e. "They are." "I am."), which it isn't, the two types of kayaks have to *be* something.

50. Answer: J.

Concept: *E203 Word Choice*

As the size is being compared between only *two* types of kayaks, "larger" is correct, not "largest." Answer choice **G** is outlandish and **H** is what "larger" replaces.

51. Answer: C.

Concept: *E104 Nonessential Information: Commas, Dashes, Parentheses*

Tip: *find the independent clause!*

The subject of the sentence is "kayaking in white water" and the verb is "appeals." (Remember: -ing words are not verbs!) The clause underlined in the question is a *nonessential clause* which means it requires either a pair of commas, parentheses, or dashes to offset them from the rest of the sentence. The nonessential information is simply a clarification of what "white water" is. Thus, the comma should be placed before "the tumultuous rapids" and after "rivers."

52. Answer: J.

Concept: *E205 Transition Words/Phrases*

Although not at the start of the sentence, this is still a transition word. The correct choice is "nevertheless" (answer choice **J**) because it presents a fact which seems to be contrary to the previous statement: that kayakers wear safety gear even though the kayaks are quite safe.

53. Answer: D.

Concept: *E205 Transition Words/Phrases*

This is essentially a *NOT* question. The three grammatically correct versions will be synonymous with what is already printed in the passage. The use of "yet" as a transition word makes answer choice **D** the *least* viable option because "yet" indicates contrary information, but the information introduced in the prior clause is causative. Answer choices **A**, **B**, and **C** correctly introduce the next sentence as *resulting* from the information that "kayaks can float in less than a foot of water."

54. Answer: F.

Concept: *E203 Word Choice: Tone*

The most appropriate name for the person in this sentence is "nature watcher" because it adequately describes what they do as well as why this is relevant to them. Answer choice **H** may seem tempting, but the phrase "a paddler can quietly paddle" would be redundant and the ACT *hates* redundancy!

55. Answer: C.

Concept: *E209 Moving Paragraphs*

The break would be most appropriate at Sentence 5 because this is where the second topic, the sea kayak, is introduced. There is no transitional word or phrase, so the ideas are best separated down the middle.

56. Answer: G.

Concept: *E101 Verbs: Agreement/Tense*

The subject of this sentence is "equipment," NOT "kayaks." As such, a singular verb conjugation is necessary.

57. Answer: B.

Concept: *E103 Independent Clauses: Period, Semicolon, Comma and FANBOYS*

Separating Independent Clauses

1. Period
2. Semicolon
3. Comma FANBOYS

Out of the answer choices available, only answer choices **B** or **C** are appropriate. Answer choice **A** is a comma splice and **D** is a run-on sentence. A conjunction is necessary here. Of course, any conjunction is *possible*, but in this case "so" (answer choice **C**) would mean that the paddle *causes* the sprayskirt to fit around the paddler, which is nonsense. Answer choice **B** correctly connects them with the simple conjunction "and."

58. Answer: J.

Concept: E206 *Modification: Moving Modifiers*

Consider each option one at a time. As it stands, there is *nothing* being pulled "*through* the water of the paddle," which doesn't make sense. Answer choice **G** would split the subject and verb with the prepositional phrase, which is incorrect without nested commas and would make this sentence difficult to understand. Answer choice **H** would put the water before the paddle that is being drawn through it, which is also incorrect. Only answer choice **J** correctly puts the paddle before the water that it is being drawn through.

59. Answer: B.

Concept: *E203 Adjectives and Adverbs*

The word "but" does not always mean that a comma is necessary. A comma-FANBOYS on the ACT means that there must be *two independent clauses* (one before and one after the comma-FANBOYS construction), but this is not the case here, so **A** is wrong. A semicolon is the same thing, so **D** is also incorrect. Hyphens or dashes indicate an explanation or list is to follow, which is not the case here so **C** is also wrong. The phrase "simple but versatile" does not require a comma as it is essentially an adjectival phrase describing the boat.

60. Answer: G.

Concept: *E201 Relevancy: Adding, Deleting, and Replacing Information*

Process of elimination is the best route for answering this question. It is not difficult to determine this paragraph is not a detailed description of muscles, nor a scientific explanation, nor a plea of safety. Even if it doesn't *seem* like a "relationship," the other three answer choices are obviously incorrect.

61. Answer: C.

Concept: *E206 Modification: Moving Modifiers*

This latter portion of the sentence is a long modifier. "Seams" is modified by "of burning rock miles beneath Earth's surface." There is no reason to punctuate within this modification.

62. Answer: J.

Concept: *E103 Independent Clauses: Period, Semicolon, Comma and FANBOYS*

As written in the passage, there is an independent and a dependent clause, but they can be combined in a variety of ways if other elements are added. Answer choices **F**, **G**, and **H** correctly conjoin these two clauses by adding a subject to the second clause to make it independent, or a comma to keep the dependent clause correctly separated. Answer choice **J** incorrectly separates an independent clause from a dependent clause with a period, but a dependent clause can't stand on its own!

63. Answer: C.

Concept: *E211 Parallel Structure*

The verb "to feed" can be assumed correct as it isn't underlined, so the same conjugation should be applied to the second "to breed" (**C**). Answer choice **B** is grammatically correct, but does not match the structure of the sentence.

64. Answer: H.

Concept: *E203 Word Choice: Tone*

Phrases such as "to a tee" or "all right" are casual and inappropriate for a formal, informative essay. Instead, the clear and concise option **H** is appropriate.

65. Answer: B.

Concept: *E211 Parallel Structure*

The list here should, first and foremost, be corrected to use "too" instead of "to." The difference between the remaining answers is the concluding comma, which should not be included as it incorrectly separates the modifications from their subject.

66. Answer: G.

Concept: *E104 Nonessential Information: Commas, Dashes, Parentheses*

The additional clause here, "called extremophiles," is not actually a functional part of the sentence. As such, a comma on each end denotes it as separate and nonessential (**G**).

67. Answer: D.

Concept: *E103 Independent Clauses: Period, Semicolon, Comma and FANBOYS*

The two independent clauses provided can be separated in a number of ways. They can be separated in the traditional way (period, semicolon, or comma-FANBOYS) or it might be apparent that the second independent clause is a clarification or explanation that can be separated with a hyphen. However, it should be immediately apparent that answer choice **D**, which doesn't punctuate at all, is a run-on sentence and incorrect.

68. Answer: J.

Concept: *E101 Verbs: Agreement/Tense*

There is no indication anywhere in the passage that thermophiles no longer exist, so the simple present-tense conjugation "flourish" is appropriate because the action is continuing in the present.

69. Answer: D.

Concept: *E204 Short and Simple*

This additional information is irrelevant and should be deleted. The same is true for the replacement options. The ACT loves clarity and conciseness and does not abide redundancy.

70. Answer: G.

Concept: *E201 Relevancy: Adding, Deleting, and Replacing Information*

Remember, it is not the "yes or no" that matters: the correct answer will have the correct supporting evidence. Answer choice **F**, while true, is not as relevant as answer choice **G** which is *functionally necessary* to understanding the passage. Without the phrase in question, the following sentence loses crucial information. Answer choices **H** and **J** are simply untrue.

71. Answer: A.

Concept: *E203 Word Choice: Tone*

The correct answer choice will be a "specific" and "vivid" description of the "underwater terrain." This usually means the correct choice will be very descriptive. Answer choices **B**, **C**, and **D** only state that the results of activity are "apparent" or "evident," whereas answer choice **A** provides a specific description of how the ocean floor is "scarred."

72. Answer: J.

Concept: E206 *Modification: Moving Modifiers*

It is important that each modification is clearly matched to its subject. The modification "from cracks" best modifies the verb "gush," and so should follow it. This also shifts the remaining words into a sensible order.

73. Answer: A.

Concept: *E205 Transition Words/Phrases*

Answer choice **A** is the LEAST correct because it does not specify the psychrophiles' affinity for cold. This is a necessary detail to provide a contrast to the previous paragraph.

74. Answer: G.

Concept: *E201 Relevancy: Adding, Deleting, and Replacing Information*

This portion of the sentence is important to making a real connection to the scientific conjecture which follows. Answer choice **G** is the only answer which accurately connects its support to both the question *and* the context.

75. Answer: D.

Concept: *E205 Transition Words/Phrases*

Answer choices **A-C** imply some sort of contradiction or seemingly contrary evidence, whereas this is in fact introducing an idea in total agreement with the preceding sentence. Only "indeed" builds off of the former sentence without implying something to the contrary will follow.

Math 64E

1. Answer: D.

Concept: *M204 Absolute Value*

$|7 - 3| - |3 - 7| = ?$

$|4| - |-4| = ?$

$4 - 4 = 0$

D. 0

Tip: *Absolute value works like parentheses or grouping symbols. You must do the work inside BEFORE taking the absolute value.*

---

2. Answer: G.

Concept: *M212 Linear Function: Rate*

$\$45/hour \ + \ \$30 \ flat \ fee$

$210 = 45(hours \ worked) + 30$

$210 = 45x + 30$
$\quad -30 \qquad\quad -30$

$180 = 45x$
$\div 45 \quad\ \div 45$

$4 = x$

G. 4

3. Answer: C.

Concept: *M109 Rate & Proportion*

$Vehicle \ A: \dfrac{1008 \ mi}{\dfrac{14 \ mi}{gal}} = 72$

$Vehicle \ B: \dfrac{1008 \ mi}{\dfrac{36 \ mi}{gal}} = 28$

$72 - 28 = 44$

C. 44

4. Answer: J.

Concept: *M201 Algebraic Operations*

$t^2 - 59t + 54 - 82t^2 + 60t$

Combine like terms:

$-81t^2 + t + 54$

J. $-81t^2 + t + 54$

5. Answer: C.

Concept: *M308 Multiple Figures*

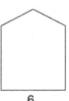

6

$5 \times 6 = 30$

C. 30

6. Answer: J.

Concept: *M217 Factoring & FOIL*

$(4z + 3)(z - 2)$

$4z^2 - 8z + 3z - 6$

J. $4z^2 - 5z - 6$

7. Answer: C.

Concept: *M110 Percent*

Given number = x

40% *of* $x = 8$

$(0.4)x = 8$

$x = \dfrac{8}{.4} = 20$

$(.15)(20) = 3$

C. 3

8. Answer: H.

Concept: *M103 Properties of Integers*

$$\begin{aligned} x - 2 \\ x - 1 \\ x \\ x + 1 \\ x + 2 \\ + \; x + 3 \end{aligned}$$

————

$6x + 3$

$6x + 3 = 447$
$\quad -3 \qquad -3$

$6x = 444$
$\div 6 \qquad \div 6$

$x = 74$

H. 74

9. Answer: D.

Concept: *M208 Coordinate Geometry & XY-plane*

Draw a picture!

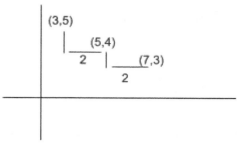

OR

$\dfrac{7 + x}{2} = 5$ $\dfrac{3 + y}{2} = 4$
$\;\times 2 \qquad\quad \times 2 \qquad\qquad\; \times 2 \qquad\quad \times 2$

$7 + x = 10$ $3 + y = 8$
$\; -7 \qquad\; -7 \qquad\qquad -3 \qquad\; -3$

$x = 3$ $y = 5$

D. $(3, 5)$

Tip: *Midpoint means average of x and y.*

10. Answer: F.

Concept: *M208 Coordinate Geometry & XY-plane*

Draw the 4th point

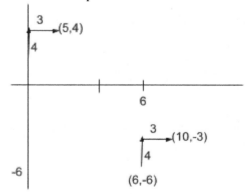

F. $(10, -3)$

11. Answer: E.

Concept: *M220 Matrix*

$$\begin{array}{c} \\ x \\ y \end{array} \begin{array}{ccc} A & B & C \\ \begin{bmatrix} 100 & 200 & 150 \\ 120 & 50 & 100 \end{bmatrix} \end{array} \quad \begin{array}{c} A \\ B \\ C \end{array} \begin{bmatrix} 5 \\ 10 \\ 15 \end{bmatrix}$$

$x = 100 \times 5 + 200 \times 10 + 150 \times 15 = 4750$

$y = 120 \times 5 + 50 \times 10 + 100 \times 15 = 2600$

$4750 + 2600 = 7350$

E. 7350

12. Answer: J.

Concept: *M301 Lines & Angles; M302 Triangles*

$y = 180 - 72 = 108$

$x = 180 - 57 = 123$

$z = 180 - 51 = 129$

$108 + 123 + 129 = 360$

J. 360

> Tip: *The sum of the EXTERIOR angles of a triangle is 360.*

13. Answer: A.

Concept: *M110 Percent; M506 Tables*

Whitney $= 30$

$\dfrac{30}{200} \times 100 = 15\%$

A. 15%

14. Answer: H.

Concept: *M508 Sampling*

$Lue = \dfrac{80}{200} = \dfrac{x}{10,000} = 4,000$

H. 4,000

15. Answer: B.

Concept: *M306 Sectors & Arcs*

$\dfrac{40}{200} = \dfrac{x^{\circ}}{360}$

$\dfrac{40 \times 360}{200} = x^{\circ}$

$72 = x^{o}$

B. 72°

> Tip: *The ACT loves 360÷5=72°; it is one of their favorite angles! Memorize!*

16. Answer: G.

Concept: *M308 Multiple Figures; M108 Ratio*

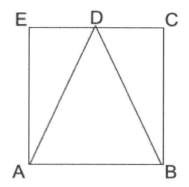

Plug in your own numbers

$\overline{AB} = 4$

$area \,\Delta ADE = (\tfrac{1}{2})(2)(4) = 4$
$area \,\Delta ADB = (\tfrac{1}{2})(4)(4) = 8$

$4 : 8 = 1 : 2$

G. 1 : 2

17. Answer: E.

Concept: *M207 Linear Functions: y=mx+b*

$y = \dfrac{2}{3}x - 4$

E. $\dfrac{2}{3}$

> Tip: *Parallel lines have the SAME slope.*

18. Answer: H.

Concept: *M108 Ratio*

Trick: Use the ratio box!

2	:	3	=	5

$x6$	$x6$	$x6$	multiplier
12	18	30	

H. 12

19. Answer: C.

Concept: *M103 Properties of Integers; M205 Exponents & Roots*

$\sqrt{58} = 7.6157$

C. 8

20. Answer: G.

Concept: *M303 Quadrilaterals*

Area of walls:
$4 \times (10 \times 15) = 600 \; sq \, ft$

$600 - window - door$

$600 - (3 \times 5) - (3.5 \times 7) = 560.5 \; sq \, ft$

$\dfrac{560.5}{300} = 1.8$

G. 2

> Tip: *Question #20 is going to be easy. When doing easy problems, estimate and don't be afraid to think it through. Usually you get to the answer quickly, saving precious time for harder problems.*

21. Answer: A.

Concept: *M217 Factoring & FOIL*

Factor:

$x^2 + 2x = 8$
$ -8 \qquad -8$

$$x^2 + 2x - 8 = 0$$

$$(x + 4)(x - 2) = 0$$

$$x = 2, \ -4$$

A. -4 and 2

> Tip: *For quadratic solutions there are words that are similar: factor, solution, root, zero, and x-intercept(s). Look at lesson M218 for a detailed explanation.*

22. Answer: K.

Concept: *M205 Exponents & Roots*

$$\frac{3a^4}{3a^6} = \frac{a^4}{a^6} = a^{4-6} = a^{-2} = \frac{1}{a^2}$$

K. $\dfrac{1}{a^2}$

> Tip: *KNOW the rules of exponents and roots. You ARE going to see them on the ACT. Watch lesson M205 on YouTube.*

23. Answer: E.

Concept: *M208 Coordinate Geometry*

M has x and y that are *opposite*.

$(-x, y)$ or $(x, -y)$

Trick: Plug in your own numbers.

$(-2, 3)$ or $(2, -3)$

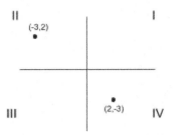

E. *II or IV only*

24. Answer: K.

Concept: *M212 Linear Function: Rate*

$fixed = \$1,400$
$variable = \$5.25$

K. $\$1,400 + 5.25b$

> Tip: *This is a common problem. Variable rate is <u>slope (m)</u>. Fixed cost is <u>y-intercept (b)</u> in slope form y=mx+b.*

25. Answer: B.

Concept: *M302 Triangles; M109 Rate & Proportion*

$$\frac{3}{7.5} = \frac{\overline{AB}}{12.5} = \frac{\overline{BC}}{15} \ Solve \ for \ AB, BC$$

$\overline{AB} = 5, \ \overline{BC} = 6$

Perimeter of ABC $= 3 + 5 + 6 = 14$

B. 14

> Tip: *Similar means congruent angles with sides in proportion to each other.*

26. Answer: G.

Concept: *M205 Exponents & Roots*

$$\frac{3\sqrt{7}}{a\sqrt{7}} = \frac{3\sqrt{7}}{7}$$

solve:

$$a\sqrt{7} = 7$$

$$\div \sqrt{7} \quad \div \sqrt{7}$$

$$a = \sqrt{7}$$

G. $\sqrt{7}$

27. Answer: C.

Concept: *M212 Linear Function: Rate*

$$70 \text{ meters} - \frac{6 \text{ meters}}{\text{second}}(x \text{ seconds}) = 10 \text{ meters} - \frac{15 \text{ meters}}{\text{second}}(x \text{ second})$$

$$70 - 6x = 10 + 15x$$
$$_{-10} \qquad _{-10}$$

$$60 - 6x = 15x$$
$$_{+6x} \quad _{+6x}$$

$$60 = 21x$$
$$_{\div 21} \quad _{\div 21}$$

$$x = 2.85$$

C. 2.9

Tip: *"Constant rate" means slope of a linear function.*

28. Answer: J.

Concept: *M504 Counting, Permutations, & Combinations*

4 roads, 2 paths, 6 trails

$$4 \times 2 \times 6 = 48$$

J. 48

29. Answer: E.

Concept: *M307 Solids; M101 Word Problems - Translation & Vocabulary*

Side of cube A is 2 inches. Cube B is <u>double</u>.

$$Side \ of \ cube \ B \ = \ 2 \times 2 \ inches \ = \ 4 \ inches$$
$$Volume \ of \ B \ = \ 4^3 = 64 \ cubic \ inches$$

E. 64

Trap*: Volume of A = 8 cubic inches. Double the <u>volume</u> of A is 16, Answer C. You must double the <u>side</u>, not the volume.*

30. Answer: G.

Concept: *M205 Exponents & Roots; M110 Percents*

Plug and chug!

$$A = 10,000(1 + .04)^5$$

Calculator!

$$A = 12,166.52$$

G. 12.167

31. Answer: D.

Concept: *M307 Solids*

$2\pi r^2 + 2\pi rh$

$r = \dfrac{20}{2} = 10 \quad h = 20$

$2\pi(10)^2 + 2\pi(10)(20)$

$200\pi + 400\pi = 600\pi$

D. 600π

32. Answer: H.

Concept: *M214 Functions f(x)*

$f(x) = 4x + 1 \quad g(x) = x^2 - 2$

$f(g(x)) = ?$

$4(x^2 - 2) + 1 = 4x^2 - 8 + 1 = 4x^2 - 7$

H. $4x^2 - 7$

> Tip: *The ACT <u>loves</u> this question. Evaluating a function is on <u>every</u> test.*

33. Answer: B.

Concept: *M501 Mean, Average*

$Games \times Games = Total\ Goals$

$(4 \times 0) + (10 \times 1) + (5 \times 2) + (9 \times 3)$
$+ (7 \times 4) + (5 \times 5) + (1 \times 6) + (2 \times 7) = 120$

Divide total goals by total games:

$\dfrac{120}{43} = 2.79$

B. 2.8

34. Answer: H.

Concept: *M301 Lines & Angles*

Supplementary means adds up to 180° or forms a straight line.

Because *A* is parallel to *B*, but *C* is not parallel to *D*, only the top part matters: *C* cutting *A* and *B*.

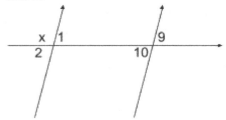

H. $\{1,\ 2,\ 9,\ 10\}$

35. Answer: E.

Concept: *M205 Exponents & Roots*

$(3x^3)^3$

Distribute exponents.

$(3)^3(x^3)^3 = 27x^9$

E. $27x^9$

36. Answer: F.

Concept: *M203 Inequalities*

$4x - 8 > 8x + 16$
$-4x \qquad\ -4x$

$-8 > 4x + 16$
$-16 \qquad\quad -16$

$-24 > 4x$
$\div 4 \qquad \div 4$

$-6 > x$

F. $x < -6$

37. Answer: C.

Concept: *M208 Coordinate Geometry & XY-Plane; M210 Systems of Equations*

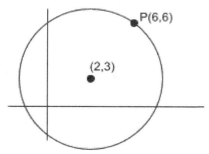

First of all, there are <u>many</u> ways to solve this problem. Plot the answer choices on the xy graph. Answer choices **A** and **B** are not even on the circle! **E** (7,3) is way off. So the only choices are **C** and **D**. Pick one and find the slope.

$$Slope\ of\ \overline{PO} = \frac{6-3}{6-2} = \frac{3}{4}$$

The right answer will have a slope of $\frac{-4}{3}$.

$$Slope\ of\ XO = \frac{-1-3}{5-2} = -\frac{4}{3}$$

C. (5,−1)

> Trick: *Use the corner of your answer sheet to measure a 90° angle. Put the corner on (2,3) and the top edge on (6,6). Draw a line from (2,3) to the circle and you will hit answer C!*

38. Answer: K.

Concept: *M401 SOHCAHTOA; M302 Triangles*

First solve for $\overline{KL}$ using the Pythagorean Theorem.

$$10^2 + \overline{KL}^2 = 12^2$$
$$100 + \overline{KL}^2 = 144$$
$$\underset{-100}{} \qquad \underset{-100}{}$$

$$\overline{KL}^2 = 44$$
$$\overline{KL}^2 = \sqrt{44}$$

$$\sin = \frac{opp}{hyp} = \frac{\sqrt{44}}{12}$$

K. $\dfrac{\sqrt{44}}{12}$

39. Answer: B.

Concept: *M301 Lines & Angles*

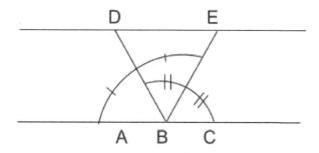

Angle DBE is half of both ∠ABE <u>and</u> ∠DBC. That makes ∠ABD≅∠EBC. It logically flows that they are all congruent.

$$\frac{180}{3} = 60°$$

B. 60°

> Tip: *"Cannot be determined" is <u>almost</u> always wrong on the second half of the test (questions higher than 30).*

40. Answer: H.

Concept: *M205 Exponents & Roots*

molecules per cm^3 means divide

$$\frac{8 \times 10^{12}}{4 \times 10^4} = 2 \times 10^{12-4} = 2 \times 10^8$$

H. 2×10^8

41. Answer: B.

Concept: *M404 Law of Sines/Cosines*

> *Trick: First look at the answers! The only thing that is different is the <u>angle</u>! Find the angle opposite the "question mark".*

To find the unknown angle subtract 170 from 300.

$$300 - 170 = 130^o$$

Yup, that's it.

B. $\sqrt{20^2 + 30^2 - 2(20)(30)cos130^o}$

> *Tip: Watch the video lesson on the Law of Sines and Cosines. The ACT only asks you to fill in the equation, NOT actually solve the problem. These are easy to do with just a little practice!*

42. Answer: J.

Concept: *M102 Operations - Order of Operations, Number Theory; M104 Fractions*

$$\frac{\frac{1}{5} + \frac{1}{3}}{2} = \frac{1}{2}\left(\frac{1}{5} + \frac{1}{3}\right)$$

If ever there was a time to use your calculator, it is now.

$$\frac{1}{2}\left(\frac{1}{5} + \frac{1}{3}\right) = \frac{1}{2}\left(\frac{3}{15} + \frac{5}{15}\right) = \frac{1}{2}\left(\frac{8}{15}\right) = \frac{4}{15}$$

J. $\dfrac{4}{15}$

> *Tip: Halfway means average.*

43. Answer: B.

Concept: *M303 Quadrilaterals*

An isosceles trapezoid has 2 pairs of equal angles and the slanted sides are congruent.

∠ADC≅∠BCD

∠BDC≅∠ACD, which is 25°

Therefore, ∠DBC looks like:

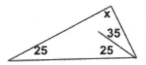

$x + 25 + 25 + 35 = 180$
$x + 85 = 180$
$x = 95$

B. 95

44. Answer: G.

Concept: *M303 Quadrilaterals; M308 Multiple Figures*

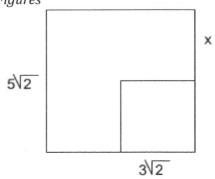

Area of large square is 50. $s_L = \sqrt{50} = 5\sqrt{2}$
Area of small square is 18. $s_S = \sqrt{18} = 3\sqrt{2}$

$x = 5\sqrt{2} - 3\sqrt{2} = 2\sqrt{2}$

G. $2\sqrt{2}$

45. Answer: E.

Concept: *M102 Operations - Order of Operations, Number Theory; M205 Exponents & Roots*

A rational number is any number that can be written in the form $\frac{a}{b}$, where a and b are integers. Rational numbers are the *ratio* of integers.

$$\sqrt{\frac{64}{49}} = \frac{\sqrt{64}}{\sqrt{49}} = \frac{8}{7}$$

E. $\sqrt{\dfrac{64}{49}}$

46. Answer: K.

Concept: *M204 Absolute Value*

$a < b$

Plug in your own numbers!

$a = 2, \ b = 3$

$|2 - 3| = |-1| = 1$

Plug $a = 2, \ b = 3$ into every answer to find which one is equal to 1.

$-(2 - 3) = -(-1) = 1$

K. $-(a - b)$

47. Answer: A.

Concept: *M501 Mean/Average*

This is a classic average problem.

$$\frac{(sum \ of \ first \ 5 \ tests)}{5} = 78$$
$$sum = 5 \times 78 = 390$$

$$\frac{(390 + 6th \ test)}{6} = 80$$
$$390 + 6th \ test = 6 \times 80 = 480$$

$$6th \ test = 480 - 390 = 90$$

A. 90

48. Answer: F.

Concept: *M219 Complex Numbers; M208: Coordinate Geometry & XY-plane*

The complex plane is an obscure topic. If you have never seen it, don't panic. It is rarely tested on the ACT.

> Trick: *"Modulus" just means the distance from the origin. Notice that it looks exactly like the solution for the hypotenuse of a right triangle—because it is!*

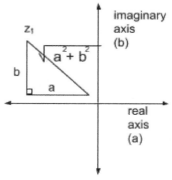

z_1 forms a right triangle with one leg (a), the real axis, and the other leg (b), the imaginary axis. Its hypotenuse is the longest; therefore, it has the greatest modulus.

F. z_1

49. Answer: C.

Concept: *M205 Exponents & Roots*

> Trick: $8 = 2^3$ and $4 = 2^2$, so substitute a base 2 for both sides.

$$8^{2x+1} = 4^{1-x}$$

$$(2^3)^{2x+1} = (2^2)^{1-x}$$

$$2^{6x+3} = 2^{2-2x}$$

The bases are now equal; thus, the exponents are also equal.

$$6x + 3 = 2 - 2x$$
$${+2x} \qquad {+2x}$$

$$8x + 3 = 2$$
$${-3} \quad {-3}$$

$$8x = -1$$
$$\div 8 \qquad \div 8$$

$$x = \frac{-1}{8}$$

C. $-\dfrac{1}{8}$

50. Answer: F.

Concept: *M403 Trig Function; M214 Functions f(x)*

> Note: This question is <u>ALL</u> about even and odd functions. It even gives the definition of even and odd functions in the answer choices. To solve, simply plug in and evaluate for x.

$$2\cos\left(\frac{1}{2}\pi\right) = 0$$

$$2\cos\left(\frac{1}{2}\cos(-\pi)\right) = 0$$

The function is even because the value of π and $-\pi$ give the same output.

F. *Even*

> Tip: An <u>even</u> function is $y = x^2$ and an <u>odd</u> function is $y = x^3$.

51. Answer: D.

Concept: *M503 Probability; M504 Counting, Permutations, & Combinations*

This problem requires making a list of all possible numbers that have *0* as one if its digits.

100	106	130	190
101	107	140	
102	108	150	
103	109	160	
104	110	170	
105	120	180	

There are 19 numbers in each set of hundreds that contain at least one zero, and 9 sets of hundreds.

$$19 \times 9 = 171$$

D. $\dfrac{171}{900}$

52. Answer: F.

Concept: *M207 Linear Functions: y=mx+b*

First find the slope of line *q*.

$$-2x + y = 1$$
$$+2x \qquad\quad +2x$$

$$y = 2x + 1$$

The slope of line *q* is positive 2.

Since $\angle a \cong \angle b$, the line reflects about the line $x = -\dfrac{1}{2}$, the x-intercept.

Reflected lines have opposite slopes, so line r has a slope of -2.

F. -2

Tip: *"Cannot be determined" is rarely a correct answer for a hard problem. If the question number is >30, the answer can be determined!*

53. Answer: D.

Concept: *M401 SOHCAHTOA*

Redraw the triangle:

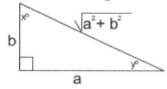

$\tan(x°) = \dfrac{a}{b}$, all the question asks is what is $\cos(x^o)$?

$\cos(x°) = \dfrac{b}{\sqrt{a^2 + b^2}}$

D. $\dfrac{b}{\sqrt{a^2 + b^2}}$

54. Answer: J.

Concept: *M305 Circles*

$A = \pi r^2$
$A = \pi(52)^2$
$A = 8494.86$

J. 8500

55. Answer: E.

Concept: *M215 Equation of a Circle*

The equation of a circle is $(x - h)^2 + (y - k)^2 = r^2$ where (h, k) is the center and r is the radius.

E. $x^2 + y^2 = 52^2$

56. Answer: G.

Concept: *M208 Coordinate Geometry & XY-plane; M305 Circles*

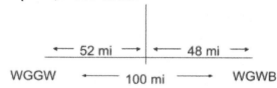

WGGW can be heard 48 miles away from WGWB, which transmits for 60 miles.

$60 - 48 = 12$

G. 12

Trap: $60 - 52 = 8$, which is choice F!

57. Answer: E.

Concept: *M210 Systems of Equations*

The question asks to solve for the solutions, or intercepts, of the two equations. Obviously the x-intercept for both equations is $x = 1$.

The second solution is $x = 2$; BACKSOLVE.

$x - 1 = (x - 1)^4$

$2 - 1 = (2 - 1)^4$

$1 = 1$

So the solution set is $1 < x < 2$. This is the region where the line has a greater y-value than the polynomial.

E. $1 < x < 2$

58. Answer: F.

Concept: *M102 Operations - Order of Operations, Number Theory*

PLUG IN! Pick a number t, u.

$x = 31 \quad t = 3 \quad u = 1$

reverse: $y = 13$

$x - y = 31 - 13 = 18$

Plug in the values for t and u to find 18.

F: $9(3 - 1) = 18$

F. $9(t - u)$

59. Answer: A.

Concept: *M302 Triangles*

$Area = \dfrac{1}{2}bh$

$base = 5 - 1 = 4$

$height = 5 - 3 = 2$

$A = \dfrac{1}{2}(2)(4) = 4$

A. 4

60. Answer: F.

Concept: *M106 Sequence*

First solve for a, because it is the first term.

$$\dfrac{a}{1 - .15} = 200$$

$$\dfrac{a}{.85} = 200$$

$a = (.85)(200)$

$a = 170$

The second term is found by multiplying the first term by .15.

$a_2 = (.15)(a)$

$a_2 = (.15)(170)$

$a_2 = (25.5)$

F. 25.5

Reading 64E

1. Answer: B.

Concept: *R104 Big Picture*

Tip: do "big picture" questions last!

To answer these big picture questions, eliminate the answers that have *anything* wrong with them. Answer choice **A** can be eliminated because both women are not sharing their dreams. Answer choice **C** can be eliminated because the narrator is one of the two people in the text. Answer choice **D** can be eliminated because the narrator does not describe several dreams in detail, only one. Answer choice **B** is the only reasonable answer.

2. Answer: F.

Concept: *R104 Big Picture*

The narrator is helpful towards her friend, so **G** and **J** can be eliminated. There is no evidence to support "lonely," nor optimistic. The first line of the passage indicates that the woman is "miserable," which aligns with what is described in answer choice **F**.

3. Answer: B.

Concept: *R201 Detail*

The passage states that the woman "thinks that by not dreaming she is unaware of things about herself," which indicates answer choice **B** is the most accurate.

4. Answer: J.

Concept: *R201 Detail*

Skim the passage for the first mention of the door. The text states in lines 1-6 that the woman "doesn't have the door of dreams,"

that she stands at the threshold. These lines support **J**: that the door is the metaphorical boundary between not-dreaming and dreaming. Answer choice **G** is a trick: it mentions dreams, but the woman has neither dreams nor nightmares. Answer choice **H** is similarly tricky, but "wakefulness" is not the same as "being awake," nor is it the same as "not-dreaming and dreaming."

5. Answer: C.

Concept: *R201 Detail; R101 Line Number*

Refer to the lines in question: the first paragraph states that the closed door of not-dreaming is a nightmare in itself. "The door to that nightmare doesn't have a latch or a knocker...our blows strike a body without an echo." If this metaphor doesn't strike the reader as "hopeless," it should be easy enough to eliminate **A** because there is no revelation about how to alter the dream, nor an explanation of what caused the nightmare (as in answer choice **B**.) The door is explicitly shut, which would not indicate that there was a possibility of escape as in answer choice **D**.

6. Answer: G.

Concept: *R201 Detail*

Line 71 states "The one she likes best is the amniotic dream." The narrator is stating this fact about the woman who enjoys listening to the narrator's dreams, which indicates answer choice **G** is correct. Answer choice **H** may be assumed, but it is not mentioned in the passage. As for answer choice **J**, the passage states the woman most strongly desires to dream about flying.

7. Answer: D.

Concept: *R201 Detail*

Read the answer choices first, then skim the passage to find which one is mentioned. The passage supports answer choice **D** in lines 31-34, which states the woman's fear that she is different from other people.

8. Answer: J.

Concept: *R201 Detail*

The passage states in lines 53-54 that the narrator knows the woman, "in the privacy of her room with the light out, hiding, she'll try to dream my dream." This describes a "self-conscious and secretive" approach.

9. Answer: C.

Concept: *R202 Vocabulary in Context*

Always go back to the text to find the answer for vocabulary in context questions. The narrator describes the woman's "envy and bad humor" being brought out, which suggests that "humor" is temporary and similar to envy. The closest answer choice is **C**: mood.

10. Answer: H.

Concept: *R201 Detail*

Skim the passage to find the description of Kafka, which is in lines 61-64. Kafka is described as being the only author who could tell dreams "without spoiling their mystery, trivializing their symbols or making them rational." Answer choice **F** and **J** should seem inappropriate. Answer choice **G** would indicate that Kafka *had* made them rational, which is contrary to what is stated in the passage. Thus, answer choice **H** is correct.

11. Answer: A.

Concept: *R104 Big Picture*

Remember: 1) skim, 2) narrow scope questions, 3) "big picture" questions.

Skim quickly to find the answer stated explicitly in the text, which can be found in lines 62-66. Here it states that it didn't drive "history in a direct and causative way," but also that it couldn't be "totally ignored."

12. Answer: H.

Concept: *R204 Main Idea/Function: Paragraph*

The first paragraph states explicitly that "the Little Ice Age… was far from a deep freeze," but rather "an irregular seesaw of rapid climatic shifts." This aligns with answer choice **H**. Don't be tricked by answer choice **J**, which is a *detail* important to understanding the main function of the paragraph, but not the main idea itself.

13. Answer: D.

Concept: *R201 Detail; R101 Line Number*

Double-check the line and its context. Evelyn's words are described as "invaluable," but with "limited" usefulness. Answer choice **A** is a trick: the writing is not completely "useless."

14. Answer: F.

Concept: *R201 Detail; R101 Line Number*

The text states that the Little Ice Age occurred "during times of remarkable change." The em dash here suggests that what follows is a further description of these times.

15. Answer: A.

Concept: *R201 Detail; R101 Line Number*

Look back in the text to read the given lines. The passage clearly states that the effects of insufficient food occurred "continent-wide," or widespread, and "could take decades to unfold," or are long-lasting.

16. Answer: J.

Concept: *R203 Inference/Assumption; R101 Line Number*

Always double-check the context of the lines in question. Immediately after 77-79, the passage reads "these crises in themselves did not threaten the continued existence of Western civilization." Therefore, answer choice **F** is incorrect. Answer choice **G** is not mentioned at all. Environmental determinism is a method of reading history, and the passage lists it as "intellectually bankrupt." Thus, answer choice **J**, broad as it may be, is the most correct answer.

17. Answer: D.

Concept: *R201 Detail; R501 Least/Not/Except*

Refer back to the text. The answer is explicitly stated in lines 83-85. Answer choice **D** is used (in modified form) in relation to "environmental determinism," not as a cause of a European food crisis.

18. Answer: G.

Concept: *R201 Detail*

The *cause* of the climate shifts is discussed at the very beginning; the rest of the passage talks about its *effects*. The answer is explicitly stated in lines 6-7: "complex and still little understood."

19. Answer: D.

Concept: *R201 Detail; R501 Least/Not/Except*

While questions that look like this are usually better answered from memory, this particular question clearly refers to a specific, easily found portion of text. The correct answers are all listed in lines 8-12, but "mild winters and an unusually calm ocean" are *not* mentioned.

20. Answer: G.

Concept: *R203 Inference/Assumption*

Hopefully, by the last question of each passage, the reader will be well-acquainted with most of the text. The explicit answer to this question is the last line in the first paragraph. Line 15-16 states: "Today's prolonged warming is an anomaly."

21. Answer: C.

Concept: *R104 Big Picture*

Remember*: do "big picture" questions last!*

Most incorrect answers in the "Reading" portion of the ACT are incorrect because the *scope* is wrong. The incorrect answer choices here are incorrect because they are *too specific*. Answer choice **C** correctly states the main idea of the passage without focusing too much details.

22. Answer: J.

Concept: *R104 Big Picture; R501 Least/Not/Except*

Answer choice **J** is correct because none of Armstrong's recorded pieces were ever mentioned, which can be confirmed by quickly scanning for quotation marks because the title of a song must have them.

23. Answer: B.

Concept: *R203 Inference/Assumption; R104 Big Picture*

This question is tricky because the answer is not stated clearly and must be inferred, but the first paragraph does state how important his "musical improvisation" was. As stated before, the incorrect answers are often *details* that the ACT is attempting to pass off as important themes or ideas.

24. Answer: G.

Concept: *R204 Main Idea/Function: Paragraph*

Refer to the lines in question and check for context. This paragraph appears to be a timeline of the 1920s and 1930s in Armstrong's life, listing only events. Answer choice **J** may be tempting, but it is only a detail in the greater context of the passage's *function*.

25. Answer: C.

Concept: *R203 Inference/Assumption; R501 Least/Not/Except*

Scan quickly for the information (it can be found in lines 51-53). The only information not mentioned is in answer choice **C**.

26. Answer: F.

Concept: *R203 Inference/Assumption; R102 Paragraph Number; R501 Least/Not/Except*

Although the answer is not stated explicitly in the paragraph, a reread shows enough evidence to eliminate choices **G**, **H**, and **J**. Answer choice **G** can be eliminated with information in lines 78-80 and 85-86; answer choice **H** can be eliminated with information in lines 75-78; answer choice **J** can be eliminated with information in lines 74-75.

27. Answer: C.

Concept: *R201 Detail; R102 Paragraph Number*

The answer is explicitly stated in the text. The last paragraph states that Armstrong wanted to provide "the kind of pleasure music gave him" (lines 79-80.)

28. Answer: G.

Concept: *R201 Detail*

Although the last paragraph is focused mainly on New Orleans and its influence on Louis Armstrong, this question asks where he *lived* last. The text states in lines 28-29 that Armstrong "finally settled in New York in 1929," with no indication that he actually *lived* anywhere else after that.

29. Answer: A.

Concept: *R203 Inference/Assumption; R101 Line Number*

Refer to the lines in question and double-check for context. The given lines discuss an example of how Armstrong was so talented that other musicians were convinced he used a special instrument. It can be inferred, then, that the passage was emphasizing his skill.

30. Answer: H.

Concept: *R201 Detail; R102 Paragraph Number*

Skim the given paragraph to find the specific detail mentioned. Lines 67-68 state that the orchestra got swinging "without them even knowing it," which is akin to saying they did so "unconsciously."

31. Answer: C.

Concept: *R103 Keyword; R501 Least/Not/Except*

Return to the explanation of qi towards the beginning of the passage. Answer choices **A** and **B** are mentioned as causing sickness in lines 28-30. Answer choice **D** is mentioned in lines 12-15.

32. Answer: F.

Concept: *R201 Detail*

The answer to this question requires a careful rereading of the given paragraph, but the answer is explicitly stated as such: "stimulation…sends impulses up the spinal cord to… the limbic system, as well as to the midbrain and the pituitary gland." Therefore, answer choice **F** is correct.

33. Answer: C.

Concept: *R203 Inference/Assumption*

The fifth paragraph states that acupuncture releases "endorphins and monoamines, chemicals that block pain signals." Of the four conditions mentioned in the question, only one refers specifically to *pain*, which is "headaches."

34. Answer: J.

Concept: *R201 Detail*

First, go back to the paragraph describing the experiment. The passage stated that the students' visual cortexes lit up when volunteers were shown a flashing light and when the vision-related point on the outside of the foot was stimulated. Answer choices **F** and **G** are tricks to suggest that the students were shown those instead of the flashing light.

35. Answer: B.

Concept: *R201 Detail; R102 Paragraph Number*

By rereading the last paragraph, it should be apparent that the research has "demonstrated new functional effects of acupuncture" but "raises more questions than it answers." This is closest to answer choice **B**.

36. Answer: J.

Concept: *R201 Detail*

Reread the paragraph that discusses yin and yang. The text states that yin reflects a lack of qi, and yang reflects an excess of qi. From this information, it is clear that the balance between yin and yang depends on the "level of qi," or answer choice **J**.

37. Answer: A.

Concept: *R201 Detail*

This information is in the same line as the question before. Line 31 mentions all of the answer choices as conditions of yang except for a pale face, answer choice **A**.

38. Answer: H.

Concept: *R202 Vocabulary in Context*

Always go back in the text to find the answer for vocabulary in context questions. The text refers to acupoints where nerves are "concentrated." If necessary, plug in the answer choices for the word "concentrated." The only answer choice that makes sense is answer choice **H**.

39. Answer: D.

Concept: *R201 Detail*

The text explicitly states that Cho eliminated the possibility of a placebo effect by stimulating an acupoint that was not associated with the visual cortex. Therefore, answer choice **D** is correct.

40. Answer: G.

Concept: *R203 Inference/Assumption*

The author states that this "study raises more questions than it answers," like many other reports, suggesting that additional studies may also raise more questions than they answer.

Science 64E

1. Answer: D.

Concept: *S203 Reading a Figure; S205 Extrapolation*

125° falls between 103° and 142° on Figure 1, which is labeled "shadow zone: neither p-waves nor s-waves received at seismographs." Therefore, 125° would not receive either type of wave.

2. Answer: G.

Concept: *S203 Reading a Figure; S207 Infer from Data*

In Figure 1, p-waves are represented by the solid lines. When the p-waves move from the mantle to the core, they continue moving (the s-waves do not), but bend slightly. The text states that the waves move and are refracted (bent) as they travel through the layers, so p-waves most likely enter the core and are refracted.

3. Answer: D.

Concept: *S205 Extrapolation*

In Figure 3, both p-waves and s-waves must make it to 10,000 km to be recorded. At 10,000, the s-waves are *above* 23 min and the p-waves are 13 min. Therefore, the time between the arrivals of the first p-waves and the first s-waves would most likely be more than 10 minutes.

4. Answer: F.

Concept: *S202 Reading a Graph*

The text defines focus as the point of origin, which would be represented by the origin on the graph in Figure 3 (0 km, 0 min).

5. Answer: A.

Concept: *S203 Reading a Figure*

Amplitude is the strength or intensity of a wave, which is shown on the seismograph in Figure 2. The first s-waves reach a higher point than the first p-waves, so the first p-waves have a lower amplitude than the first s-waves.

6. Answer: F.

Concept: *S203 Reading a Figure*

In Figure 2, the clay is represented by the lighter gray area. There are five points at which it could be measured: Winnipeg, Site 1, Site 2, Site 3, and Grand Forks. The clay is thinner at Winnipeg (about 10 m) than any other location.

7. Answer: C.

Concept: *S202 Reading a Graph*

In Figure 3, the dot representing the data point for the lowest $\delta^{18}O$ value is the point furthest to the left of each graph, which falls at around -25 and at a depth of between 25 and 30 m.

8. Answer: J.

Concept: *S203 Reading a Figure*

In Figure 2, the lake clay (lighter gray) increases in thickness from Grand Forks to Site 3 (right to left), while the glacial till (stripes) gets thinner.

9. Answer: C.

Concept: *S208 Conversion*

In Figure 2, the top glacial till (stripes) is around 200 at Site 1, 203 at Site 2, and 190 at

Site 3. The only graph that shows Site 2 as the highest elevation is C.

10. Answer: J.

Concept: *S202 Reading a Graph*

The question is asking for the $\delta^{18}O$ value around 3 m below the surface. In each graph in Figure 3, when the depth is between 0 and 5 m, the $\delta^{18}O$ value is between -14 and -16.

11. Answer: B.

Concept: *S104 Inference*

Experiment 3 is the only experiment that mentions visible bubbles, so the students likely used plastic bottles so they could see the bubbles in the liquid.

12. Answer: J.

Concept: *S201 Reading a Table*

In Table 1, the time before shaking is the same (1.75) in Trials 1, 3, and 5.

13. Answer: D.

Concept: *S201 Reading a Table*

In Table 2, the roll time increased after shaking in both trials.

14. Answer: H.

Concept: *S102 Experimental Design/Parameters*

In Experiment 3, the text states there were no bubbles visible after 2 hours. In Experiment 2, Trial 5 was done after waiting 2 hours, when the bubbles created in Trial 4 were likely no longer present.

15. Answer: A.

Concept: *S207 Infer from Data*

In Experiment 3, the text states there were no bubbles visible after 2 hours. Trial 5 should have had no bubbles before shaking, which gave a roll time of 1.75. Two hours later, there would also be no bubbles before shaking, so the roll time would also have been around 1.75.

16. Answer: H.

Concept: *S102 Experimental Design/Parameters*

In Experiment 3, the text states that bubbles were present after 15 min, but not after 2 hr. Similarly, Trial 4 (after 15 min) shows an increase in roll time compared to water, but Trial 5 (after 2 hr) doesn't. Thus, it likely would have taken between 15 min and 2 hr for the bubbles to become too few to affect the roll time.

17. Answer: A.

Concept: *S202 Reading a Graph; S201 Reading a Table*

In Figure 1, chlorophyll b (solid line) hits the highest absorption around 85 absorption, which is around 480 nm wavelength. In Table 1, 480 nm falls within the Blue category.

18. Answer: F.

Concept: *S303 Biology*

The chemical equation in the passage describes photosynthesis, because carbon dioxide, water, and energy are converted into glucose (sugar), oxygen, and water. The reader must know that photosynthesis occurs in the chloroplasts.

19. Answer: B.

Concept: *S202 Reading a Graph*

In Figure 2, the rate of photosynthesis at 670 nm is around 95%. The only area of the graph where the rate of photosynthesis is higher *of the given answer choices* is 430 nm.

20. Answer: G.

Concept: *S303 Biology*

In the chemical equation, carbon is represented by C. The 6 carbons in 6 CO_2 on the left side of the equation (carbon dioxide), are transferred, on the right side of the equation (the products), into glucose ($C_6H_{12}O_6$), or sugar.

21. Answer: C.

Concept: *S202 Reading a Graph*

In Figure 2, the highest rate of photosynthesis (around 100%) occurs at 440 nm wavelength. In Figure 1, 440 nm wavelength occurs near the maximum of chlorophyll (dotted line).

22. Answer: G.

Concept: *S201 Reading a Table; S102 Experimental Design/Parameters*

In Table 1, the density of ethanol was 0.793, because liquid 1 was entirely ethanol and no water.

23. Answer: C.

Concept: *S201 Reading a Table; S304 Chemistry*

An object will sink in a liquid with a lower density, but float in a liquid with a higher density. PA-11 sank in liquids 1-5 and floated in liquids 6-10, so has a density between 0.999 and 1.05.

24. Answer: H.

Concept: *S205 Extrapolation*

In Table 2, the mass of the solution increases as density increases. For every 3-4 the mass increases, the density increases around 0.05. When the mass is 64.64, the density is 1.29. When the mass is 67.54, the density will likely be around 1.35. (Density can also be calculated directly using the formula density = mass/volume, and using a mass of 67.54 and volume of 50 mL.)

25. Answer: B.

Concept: *S304 Chemistry; S207 Infer from Data*

Liquids 1 and 2 had a lower density than liquids 3 and 4. An object will sink in a liquid with a lower density, but float in a liquid with a higher density. Object B shows an impossible scenario, because the object would be floating in less dense liquids and sinking in more dense liquids.

26. Answer: F.

Concept: *S301 Inquiry Process*

In experiment 1, the text defines taring as resetting the balance to 0. This allows the students to accurately measure the mass of the liquids in the cylinder.

27. Answer: B.

Concept: *S201 Reading a Table; S304 Chemistry*

An object will sink in a liquid with a lower density, but float in a liquid with a higher density. PA-6 floated in liquids 8-10 and polycarbonate floated in liquids 9-10. Polycarbonate was "harder" to float (floated in fewer liquids), and so must be denser.

28. Answer: H.

Concept: *S101 Find in Text; S201 Reading a Table*

According to the first paragraph of the text, fermentation produces either CO_2 and acid or only acid. In Table 1, B makes acid and CO_2, and D makes acid, so both B and D are undergoing fermentation.

29. Answer: C.

Concept: *S207 Infer from Data; S102 Experimental Design/Parameters*

According to Table 1, B produces acid and CO_2 in lactose, and C produces acid and CO_2 in sucrose. If both species were present, there would be acid and CO_2 in both sucrose and lactose.

30. Answer: G.

Concept: *S201 Reading a Table*

In Table 1, B did not produce anything in sucrose but produced acid and CO_2 in lactose. The species is likely B.

31. Answer: D.

Concept: *S207 Infer from Data; S102 Experimental Design/Parameters*

In Table 1, neither C nor D produced CO_2 in lactose. In Table 2, C and D did produce CO_2 in lactose, so they must have acted synergistically.

32. Answer: G.

Concept: *S201 Reading a Table; S102 Experimental Design/Parameters*

According to Table 1, species D in sucrose produces acid but no CO_2. The text states that "if acid was produced, the solution was yellow" and "if CO_2 was produced, a gas bubble was observed at the top of the Durham tube." Species D in sucrose would produce yellow coloration but no gas bubble.

33. Answer: D.

Concept: *S103 Argumentation and Evidence; S201 Reading a Table*

In Table 1, neither A nor C produces acid or CO_2 in lactose, but C produces acid and CO_2 in sucrose. A and C together (in Table 2) produced nothing in lactose, but in sucrose produced acid and CO_2, which is the same as what C would have done alone.

34. Answer: H.

Concept: *S104 Inference*

Scientists agreed that genetic material (genes) were in chromosomes in the nucleus. If genes are made only of DNA, which is the first sentence in the DNA Hypothesis, DNA would increase as chromosomes in the nucleus increased.

35. Answer: D.

Concept: *S104 Inference*

The first paragraph of the text states that in the 1940s, chromosomes had only been found in the nucleus of the cell. By stating that DNA is found only in the nucleus, the scientist is suggesting that genes are made up of only DNA because protein is also found elsewhere in the cell.

36. Answer: J.

Concept: *S102 Experimental Design/Parameters*

The second paragraph of the text describes the subunits that compose both DNA and proteins.

37. Answer: A.

Concept: *S102 Experimental Design/Parameters*

The Protein Hypothesis is summed up by comparing the small number of combinations in DNA to the large number of combinations in protein, which is due to the fact that DNA is composed of only 4 types of nucleotides whereas protein is composed of 20 amino acids.

38. Answer: F.

Concept: *S103 Argumentation and Evidence*

The text states that in the 1940s, chromosomes had only been found in the nucleus. The DNA Hypothesis mentions a key argument that DNA is only found in the nucleus, so must be the source material for genes. However, if DNA was found outside the nucleus, this would contradict the DNA Hypothesis, because it would show that genes/DNA were found outside the nucleus.

39. Answer: B.

Concept: *S103 Argumentation and Evidence*

The DNA Hypothesis adds on the argument that the amount of protein in a cell differs from cell type to cell type.

40. Answer: J.

Concept: *S101 Find in Text; S203 Reading a Figure*

The text states that DNA is composed of subunits called nucleotides, which would be a string of only N.

ACT 61C (2006)

English

1. Answer: D.

Concept: *E204 Short and Simple*

The words "associated" and "connected" are synonyms, so there is no reason to include both. For this reason, both answer choices **A** and **C** are incorrect and redundant. Answer choice **B** has a pronoun that does not agree with any noun ("them"), which is incorrect. So, answer choice **D** is the only possible answer. As a shortcut, one could also recognize that it is the shortest and simplest answer, which is a strong indicator that it is correct.

2. Answer: F.

Concept: *E204 Short and Simple*

As in Question 1, all of the answer choices other than **F** are unnecessarily complicated and add no new ideas to the statement. Therefore, the shortest and simplest choice is correct.

3. Answer: B.

Concept: *E103 Independent Clauses: Period, Semicolon, Comma and FANBOYS*

Separating Independent Clauses
1. Period
2. Semicolon
3. Comma FANBOYS

Each answer choice must be considered separately, as some words are added or removed. However, based on the answers provided, it should be clear that there are two independent clauses being separated. The only answer choice where two independent clauses are not validly separated is **C**, which lacks the necessary FANBOYS conjunction after the comma.

4. Answer: J.

Concept: *E101 Verbs: Agreement/Tense; E102 Commas*

Tip: *find the independent clause!*

The main portion of the sentence is "It is a social music" - anything after that is dependent information. Only answer choice **J** correctly inserts a comma and makes the second clause dependent, requiring no other changes.

5. Answer: A.

Concept: *E102 Commas*

Know this rule: reflexive pronouns do not require commas. Simply put, no new clause or article is being presented. Reflexive pronouns are used for emphasis and do not require a comma to separate them.

6. Answer: G.

Concept: *E206 Modification: Dangling Modifiers*

These questions are tricky! What is being tested here is whether or not the reader recognizes that the active verb ("dance") must match the subject ("the couples"). The dance does not perform itself, nor dance itself. Only answer choice **G** correctly matches the verb to the subject.

7. Answer: A.

Concept: *E206 Modification: Dangling Modifiers*

"Long past" is describing "midnight." They are adjectives within a modification, requiring no punctuation.

8. Answer: G.

Concept: *E101 Verbs: Agreement/Tense*

Look for another verb in the sentence for a quick indication of what tense the verb should be in. The first verb in the sentence is "step," and it is in the present tense. Answer choices **A**, **H**, and **J** all state "were stepping," "have stepped," and "will step," which put them in the incorrect tense.

9. Answer: A.

Concept: *E106 Apostrophes: Possessive, Plural, Contractions*

The plural possessive "their" is correct because the nouns it is replacing is "the dancers." Notice that later in the sentence the pronoun "their" repeats ("their music").

10. Answer: J.

Concept: *E201 Relevancy: Adding, Deleting, and Replacing Information*

In these questions, remember to prioritize the supporting evidence, *not* the "yes or no" portion. Answer choice **J** correctly states that the added sentence would "distract from the paragraph's focus on waila's uses and influences."

11. Answer: C.

Concept: E206 *Modification: Moving Modifiers*

This one is a little tough. Notice that the phrase "of Spanish missionaries" is a modifier of "guitars," which necessitates that they stay together. So, the phrase "in the 1700s" may not be placed between them, lest the modification be invalidated.

12. Answer: J.

Concept: *E101 Verbs: Agreement/Tense*

The simple past tense, conjugated with only the "-ed" ending, is correct in this sentence. There is no ongoing action (**F** and **G**), nor any need for the reflexive "were borrowed" (**H**) which would cause the O'odham to no longer be the acting subject but instead the acted-upon object.

13. Answer: A.

Concept: *E201 Relevancy: Adding, Deleting, and Replacing Information*

This paragraph is discussing all of the different ways that the O'odham borrowed musical influences. This sentence in particular explains the introduction of *woodwinds* to waila. Only answer choice **A** includes *relevant* information by mentioning the "presence of saxophones," which are woodwind instruments. Answer choice **B** is irrelevant; **C** is about the construction of saxophones, which is less relevant than **A**, and **D** focuses on jazz bands, which is not relevant.

14. Answer: G.

Concept: *E102 Commas*

This sentence has a very simple structure despite the compound subject. "Around this time" is a prepositional phrase; "the polka music and button accordion" is a compound subject; "played by German immigrant railroad workers" is a modifier, and "left their mark on waila" is the predicate. Though the subject is very large, this sentence essentially follows basic subject-predicate structure and thus has no need for a comma to separate any of the information.

15. Answer: C.

Concept: *E209 Moving Paragraphs*

The pronoun "those" in the added sentence indicates some prior information, and it even states that "those" are "German influences." It is up to the reader to discover *where else* in the passage "German influences" are mentioned. The last sentence of paragraph 3 mentions the influence of "German immigrant railroad workers" which indicates the correct placement of the sentence.

16. Answer: J.

Concept: *E202 Word Choice: Correct Word*

The narrator is describing the "difference" between the two cultures' ways of computing age. "Contest" and "dispute" (**F** and **H**) would suggest that a battle was ensuing where one can take over the other, but they are simply two ways of doing things. "Change" would mean that the methods of one changed to another, but that's not true, either. There is simply a "difference" between the two methods.

17. Answer: B.

Concept: *E104 Nonessential Information: Commas, Dashes, Parentheses*

The extra clause "according...system" should be nested within commas to separate it from the necessary parts of the sentence.

Remember: *if the information can be removed from the sentence without changing the meaning of the sentence, then it is correct!*

18. Answer: J.

Concept: *E201 Relevancy: Adding, Deleting, and Replacing Information*

It is not relevant to this paragraph to make this statement about the importance of birthdays. As such, it is better removed. The replacement options are no better, as they offer similarly irrelevant statements regarding the universal popularity of birthdays.

19. Answer: A.

Concept: *E202 Word Choice: Correct Word*

The difference is subtle, but "heightened" is the most correct option. "Raised" and "lifted" imply an actual vertical movement, and "lighted" is akin to "illumination." "Heightened" is used as an intensifier rather than a measure of height.

20. Answer: F.

Concept: *E201 Relevancy: Adding, Deleting, and Replacing Information*

To find what would be lost, one must consider what is added by this sentence. It explains the added importance of New Year's Day in Korea. It is not a "repetitive reminder," nor a "defense," nor an "illustration of counting." The only valid option is that it comments on the significance of New Year's in Korea.

21. Answer: C.

Concept: *E205 Transition Words/Phrases*

Transition words indicate *how* information is linked, and greatly impact the meaning of the sentence. The correct answer, "in fact," builds off of the prior point and adds a new point or example. "Though" implies contradiction; "otherwise" similarly notes an exception, while "then" implies a chronological ordering.

22. Answer: F.

Concept: *E202 Word Choice: Correct Word*

Prepositions can be difficult to differentiate. They are often best determined through common-sense, familiarity, and idiomatic use. It should be clear that in the English language it is not common to "point on." Deleting the underlined portion would mean that there is no object being "pointed" at, which doesn't make sense. It can be pointed "at" or "to." In common usage, humans *at* things, while ideas point *to* other things.

23. Answer: A.

Concept: *E106 Apostrophes: Possessive, Plural, Contractions*

Because "a person" is singular and this person is in ownership of "age," a singular possessive is necessary. Therefore, a simple apostrophe-S is necessary. Answer choice **D** incorrectly adds a comma and breaks up the subject from the verb.

24. Answer: J.

Concept: *E105 Pronouns: Agreement/Case*

Always find the noun that the pronoun is replacing. In this case, the pronoun is replacing an *idea* ("the value a society places on life experience and longevity"). Therefore, answer choices **F** and **G** are incorrect because they replace people. Answer choice **H** would mean that some object was in possession of the idea. Instead, the sentence is emphasizing a *time* when the idea was being demonstrated.

25. Answer: B.

Concept: *E206 Modification: Dangling Modifiers*

This question is easier to answer after discovering the correct pronoun in the previous answer. "This idea" must be demonstrated "by" some subject. Any other phrase or word inserted in the underlined portion would render the entire sentence incomplete.

26. Answer: F.

Concept: *E202 Word Choice: Correct Word*

The keyword in the question is "positive." Answer choices **G-J** do not provide any indication of a "positive attitude." The "great enthusiasm" mentioned in **F**, however, does have a positive connotation.

27. Answer: A.

Concept: *E109 Relative Pronouns*

The relative pronoun here will refer to "American society." "Whose" is incorrectly possessive and would refer to a person. "Whom" is also used in reference to people. "This" is not a relative pronoun, as is necessary here. Answer choice **A** correctly uses "that" in order to create a restrictive clause which is necessary to understanding how American society has been described.

28. Answer: H.

Concept: *E201 Relevancy: Adding, Deleting, and Replacing Information*

The most significant indicator here is the "details" mentioned in answer choice **H**. It should be apparent that both phrases in question are details, so this should stand out as a strong option. The others can be ruled out due to lack of humor, preference, and personal input from the author. Furthermore, the details are "contrasting," which should make the answer choice fairly obvious.

29. Answer: D.

Concept: *E204 Short and Simple*

The words "refuse" and "hesitate" are synonymous with "balk"; they all indicate a sense of reluctance. In questions like these, take the shortest and simplest answer. In this case, all that is necessary is "balk," so answer choice **D** is correct.

30. Answer: G.

Concept: *E202 Word Choice: Correct Word*

The word "apparently" implies something not being as it appears, or only *appears* that way on the surface, which is precisely what this sentence discusses. "Visibly" might be enticing, but actually suggests something that can be *seen* with the eyes rather than something being intellectually understood.

31. Answer: C.

Concept: *E202 Word Choice: Correct Word*

Read the question! Only answer choice **C** actually "illustrates the term dress code" as requested in the question! The other options do not help promote understanding of the term because they offer no insight into *what* was being prohibited.

32. Answer: J.

Concept: *E203 Word Choice: Tone*

In this essay, it is inappropriate to include slang terms and colloquialisms such as "blow off" or "bored to tears." The phrase "inefficient toward" is not idiomatic and should strike the reader as strange. Notice also that the correct phrase will be contrasted with "a positive educational climate."

33. Answer: A.

Concept: *E201 Relevancy: Adding, Deleting, and Replacing Information*

Since the correct answer will "effectively introduce the main idea of the paragraph," it is necessary to read ahead. The rest of the paragraph deals with the constitutional implications of the case. Answer choices **B-D** do not address this.

34. Answer: H.

Concept: *E102 Commas*

"The United States District Court of New Hampshire" is the subject of this sentence and does not require any internal commas. The verb is "agreed," and no comma is required between the subject and predicate.

35. Answer: C.

Concept: *E202 Word Choice: Correct Word*

Rights are stated as a "right *to do* something." Consider reading the sentence as "a person's *freedom* to wear clothing." In this context, it would be silly to say "freedom of wearing" or "freedom for wearing." Answer choice **D**, without any preposition at all, is clearly incorrect.

36. Answer: G.

Concept: *E104 Nonessential Information: Commas, Dashes, Parentheses*

The "however" in question is not a necessary clause, and is best nested between commas to denote its properties as a nonessential clause. Answer choice **G** correctly places the transition word in between two commas, indicating it can be removed without changing the rest of the sentence.

37. Answer: D.

Concept: *E204 Short and Simple*

The dependent clauses suggested by answer choices **A-C** are unnecessary and irrelevant.

Tip: *Shorter is better! If a short option seems just as valid as a long option, the short option is almost always correct.*

38. Answer: H.

Concept: *E106 Apostrophes: Possessive, Plural, Contractions*

The pronoun is referring to "the board," which is singular, and the claim the board is making is owned by them. So, the correct answer is "its," the possessive form of "it." The word "it's" is a contraction meaning "it is."

39. Answer: A.

Concept: *E202 Word Choice: Correct Word*

The correct option is the existing "that," as it is expanding upon the word "claim" in such a way as to require this relative pronoun. Forms of "which" are not correct because there is not a question of specification (as in: "which one"), nor is "where" because it unduly implies location (physical or not).

40. Answer: J.

Concept: *E205 Transition Words/Phrases*

Although moved into the middle of the sentence, this is still a transition word, which means the reader should return to the previous sentence for context. "However" is appropriate because it shows an unexpected contrast to the information just presented, whereas "thus," "therefore," and "moreover" would all show some sort of result or further example. (A smart test-taker will recognize that the three incorrect answers are all synonymous!)

41. Answer: C.

Concept: *E101 Verbs: Agreement/Tense*

The simple present conjugation "wearing" is adequate for this sentence because it presents the action as a noun, as in "the act of wearing." This is the only correct option in this context.

42. Answer: F.

Concept: *E201 Relevancy: Adding, Deleting, and Replacing Information*

In this paragraph, the existing sentence is the best option. The question looks both for a strong opener and a conveyance of "the importance of this case." The only option which addresses both aspects of this question correctly is answer choice **F** - the others fail to meet one or both requirements.

43. Answer: C.

Concept: *E102 Commas*

Big 3 Comma Rules

1. No commas between subject and verb
2. No commas before or after prepositions
3. No commas between describing words and the things they describe

Since none of the words are changing in the answers, the preposition "of" must be correct. Prepositions do not have a comma before or after them, so answer choices **A** and **B** are incorrect. Answer choice **D** baits the reader into thinking that the second half of the sentence is an independent clause needing a comma and a conjunction, but it is not.

44. Answer: F.

Concept: *E202 Word Choice: Correct Word*

The correct preposition here is "in," because one does not have responsibility "on," "with," or "about" public education. It is the only answer which makes sense in context.

45. Answer: D.

Concept: *E210 Writer's Goal*

Remember, the correctness of each answer choice will be determined by the supporting evidence, not the "yes or no." The only option which both addresses the question "urging students" and correctly connects it to the passage is answer choice **D**. While the other answer choices may do one thing or another, they do not adequately fulfill both requirements.

46. Answer: G.

Concept: *E205 Transition Words/Phrases*

"Because of" correctly portrays the correlation (or cause and effect) of the information presented in the prior sentence and the present sentence. The other options do not and make the sentence confusing.

47. Answer: A.

Concept: *E201 Relevancy: Adding, Deleting, and Replacing Information*

While answer choice **D** is almost correct, in that it does provide an important description, it is not one of "setting." As such, only answer choice **A** is the best answer because the contrast is indeed very important to the paragraph and almost entirely set up by the opening sentence.

48. Answer: G.

Concept: *E106 Apostrophes: Possessive, Plural, Contractions*

Notice that there are multiple faces, so there must be multiple girls. Because the noun is plural (multiple girls) and possessive (faces belonging to them), there must be an apostrophe following the letter *S*. Therefore, answer choice **G** is correct.

49. Answer: D.

Concept: *E204 Short and Simple*

The shortest, simplest answer is often correct. When it does not lose out on any important meanings, it is definitely correct. In this case, "apparent" is a single word which is just as appropriate as the entire phrases in other options, making the sentence much more concise and readable.

50. Answer: G.

Concept: *E109 Relative Pronouns*

The pronoun "who" is appropriate here to refer to a human antecedent. While "they" can also be used for humans, it is not a relative pronoun and thus creates a new independent clause. Without a conjunction to make a compound sentence, both answer choices **F** and **J** are incorrect.

51. Answer: C.

Concept: *E202 Word Choice: Correct Word; E204 Short and Simple*

There are a lot of issues with the wrong answers, both grammatically and idiomatically. **A** is overly verbose and **B** is redundant because it repeats "magazine." (Redundancy is always wrong on the ACT.) Between **C** and **D**, articles are simply "in" magazines.

Note: *answer choices with "being" in them are almost always wrong!*

52. Answer: H.

Concept: *E104 Nonessential Information: Commas, Dashes, Parentheses*

It is best to find the subject and predicate in the sentence first. In this case, "Houdini" is the subject and "was" is the predicate. The clause beginning with "who devoted" is a nonessential clause clarifying information about the subject. Any other predicate, like in answer choice **G**, or without it, as in answer choice **J**, would render the entire sentence incomplete. Answer choice **F** doesn't have the necessary comma to offset the nonessential clause.

53. Answer: B.

Concept: *E201 Relevancy: Adding, Deleting, and Replacing Information*

This question is best solved through elimination. There is simply no explanation of Doyle and Houdini's friendship, nor is there an explanation for Houdini's skepticism. Out of answer choices **B** and **D**, one can simply read on to discover that the information is not "irrelevant," but rather is quite relevant to how their friendship was later damaged.

54. Answer: J.

Concept: *E205 Transition Words/Phrases; E103 Independent Clauses: Period, Semicolon, Comma and FANBOYS*

Any sentence that begins with "though," is likely *not* the main sentence (or independent clause), but a dependent clause. This introductory clause is being used to present contrary information after it in the main sentence. This dependent clause simply needs a comma to offset it from the independent clause.

55. Answer: D.

Concept: *E204 Short and Simple*

The correct option is significantly shorter than the others, which should immediately strike the reader as a hint. The wordiness of answer choices **A** and **B** is absurd. Though answer choice **C** is a little shorter, it is still unnecessarily wordy.

56. Answer: J.

Concept: *E205 Transition Words/Phrases*

Transitioning also means knowing when, where, and how to split up ideas. In this case, the shift of focus from Houdini to the hoax's reveal is cause enough to create a new paragraph. The transition "since" is unnecessary, and while another, more appropriate, transition word could be included, it is optional.

57. Answer: C.

Concept: *E105 Pronouns: Agreement/Case*

When determining the correct pronoun for a situation with multiple pronouns, remove one and determine if it is correct. Restated: "...Frances Griffiths publicly admitted that *her* had staged..." This is clearly incorrect, as is every other answer choice which doesn't include "she." Therefore, answer choice **C** is correct.

58. Answer: H.

Concept: *E101 Verbs: Agreement/Tense*

Four out of the five options use the same past-tense form of the verb "to use"; this should be a pretty strong indicator to look at the fifth. The present-tense "using" is not correct for an action which took place in the past.

59. Answer: B.

Concept: *E201 Relevancy: Adding, Deleting, and Replacing Information*

The question specifically seeks a link to the opening sentence, so double-check the first sentence of the passage. The passage began with Sherlock Holmes; as such, answer choice **B** is the appropriate link.

60. Answer: J.

Concept: *E210 Writer's Goal*

Remember to prioritize the *supporting evidence* when analyzing these answers. Answer choice **J** is correct because its evidence correctly states that Sir Arthur Conan Doyle is only "one author" instead of "famous authors."

Tip: *this is common on "Writer's Goal" questions - the answer choices incorrectly focus on a group of people rather than on one person or vice versa.*

61. Answer: C.

Concept: *E105 Pronouns: Agreement/Case*

It is necessary to note that the first clause is a *dependent clause*, and does not contain the subject and predicate of the sentence. Without stating "Dickinson," the sentence has no subject and the pronoun "her" in the first clause has no clear reference.

62. Answer: F.

Concept: *E107 Colons and Dashes*

The colon is used following an independent clause to lead into an example or explanation. In this case, the count of letters and recipients

furthers the explanation of the preceding independent clause.

63. Answer: B.

Concept: *E205 Transition Words/Phrases*

There is no reason to create a new paragraph here. Leaving one sentence by itself is poor form, and should be a good clue that this should remain one paragraph. Between answer choices **A** and **B**, only **B** correctly places the comma after the transitional modification phrase.

64. Answer: F.

Concept: *E211 Parallel Structure*

When multiple prepositions are used like this (both linked to the same action), they should be in the same form. As such, Dickinson "wrote of ___ and of ___" is the correct wording. Answer choices **H** and **J** are too wordy and easily eliminated.

65. Answer: D.

Concept: *E201 Relevancy: Adding, Deleting, and Replacing Information*

The question states the paragraph's focus ("roles that letters played in Emily Dickinson's life"), so the correct sentence will state what those roles are. Only answer choice **D** indicates what letters *did for her*.

66. Answer: H.

Concept: *E102 Commas*

The underlined portion separates a modification from its subject. As such, all that is necessary is a comma.

67. Answer: B.

Concept: *E109 Relative Pronoun*

"Whom" is only used after a preposition. "Who" is correct here as a relative pronoun introducing a restrictive clause. Answer choice **C** creates an entirely new meaning, and **D** incorrectly changes the subject of the verb phrase "had died."

68. Answer: G.

Concept: *E102: Commas; E103 Independent Clauses: Period, Semicolon, Comma and FANBOYS*

There is no need to include any punctuation in the underlined portion. "One significant aspect of this relationship" is the subject of the sentence and "was" is the predicate. It is organized in a basic subject-predicate order with no extra clauses or modifications.

69. Answer: C.

Concept: *E105 Pronouns: Agreement/Case*

The fact that Susan and Emily are both mentioned in the prior sentence means the pronoun "her" is ambiguous as it could refer to either. Whenever an ambiguous pronoun is present, it is best resolved by including the proper noun, as in answer choice **C**.

70. Answer: J.

Concept: *E204 Short and Simple*

None of the additional descriptions provided are relevant to the sentence. While they may well be factual, this is not the place to include them. Answer choice **J** is the most clear and concise. It's also the shortest!

71. Answer: D.

Concept: *E201 Relevancy: Adding, Deleting, and Replacing Information*

The question asks for a replacement which "clearly describe[s] the interaction. . . during the writing process." Only answer choice **D** shows an interaction and not just an action; that is, it shows both women taking part in different ways.

Tip: *the following sentence states "As a result, Emily wrote two other versions," which indicates that Susan suggested revisions!*

72. Answer: F.

Concept: *E204 Short and Simple*

The other options here are redundant and wordy. None of them offer any extra insight, only unnecessary restatements and phrasing.

73. Answer: B.

Concept: *E101 Verbs: Agreement/Tense*

The plural "years" needs to have a plural verb conjugation ("reveal") to match. Answer choices **C** and **D** can be immediately ruled out because they said "would/will of" instead of "could/will have."

74. Answer: H.

Concept: *E105 Pronouns: Agreement/Case*

"Her" is the correct pronoun because the intended antecedent is Dickinson. The other options incorrectly change the meaning of the sentence.

75. Answer: D.

Concept: *E102 Commas*

There is no need to include any commas in the underlined portion. Do not be tempted to put a comma after "perhaps" as with most transitions words.

Math 61C

1. Answer: A.

Concept: *M212 Linear Function: Rate*

Pick an equation!

This is a linear function with $2.00 to make <u>each</u> balloon bouquet. The $39.99 is the y-intercept, a one-time cost.

A. $2.00b + $39.99

2. Answer: K.

Concept: *M201 Algebraic Operations*

$(x - y)^2$, $x = 5$, $y = -1$

$(5 - (-1))^2 = 6^2 = 36$

K. 36

> Tip: *Be careful when substituting negative numbers. Use parentheses!*

3. Answer: B.

Concept: *M212 Linear Function: Rate*

5 words on day one. 3 words each day after for 20 days.

$5 + 3(19) = 62$

B. 62

4. Answer: G.

Concept: *M205 Exponents & Roots*

$(4x^2)^3 = 4^3 \times x^{2 \times 3} = 64x^6$

G. $64x^6$

5. Answer: E.

Concept: *M103 Properties of Integers*

E. 1, 2, 4, 8

> Tip: *Factors are integers that divide evenly into integers. Don't get mixed up between multiples and factors. Multiples and factors are only integers - they never have remainders, decimals, or fractions.*

6. Answer: H.

Concept: *M201 Algebraic Operations*

Distribute:

$2(4x + 7) - 3(2x - 4)$

Combine like terms (CLT):

$8x + 14 - 6x + 12$

$2x + 26$

H. $2x + 6$

7. Answer: E.

Concept: *M501 Mean, Average*

62, 78, 83, 84, 93

$\frac{62 + 78 + 83 + 84 + 93}{5} = 84.5$

E. 84.5

8. Answer: G.

Concept: *M211 System Word Problems*

$Uptown = \$120 + \$25/month$
$Downtown = \$60 + \$35/month$

$120 + 25x = 60 + 35x$
${\scriptstyle -60} {\scriptstyle -60}$

$60 + 25x = 35x$
${\scriptstyle -25x} {\scriptstyle -25x}$

$60 = 10x$
${\scriptstyle \div 10} {\scriptstyle \div 10}$

$6 = x$

G. 6

9. Answer: B.

Concept: *M308 Multiple Figures*

Since all the sides meet at right angles, the perimeter is no different than that of a rectangle: $2l + 2w$.

$12 + 8 = 20$

$2(20) + 2(20) = 80$

B. 80

> Tip: *Know the above problem; it shows up a lot!*

10. Answer: J.

Concept: *M101 Word Problems - Translation & Vocabulary; M210 Systems of Equations*

$\begin{aligned} x + y &= 11 \\ + \; x - y &= 5 \\ \hline 2x + 0y &= 16 \end{aligned}$

$2x = 16$
${\scriptstyle \div 2} {\scriptstyle \div 2}$

$x = 8$
$y = 3$

$8 \times 3 = 24$

J. 24

11. Answer: E.

Concept: *M217 Factoring & FOIL*

$(3x + 7)^2$

$(3x + 7)(3x + 7)$

$9x^2 + 21x + 21x + 49$

$9x^2 + 42x + 49$

E. $9x^2 + 42x + 49$

12. Answer: J.

Concept: *M207 Linear Functions: Slope*

$$m = \frac{7 - 2}{6 - (-5)} = \frac{5}{11}$$

J. $\dfrac{5}{11}$

13. Answer: B.

Concept: *M202 Solving Equations; M104 Fractions*

$$\frac{1}{3}k + \frac{1}{4}k = 1$$

$$\frac{4}{12}k + \frac{3}{12}k = 1$$

$$\frac{7}{12}k = 1$$

$$\div \frac{7}{12} \qquad \div \frac{7}{12}$$

$$k = \frac{12}{7}$$

B. $\frac{12}{7}$

14. Answer: G.

Concept: *M302 Triangles*

Pythagorean Theorem:
$a^2 + b^2 = c^2$

$$c = \sqrt{a^2 + b^2}$$

$$c = \sqrt{6^2 + 7^2}$$

$$c = \sqrt{36 + 49}$$

$$c = \sqrt{85}$$

G. $\sqrt{85}$

15. Answer: C.

Concept: *M308 Multiple Figures*

The easiest way to do this problem is to isolate the two right triangles with hypotenuses $\overline{ED}$ and $\overline{DC}$.

Count the remaining square units = 17.

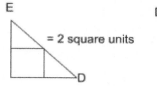 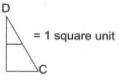

$17 + 2 + 1 = 20$

C. 20

16. Answer: G.

Concept: *M308 Multiple Figures; M302 Triangles*

The answer is **G** because ΔADE is a right triangle with $\overline{AE}$ as the hypotenuse. The hypotenuse is <u>always</u> the longest side of a right triangle and <u>never</u> congruent with either leg.

G. $\overline{AD} \cong \overline{AE}$

17. Answer: A.

Concept: *M110 Percent*

(Wow, this is an old test: Leticia is buying CD's!)

23% off → D=.23p

A. $p - .23p$

18. Answer: H.

Concept: *M308 Multiple Figures; M302 Triangles*

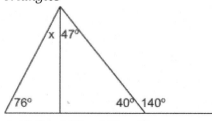

$\angle ABC = 180 - 140 = 40$

$180 - (47 + 76 + 40) = 17$

$180 - (47 + 76 + 40)$

$7 + 6 = 13$

The last digit is 3. $10 - 3 = 7$, so the answer HAS to end in 7. So, H has to be correct.

Practice this technique; it often works!

H. 17°

19. Answer: C.

Concept: *M213 Distance/Rate/Time*

$D = RT$

900 *miles at* $50mph$

$900 = 50t$
$\div 50 \qquad \div 50$

$18 = t$

To <u>reduce</u> her time by 3 hours:

$18 - 3 = 15$

$D = RT$

$900 = R(15)$
$\div 15 \qquad \div 15$

$60 = R$

How much faster?

$60 - 50 = 10$

C. 10

20. Answer: K.

Concept: *M103 Properties of Integers*

Use the calculator!

$9 : gcd(216, \ 180) = 36$

To solve the old-school way, notice that both numbers are even and multiples of 3 (you know this by the sum of the digits).

Divide both by 6.

$216 \div 6 = 36 \quad$ and $\quad 180 \div 6 = 30$

36 and 30 are both multiples of 6.

$36 \div 6 = 6 \quad$ and $\quad 30 \div 6 = 5$

Therefore, 216 and 180 are multiples of $6 \times 6 = 36$.

K. $36x$

21. Answer: B.

Concept: *M212 Linear Function: Rate; M506 Tables*

To spend the <u>least</u> amount of money you need to buy 1 bag of 12, 1 bag of 6, and 2 single lemons.

$12 + 6 + 2 = 20$

$1 \times (2.10) + 1 \times (1.20) + 2 \times (.30) = \$3.90$

B. $3.90

22. Answer: K.

Concept: *M204 Absolute Value; M203 Inequalities*

Maximum:
$|d - 3| \leq 0.001$

$d - 3 = 0.001$
$ \underset{+3}{} \underset{+3}{}$
$d = 3.001$

> Trap: *H. 2.999 is the <u>minimum</u> diameter.*

K. 3.001

23. Answer: A.

Concept: *M217 Factoring & FOIL*

$5x^2 - 13x - 6$

$(x - 3)(5x + 2)$

> Trick: *Plug in your own numbers. When there is a variable in the question and variables in the answers, plug in a number for x.*

Pick $x = 1$

$5(1)^2 - 13(1) - 6 = -14$

Now find the answer that equals -14 when $x = 1$.

A. $(1 - 3)(5 + 2) = -14$ ✓
B. $(1 - 2)(5 - 3) = -2$ ✗
C. $(1 - 2)(5 - 3) = -8$ ✗
D. $(1 + 2)(5 - 3) = 6$ ✗
E. $(1 + 3)(5 - 2) = 12$ ✗

A. $(x - 3)(5x + 2)$

24. Answer: F.

Concept: *M503 Probability*

6 *red*, 5 *yellow*, 7 *green* = 18 *total*

x = *new red marbles*

$\dfrac{(6 + x)}{(18 + x)} = \dfrac{3}{5}$ *cross multiply*

$5(6 + x) = 3(18 + x)$

$30 + 5x = 54 + 3x$
$\underset{-30}{} \underset{-3x}{} \underset{-30}{} \underset{-3x}{}$

$2x = 24$
$\underset{\div 2}{} \underset{\div 2}{}$

$x = 12$

> Trick: *Last digit math. WARNING! Only for students with math scores >30 (or for sneaky students who love to go quickly. This solution is <u>fast</u>!*

It is given that there are 6 red marbles and 18 total.

Probability is $\frac{6}{18}$ or $\frac{1}{3}$ to randomly pull a red.

To change the probability to $\frac{3}{5}$, the denominator <u>must</u> be a multiple of 5 because it is reduced to 5.

Let's use the Last Digit Math technique to get to a multiple of 5 before most students can even pick up their calculators!

Denom.   Last digit of answer choice

F. 1<u>2</u> $8 + 2 = 10$ (winner)
G. 1<u>6</u> $8 + 6 = 14$ (loser)
H. 1<u>8</u> $8 + 8 = 16$ (loser)
J. 2<u>4</u> $8 + 4 = 12$ (loser)
K. 3<u>6</u>   already know it's a loser from B.

Also works for $\frac{1}{3}$. (Why? Because it HAS to!)

F. $3 + 2 = 5$
G. $3 + 6 = 9$
H. $3 + 8 = 1$
J. $3 + 4 = 7$

(This trick is not for the faint of heart, but if you want a lot of extra time, look for opportunities like this. The ACT is super-friendly to this trick because they often make the answer choices end in different digits.)

F. 12

25. Answer: D.

Concept: *M401 SOHCAHTOA*

S $\frac{O}{H}$ C $\frac{A}{H}$ T $\frac{O}{A}$

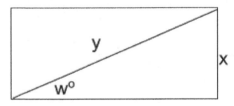

$\frac{x}{y}$ *is* $\frac{opposite}{hypotenuse}$ *which is* $\sin(w°)$

D. $\sin(w°) = \frac{x}{y}$

Tip: *You can do right triangle trigonometry with just a short lesson and a few practice problems. Watch my video on Youtube!*

26. Answer: J.

Concept: *M207 Linear Functions: y=mx+b*

$y = ax + b$ vs $y = cx + b$

Slope of a line is <u>greater</u> than c.

$a > c$

Note: *YES, it is actually this easy! Don't overthink it. Pick the correct answer and move on!*

J. $a > c$

27. Answer: A.

Concept: *M304 Polygon*
Draw!

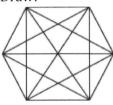

6 on the outside (obviously; it's a hexagon) plus 9 on the inside is 15.

A. 15

Tip: $\frac{n(n - 3)}{2}$ *is the formula for the distinct diagonals of a polygon. Do you need to know this? Not really, unless you want a 34+, in which case you should know it.*

28. Answer: H.

Concept: *M109 Rate & Proportion; M506 Tables*

$\frac{60}{280} = \frac{x}{112}$ *cross multiply*

$6720 = 280x$
$\div 280 \qquad \div 280$

$24 = x$

H. 24

29. Answer: C.

Concept: *M307 Solids*

$$volume = \pi r^2 h$$
$$= \pi (12)^2 (5)$$
$$= 2261.9$$

C. 2262

30. Answer: G.

Concept: *M306 Sectors & Arcs*

Length of zipper = radius + arc length

$$radius + \frac{45°}{360°} (circumference)$$

$$12 + \frac{45}{360}(24\pi) = 21.42$$

G. 22

31. Answer: E.

Concept: *M207 Linear Functions: y=mx+b;*
M208 Coordinate Geometry & XY-plane

A faster rate means a steeper slope! When the faster hose stops the slope becomes less.

E.

32. Answer: F.

Concept: *M401 SOHCAHTOA*

$$S\frac{O}{H} \; C\frac{A}{H} \; T\frac{O}{A}$$

Solve for x:

$$\tan(75°) = \frac{6'}{x}$$
$$\times x \qquad\qquad \times x$$

$$x\tan(75^o) = 6$$
$$\div \tan 75 \qquad \div \tan 75$$

$$x = \frac{6}{\tan 75°}$$

F. $\dfrac{6}{\tan 75°}$

33. Answer: C.

Concept: *M110 Percent; M205 Exponents &*
Roots

$$P(t) = p_0 \left(1 + \frac{r}{100}\right)^t$$

$$P(10) = 782{,}000 \left(1 + \frac{5}{100}\right)^t$$

C. $782{,}000(1.05)^{10}$

34. Answer: J.

Concept: *M212 Linear Function: Rate; M506 Tables*

1. 11/22: $(8)(.25) = 2.00$
2. 11/23: $(10)(.25) = 2.50$
3. 11/24: $(15)(.10) = 1.50$
4. 11/26: $(17)(.10) = 1.70$
5. 11/27: $(22)(.05) = 1.10$

Total $8.80

J. $8.80

35. Answer: B.

Concept: *M303 Quadrilaterals; M302 Triangles*

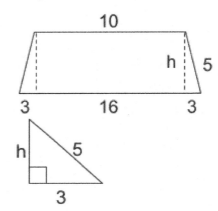

It's a 3-4-5- right triangle!

B. 4

Tip: *The slant side of a trapezoid forms the hypotenuse of a right triangle with the height as a leg. Legs __MUST__ be shorter than the hypotenuse! In the previous question, this allows you to immediately eliminate C, D, and E.*

36. Answer: K.

Concept: *M203 Inequalities*

$$3(x + 2) > 4(x - 3)$$

$$3x + 6 > 4x - 12$$
$$-3x \qquad -3x$$

$$6 > x - 12$$
$$+12 \qquad +12$$

$$18 > x$$

K. $x < 18$

37. Answer: C.

Concept: *M208 Coordinate Geometry & XY-plane*

The midpoint is the average!

midpoint of $\overline{AB} = (4, -3)$

$A = (1, -5)$

$$x_B = \frac{1 + x_B}{2} = 4$$
$$\qquad \times 2 \qquad \times 2$$

$$1 + x_B = 8$$
$$-1 \qquad -1$$

$$x_B = 7$$

$$y_B = \frac{-5 + y_B}{2} = -3$$
$$\qquad \times 2 \qquad \times 2$$

$$-5 + y_B = -6$$
$$+5 \qquad +5$$

$$y_B = -1$$

$$x_B + y_B = 7 + (-1) = 6$$

C. 6

38. Answer: J.

Concept: *M218 Rational Functions & PLD*

Two Solutions: 1) Algebra, 2) Plug-in

1) Algebra:

$$\frac{x+1}{x^3-x} = \frac{x+1}{x(x^2-1)} = \frac{x+1}{x(x-1)(x+1)}$$

Cancel out x+1:

$$= \frac{1}{x(x-1)} = \frac{1}{x^2-x}$$

2) Plug-in:

Let x=2

$$\frac{x+1}{x^3-3} = \frac{2+1}{2^3-2} = \frac{3}{6} = \frac{1}{2}$$

F. $\frac{1}{4} - \frac{1}{8} = \frac{1}{8}$ No

G. $\frac{1}{8} - \frac{1}{2} = \frac{-3}{8}$ No

H. $\frac{1}{4-1} = \frac{1}{3}$ No

J. $\frac{1}{4-2} = \frac{1}{2}$ Yes!

K. $\frac{1}{8}$ No

39. Answer: C.

Concept: *M301 Lines & Angles; M302 Triangles*

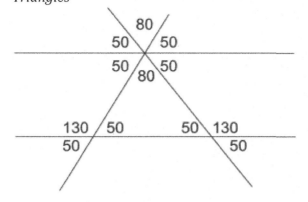

C. 8

40. Answer: H.

Concept: *M207 Linear Functions: y=mx+b; M203 Inequalities*

To solve, find $600 worth of sales each for students

y-axis: <u>student</u> $\dfrac{\$600}{\$2} = 300\ tickets$

x-axis: <u>adults</u> $\dfrac{\$600}{\$3} = 200\ tickets$

Plot y-intercept $(0, 300)$ and x-intercept $(200, 0)$.

H.

41. Answer: A.

Concept: *M502 Median, Mode*

Put in order:

21, 33, 33, 42, 67, 79, 89

Median = 42

A. 42

42. Answer: F.

Concept: *M204 Absolute Value*

$|x|^2 + 2\,|x| - 3 = 0$

Backsolve by plugging in answers:

$|1|^2 + 2\,|1| - 3 = 0$
$1 + 2 - 3 = 0$
$3 - 3 = 0$
$0 = 0$
Yes

$|-1|^2 + 2\,|-1| - 3 = 0$
$1 + 2 - 3 = 0$
$3 - 3 = 0$
$0 = 0$
Yes

$|3|^2 + 2\,|3| - 3 = 0$
$9 + 6 - 3 = 0$
$15 - 3 = 0$
$12 = 0$
No

$|-3|^2 + 2\,|-3| - 3 = 0$
$9 + 6 - 3 = 0$
$15 - 3 = 0$
$12 = 0$
No

F. ± 1

43. Answer: D.

Concept: *M208 Coordinate Geometry & XY-plane; M207 Linear Functions: y=mx+b*

The point $(2, 5)$ is still on a line with slope $-\dfrac{2}{3}$.

There are several solutions but the fastest is to know that slope = $\dfrac{rise}{run}$. A slope of $-\dfrac{2}{3}$ means <u>down</u> 2 in y and over 3 in x, so the answer is $(x + 3,\ y - 2)$. $(2 + 3,\ 5 - 2) = (5, 3)$, point D.

D. $(5, 3)$

44. Answer: F.

Concept: *M108 Ratio; M302 Triangles*

Re-draw the triangle.

$\overline{BA}$ is part of both, so make it equal to 1.

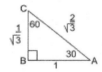 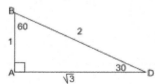

Good news! You don't have to add up the sides, you just have to compare the sides of a 30-60-90 right triangle:

$BC : AB,\ AC : BD,\ AB : AD$

F. $AB : AD$

Tip: *Know the sides of a 30-60-90 and 45-45-90 right triangle. You <u>will</u> see them on the ACT.*

45. Answer: C.

Concept: *M308 Multiple Figures*

The measure of an interior angle of a regular n-sided polygon is $\dfrac{180(n-2)}{n}$.

An interior angle of a pentagon is

$$\frac{180\,(5-2)}{5} = 108 \,.$$

The supplement to 108 is 72.

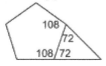

The triangle is therefore isosceles.

$$72 + 72 + x = 180$$

$$144 + x = 180$$
$$\underset{-144}{} \qquad \underset{-144}{}$$

$$x = 36$$

C. 36

Tip: *Know the angles of regular polygons, triangles to hexagons:*		

Sides	Total Angles	Regular Angle
3	180	60
4	360	90
5	540	108
6	720	120

46. Answer: K.

Concept: *M307 Solids*

Surface area of a cube is $6x^2$.

$$6 \times 3^2 = 6 \times 9 = 54$$

K. 54

47. Answer: C.

Concept: *M110 Percent*

When no number is given in a percentage problem, pick 100!

$$100 + 25\% = 125$$
$$125 - 20\% = 100$$

Know how to do this:

$$(100)(1.25)(.8) = 100$$

C. 100%

Trap: *Answer D is a huge trap. <u>Never</u> add or subtract percentages. ALWAYS multiply.*

48. Answer: J.

Concept: *M102 Operations - Order of Operations, Number Theory*

To solve, <u>PLUG IN</u>!

If $x > 1$, make $x = 2$.

The reciprocal of 2 is $\dfrac{1}{2}$.

J. *between* 0 *and* 1.

49. Answer: D.

Concept: *M203 Inequalities; M105 Number Line*

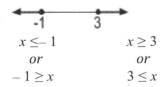

$x \leq -1$ $x \geq 3$
or   *or*
$-1 \geq x$ $3 \leq x$

> **Trap:** *A number cannot be less than* -1 *and greater than 3. Answer choices* **A** *and* **B** *are traps.*

D. $-1 \geq x \text{ or } 3 \leq x$

> **Tip:** *Know how to flip inequalities!*

> **Tip:** *Know the difference between* AND *and* OR. AND *means both have to be true.* OR *means either one is true.*

50. Answer: J.

Concept: *M101 Word Problems - Translation & Vocabulary; M208 Coordinate Geometry & XY-plane*

y is <u>1 less than</u> *the square of x translates to:*

$y = x^2 - 1$

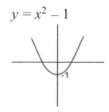

J.

51. Answer: E.

Concept: *M104 Fractions; M103 Properties of Integers*

Why is this an integer problem? Because Ms. Chu does not break any disks, so it is whole numbers and multiples that are really being tested. You have to do this the hard way checking each answer. To do it four times, start with the biggest number.

Backsolve
(1). $81 - \frac{81}{3} = 54$ (2). $54 - \frac{54}{3} = 36$
(3). $36 - \frac{36}{3} = 24$ (4). $24 - \frac{24}{3} = 16$

E. 81

52. Answer: J.

Concept: *M103 Properties of Integers*

Plug-in: *When asked about integers use numbers!*

$m = 2 < n = 3$ or $m = 3 < n = 4$

F. $m = 2 \text{ or } 3$ No

G. $n = 2 \text{ or } 4$ No

H. $n - m = 4 - 3 = 1 \text{ or } 3 - 2 = 1$ No

J. $n^2 - m^2 = 4^2 - 3^2 = 16 - 9 = 7$
or $3^2 - 2^2 = 9 - 4 = 5$ Yes!

K. $n^2 + m^2 = 4^2 + 3^2 = 16 + 9 = 25$ No

J. $n^2 - m^2$ *is odd*

53. Answer: A.

Concept: *M214 Functions f(x)*

> Note: *This is the hardest evaluate f(x) for some value of x type of problem we have ever seen. (Yes, it is ridiculously easy.)*

$P(-1)$

Look at $x < 0$

$P(x) = -(x)^5 + (x)^4 + 36(x) - 36$

Use parentheses!

$P(-1) = -(-1)^5 + (-1)^4 + 36(-1) - 36$

This is a great time to be <u>very</u> good with your TI-84/83.

$P(-1) = 1 + 1 - 36 - 36 = 2 - 72 = -70$

A. -70

> Tip: <u>*Always*</u> *use parentheses when evaluating a function. This is especially true for a negative number.*

54. Answer: K.

Concept: *M305 Circles; M111 Units*

3 *feet* = 36 *inches*

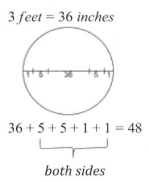

$36 + 5 + 5 + 1 + 1 = 48$

both sides

This is a #54, so it simply cannot be as easy as adding up the numbers in the problem.

Diameter means <u>both</u> sides of the circle. Anything added to one side, must be added to the other.

K. 48

55. Answer: B.

Concept: *M403 Trig Function*

We <u>love</u> this problem. It is <u>so</u> easy... <u>if</u> you know how to graph $f(x) = a\sin(x)$.

The question asks which has a bigger <u>amplitude</u>.

The amplitude of the graph of $\sin(x)$ or $\cos(x)$ is $\frac{1}{2}$ the height/distance from the max to the min.

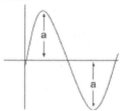

The sine wave $y(t)$ is <u>higher</u>, therefore it has a greater amplitude. See our lessons on trig functions.

B. $0 < a_2 < a_1$

56. Answer: H.

Concept: *M403 Trig Function*

$\sin^2(x) + \cos^2(x) = 1$

$\sin^2(x) = 1 - \cos^2(x)$

$\cos^2(x) = 1 - \sin^2(x)$

$$\frac{\sqrt{1 - \cos^2 x}}{\sin x} + \frac{\sqrt{1 - \sin^2 x}}{\cos x}$$

$$\frac{\sqrt{\sin^2 x}}{\sin x} + \frac{\sqrt{\cos^2 x}}{\cos x}$$

$$\frac{\sin x}{\sin x} + \frac{\cos x}{\cos x}$$

$$1 + 1 = 2$$

H. 2

57. Answer: A.

Concept: *M214 Functions f(x)*

$f(x) = \sqrt{x}$

$g(x) = 7x + b$

$y = f(g(x))$ passes through $(4, 6)$

Substitute:

$6 = f(g(4))$

Put the 4 into g(x) and the g(4) into f(x)

$6 = \sqrt{7(4) + b}$

$6 = \sqrt{28 + b}$

Square both sides:

$$36 = 28 + b$$
$$\underline{-28 \quad -28}$$
$$8 = b$$

A. 8

58. Answer: K.

Concept: *M309 Rotate a Figure*

Reflect $\triangle XYZ$ about side $\overline{yz}$.
Draw!

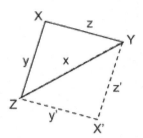

The perimeter of the quadrilateral formed by the reflection is $y + y + z + z$ or $2(y + z)$.

K. $2(y + z)$

Tip: *Know how to __reflect!__*

---

59. Answer: E.

Concept: *M214 Functions f(x)*

Odd function means $f(-x) = -f(x)$.
For example, $f(-2) = -f(2)$.
Let's make $f(x) = x^3$, so $f(2) = 8$ and
$f(-2) = -8$.
It is an odd function because $f(-2) = -f(2)$.

E.

Tip: *An EVEN function is where $f(x) = f(-x)$, such as $f(x) = x^2$. An ODD function is where $f(-x) = -f(x)$, such as $f(x) = x^3$.*

---

60. Answer: J.

Concept: *M206 Logarithm*

$log_2 24 - log_2 3 = log_5 x$

Quotient Rule: $log(x) - log(y) = log\left(\dfrac{x}{y}\right)$

$log_2 24 - log_2 3 = log_2\left(\dfrac{24}{3}\right) = log_2(8) = 3$

$3 = log_5 x$

$5^3 = 125$ so $x = 125$

J. 125

Reading 61C

1. Answer: B.

Concept: *R104 Big Picture*

Remember: *save "Big Picture" questions for last!*

It is often easiest (and quickest!) to eliminate answer choices which are absolutely incorrect. Stick to the information related in the passage. There is no indication that the narrator had difficulties dealing with the loss of their former neighbor, nor that the narrator is an adult or talking about pairs of adults for any length. So, answer choices **C** and **D** are clearly incorrect. Answer choice **A** would mean that the narrator's nervousness about meeting Eugene was the "main theme" of the passage, but it is only part of the greater story of their friendship. Answer choice **B** correctly states that the main theme of the passage is the narrator's making of a new friend and the effect of that friendship on her.

2. Answer: J.

Concept: *R201 Detail; R501 Least/Not/Except*

This is a *NOT* question, so the correct answer will have no information about it in the passage or will be completely irrelevant. Although the narrator has a good view of Eugene's house and is familiar with it, there is *no indication that she ever entered his home*. Thus, answer choice **F** is incorrect. It is explicitly stated that the narrator and Eugene share a love of reading, so answer choice **G** is incorrect. Answer choice **H** is stated in lines 5-6 ("the only house on the block that had a yard and trees"), so it is incorrect. As for answer choice **J**, no other careers are mentioned except for one, which makes it correct.

3. Answer: C.

Concept: *R201 Detail*

This question is tricky because the two sets of parents are never *directly* contrasted in the same sentence. The trick is making sure that the information in the answer choices is stated in the passage. Only answer choice **C** correctly states that the old couple spent lots of time together and that Eugene's parents do not. Regarding the other answer choices, there is no indication that the old couple were socialites, nor that Eugene's parents enjoyed tending the flowers (they didn't replant them), or that the old couple worked outside the house.

4. Answer: F.

Concept: *R204 Main Idea/Function: Paragraph; R102 Paragraph Number*

For questions like these, always look back at the paragraphs mentioned. The penultimate paragraph describes her family members' thoughts about their current living situation, and the final paragraph describes how the narrator's thinking began to change after meeting Eugene. Thus, answer choice **F** correctly indicates that before-and-after relationship.

5. Answer: C.

Concept: *R203 Inference/Assumption*

Although the answer is not explicitly stated, there is clear evidence that will help make an inference. The narrator mentions seeing the father mowing, "and when he finished" the narrator didn't see the flowers anymore. This clearly implies the father mowed down the flowers, which makes answer choice **C** correct.

6. Answer: J.

Concept: R203 Inference/Assumption

The text states in lines 56-57 that Eugene was blushing and liked the narrator when they first spoke. This clearly implies that he had taken notice of the narrator ahead of their first meeting, as indicated in answer choice **J**.

7. Answer: A.

Concept: R201 Detail; R102 Paragraph Number

Always refer back to the given line to see where it fits into the rest of the passage. The line in question separates the narrator's career plans and her desire to explore Eugene's house and spend time with him. The only answer choice that mentions getting to know Eugene is **A**.

8. Answer: H.

Concept: R201 Detail

Reread the paragraph (lines 67-79) that mentions her parents' dreams, and it will be apparent that her parents "talked constantly" about plans for "someday," which describes something she has heard many times but that seems far off: answer choice **H**.

9. Answer: D.

Concept: R201 Detail

In lines 11-16, the narrator describes her growing familiarity with the elderly couple's life. She states, "Over the years I had become part of their family" and that she "knew all this by watching them at mealtimes." Therefore, answer choice **D** is correct.

10. Answer: G.

Concept: R201 Detail

This question can be tricky since it refers to details that may have been overlooked on the first read-through. Skim the entire passage to find the narrator's feelings about looking into Eugene's house. In line 63, the narrator mentions feeling slightly dishonest, which only matches choice **G**.

11. Answer: B.

Concept: R104 Big Picture

There is nothing in the passage to suggest Eleanor Roosevelt is quiet (**A**), traditional (**C**), or calm (**D**), so they can be eliminated. Thus, answer choice **B** is correct.

Tip: *this is the most efficient process if the answer is not explicitly stated in the passage.*

12. Answer: F.

Concept: R203 Inference/Assumption

The last paragraph sums up the passage well. It states that she "refused to withdraw from controversy and brought… agitators and activists into the White House." From these details, it can be inferred that she was exceptional because she raised unpopular views to the forefront of politics.

13. Answer: D.

Concept: R201 Detail; R501 Least/Not/Except

This is a tough question if the word "theories" didn't jump out on the first read. If not, take a quick skim through the passage. The word can be found in the passage (lines 48-49), where it states ER was not interested in complex theories.

14. Answer: J.

Concept: *R203 Inference/Assumption*

There is no specific place to find an answer like this, so, rather than reread the entire passage, see if the answer choices can be eliminated by logical assumptions. The text states explicitly that she was "uninterested in complex theories," which eliminates answer choice **F**. It also states that ER moved away from "isolationist positions" (**H**) and that she "refused to withdraw from controversy," which would not reflect a "flexible" personality (**G**). Her determination is frequently suggested and her progressive attitudes (courting activists, socialists, favoring race relations, etc.) are the focus of the entire passage, so **J** is the best choice.

Tip: *if answer choice* **F** *can be eliminated in this question, it should indicate an incorrect answer in the previous question as well!*

15. Answer: D.

Concept: *R203 Inference/Assumption*

In lines 34-38, ER is described as battling "on the margins of national politics" while fighting for social justice, which implies that the U.S. was "unsupportive" of her social views on welfare.

16. Answer: G.

Concept: *R203 Inference/Assumption; R102 Paragraph Number*

When asked about the paragraph as a whole, always reread the given paragraph. By process of elimination, it should seem clear that although the word "game" is mentioned, ER did not "only" play when she could win (**F**). She never attempted to replace her husband as president, but made her decisions *despite* her husband's important position (**H**). Answer choice **J** may be tempting, but based

on the last paragraph, there is little to suggest her saw herself as "the country's role model." Only answer choice **G** maintains the focus of the paragraph regarding her work with activists and "worked with movements for justice and peace," as stated in the paragraph.

17. Answer: A.

Concept: *R204 Main Idea/Function: Paragraph; R102 Paragraph Number*

Always reread the given paragraph, which lists ER's accomplishments *by the time she became First Lady*, suggesting that these early successes helped prepare her for her role as First Lady, as stated in answer choice **A**.

18. Answer: F.

Concept: *R201 Detail*

This small detail is explicitly stated in lines 48-49: "Her goal was simple, a life of dignity and decency for all." This is almost verbatim repeated in answer choice **F**. (This answer could also be arrived at rather easily through elimination.)

19. Answer: C.

Concept: *R201 Detail*

Again, this answer is explicitly stated in lines 58-59. Furthermore, as in question 18, the incorrect answer choices should appear completely inappropriate. ER is explicitly anti-isolationist (**A**). Answer choice **B** states that the White House models the relationship between the people and their government, which does not align with ER's interest in including activists in government. Although she utilized the media, there's no indication that she believed it should "control" the relationship between people and their government.

20. Answer: H.

Concept: *R203 Inference/Assumption*

This is an inference that must be made from the flow of information. The author talks about ER's enjoyment of the game immediately following her setbacks and obstacles, which implies that she "embraced" the challenge of criticism and obstacles.

21. Answer: A.

Concept: *R104 Big Picture*

Remember: *questions 21 and 22 are "big picture" questions, so return to them after completing some "narrow scope" questions.*

Although the text is particularly tricky, read through the answer choices to see if any can easily be eliminated. Answer choice **D** can be eliminated because the story is not about a "recent event," and **C** can be eliminated because the narrator doesn't mention the perspectives of her parents. Between the remaining answer choices, **A** is more accurate because the passage does begin and end with assertions, and the story illustrates those assertions. **B** is incorrect because she doesn't disprove anything she states in the first paragraph.

22. Answer: H.

Concept: *R104 Big Picture*

Always refer to the lines in question. In lines 9-44, the passage describes the narrator's experience with the "thing," but the given lines end with the reveal that the "thing" was light reflected on a passing car. This is the logical way to come to the conclusion that the tension grew, but was "broken" by the realization about the car.

23. Answer: C.

Concept: *R102 Paragraph Number*

The paragraph in question is a description of the light on the wall and how it moved around. There's no indication that the narrator attempted to do anything about it or a philosophical musing on the nature of the object, which render answer choices **A** and **B** incorrect. Answer choice **D** only comes later in the passage, not in the paragraph in question, so it is wrong. Answer choice **C** correctly states that the paragraph provides lots of "sensory details... depicting the object and its movements."

24. Answer: J.

Concept: *R201 Detail; R203 Inference/Assumption*

Hopefully the reader remembers that Amy was only mentioned near the beginning of the passage. The passage states that she couldn't "blink or breathe" or she would be found by the "thing." This suggests that the narrator was "afraid of alerting the thing," as in answer choice **J**.

25. Answer: D.

Concept: *R203 Inference/Assumption; R104 Big Picture*

Immediately after discovering the truth about the light, the narrator states "Figuring it out was as memorable as the oblong itself." Neither here nor anywhere else in the passage does the narrator state that her discovery was "deflating" or "disappointing." It could be inferred that she was satisfied, but *not* because she could now go to sleep. Rather, the discovery is the basis for the narrator's argument about the importance of reason, which indicates answer choice **D** is correct.

26. Answer: G.

Concept: *R203 Inference/Assumption; R101 Line Number*

The entirety of the paragraph from 45-55 is about the metaphor of swimming towards the surface. The membrane mentioned in line 52 is also mentioned earlier in the paragraph (line 47) where the narrator refers to it as "the membrane of skin that both separates and connects the inner life and the outer world." Thus, answer choice **G** is correct.

27. Answer: D.

Concept: *R201 Detail*

Always refer to the line in question. The author states that she can connect to the "outer world by reason" or the "show in light," which suggests it is neither outer nor reasonable: it is a fantasy.

28. Answer: F.

Concept: *R101 Line Number*

Referring to the line in question, the line prior indicates the author is talking about "blind egoism," which is remarkably similar to "deceptive self-absorption" (**F**).

29. Answer: C.

Concept: *R101 Line Number*

This is a particularly tricky question. The lines state that an enriched imagination is not worth the risk of possible ignorance, but rather that the "trick of reason is to get the imagination to seize the actual world." Answer choices **A** and **D** are too disparaging of the imagination, and **B** *inverts* what the lines are attempting to say.

30. Answer: G.

Concept: *R203 Inference/Assumption*

The narrator states that the world "was a coincidental collection of things and people... and I myself was one such item." There is no indication of a *comparison*, so answer choices **F** and **J** are incorrect. Answer choice **H** is entirely irrelevant and **G** correctly states what the essence of the statement is.

31. Answer: B.

Concept: *R201 Detail; R203 Inference/Assumption*

This question is best done through elimination because at first glance it is not obvious. However, answer choices **A**, **C**, and **D** are really only restating the same thing: that scientific discoveries are met with just as much skepticism by scientists as by the rest of the world! Only answer choice **B** makes the distinction that new theories are better received when the scientist is "well-respected."

32. Answer: J.

Concept: *R203 Inference/Assumption*

At the end of the second paragraph, the author states Frank's work "caused the widely respected scientist to acquire a certain reputation... as a bit unstable," which indicates any of the answers. However, later on in lines 73-78, the passage states that "despite the derision, colleagues continued to respect Frank's mainstream work" on particles. This indicates answer choice **J** is correct.

33. Answer: B.

Concept: *R201 Detail*

While it might be tricky to find the support for the correct answer, since the chronology of the passage is not always in order, the answer is clearly supported in lines 20-21. The passage states Frank "seemed relieved that part of a long ordeal was ending." Although the word "relieved" is mentioned, Frank was not "bitter" about his treatment, so **A** is wrong. **C** is a trick because his *theory* had actually not proven anything quite yet, although it was well-respected. The text states clearly that Frank was not "gloating or anticipating glory," so **D** is also incorrect. He may seem more "relieved" than "grateful," but the other three answer choices are clearly incorrect.

34. Answer: H.

Concept: *R204 Main Idea/Function: Paragraph; R102 Paragraph Number*

For questions like these, always go back and reread the given paragraph. Answer choice **F** can be eliminated because there is no "earlier criticism of scientists." Answer choices **G** and **J** are definitely untrue because there is no connection to the role of science in society or the difference between theoretical and practical research. Answer choice **H** is the only reasonable answer.

35. Answer: A.

Concept: *R201 Detail*

Quickly skim the passage to find the required detail. The answer is mentioned in lines 45-47: they "analyzed photos of the electrical phenomena that accompany sunspots" and noticed dark specks that they decided to explore further.

36. Answer: F.

Concept: *R102 Paragraph Number*

Double-check the lines in question for context and note that the question states "in terms of the eighth paragraph as a whole." Answer choice **G** is irrelevant, and answer choice **J** should seem silly. Answers **F** and **H** are relevant to the paragraph, but **H** incorrectly states that the information is about the comets, rather than the vapor. Only answer choice **F** correctly states, in broad enough terms, that the lines in question were about providing sense to the information in the paragraph.

37. Answer: C.

Concept: *R203 Inference/Assumption*

Although the answer is not stated in the text, it can be inferred based on the information provided. It states that their "new evidence... leaves little doubt Earth is indeed being bombarded by *something*," which indicates that when their research was published there was a degree of understanding. Furthermore, the final paragraph states "it has not proved that they are comets... But Frank's evidence opens the matter up to study." Answer choices **A**, **B**, and **D** are noticeably positive or negative, whereas **C** simply states that Frank's work was early in its development, but "worthy of consideration."

38. Answer: G.

Concept: *R201 Detail; R101 Line Number*

Always look back in the passage at the line in question. The author mentions that it was clear that objects were bombarding Earth. "Something" is italicized to emphasize that it may or may not have been small comets, as Frank is attempting to prove.

39. Answer: D.

Concept: *R101 Line Number*

After mentioning the "schizophrenic existence," Zare goes on to describe how a scientist has to think contradictory thoughts in a proper balance to succeed in the profession. Answer choice **A** should seem too extreme and unrelated. Answer choices **B** and **C** can be ruled out because they emphasize an "either/or" mindset rather than one that includes both sides, as indicated in answer choice **D**, which is correct.

40. Answer: H.

Concept: *R201 Detail*

Skim the passage to find mention of the scientists first finding the dark specks. The answer is found in lines 51-52, which states their curiosity grew, eventually into an "obsession." Answer choice **G** is not extreme enough, whereas answer choice **H** states that the level of involvement increased, but doesn't limit it.

Science 61C

1. Answer: B.

Concept: *S102 Experimental Design/Parameters*

The text states that 1 gene is transferred every 15 minutes. So, after 45 minutes, 3 complete genes would have transferred. In the final 5 minutes, a part of the 4th gene would be transferred, but the process would not be complete - only 3 complete genes would have been transferred.

2. Answer: J.

Concept: *S101 Find in Text; S203 Reading a Figure*

Student 3 states that replication can begin anywhere, but always proceeds clockwise (such as S, A, G, F, X, R). If the first gene replicated is G, the second is F and the third is X.

3. Answer: C.

Concept: *S101 Find in Text*

Both students 3 and 4 state that "replication can begin between any 2 genes."

4. Answer: F.

Concept: *S101 Find in Text; S203 Reading a Figure*

Student 1 states that replication begins between Gene F and X, with Gene X being replicated first and Gene F being replicated last. The genes would replicate in this order: X, R, S, A, G, F. After 45 minutes, 3 genes would have transferred, so X, R, and S would've transferred and A, G, and F would not have been transferred.

5. Answer: A.

Concept: *S101 Find in Text; S203 Reading a Figure*

Student 2 states that replication begins between Gene F and X, but the direction can vary. Genes can be transferred F, G, A, S, R, X or X, R, S, A, G, F. After 30 min, 2 genes would have transferred: either F, G or X, R. Thus, A and S would definitely not have transferred.

6. Answer: J.

Concept: *S101 Find in Text*

According to Students 1 and 2, only F or X could be the last gene transferred. Students 3 and 4 state that gene transfer can start anywhere, so it is possible that A could be the last transferred.

7. Answer: D.

Concept: *S104 Inference; S203 Reading a Figure*

Student 1 states that gene transfer begins with X and goes X, R, S, A, G, F. If X, R, S, and A were transferred, and it takes 15 min per gene (according to the text), then 60 minutes would've passed.

8. Answer: G.

Concept: *S204 Trends*

In Figure 1, as the wavelength of the different S colors increases, the reflectance increases, as shown by the upward-sloping lines. For SO_2 the reflectance increases then decreases.

9. Answer: C.

Concept: *S204 Trends; S202 Reading a Graph*

In Figure 4, the small plume line (dotted) is always higher than the large plume line (solid) for each wavelength. So, the large plume reflectance is always lower.

10. Answer: H.

Concept: *S202 Reading a Graph*

In Figure 1, the white S line at 0.40 μm is around 0.2 reflectance.

11. Answer: D.

Concept: *S206 Correlation*

The line for the Pele crater floor in Figure 3 is shallow, and is most similar to the brown S line in Figure 1.

12. Answer: H.

Concept: *S202 Reading a Graph*

In Figure 4, the large plume line (solid) is steadily increasing until it levels off around 0.60 μm and 0.5 reflectance. The small plume line (dotted) is steadily increasing the entire time, so if it is around 0.85 reflectance at 0.60 μm, it will be at a slightly higher reflectance at 0.61 μm.

13. Answer: B.

Concept: *S101 Find in Text*

The text defines reflectance as the fraction of light that is reflected by a surface, so a reflectance of 0.98 at 0.60 μm means that 98% of light is reflected, and that light is 0.60 μm.

14. Answer: F.

Concept: *S205 Extrapolation*

In Table 1, V starts at 0 and is 8.4 after 12 sec. Thus, V must reach 7.6 some time between 0 and 12 sec.

15. Answer: C.

Concept: *S205 Extrapolation*

In Table 2, time increases as capacitance increases. At 0.6, the time is 4.2 sec and at 1.2, the time is 8.3 sec. From this, it can be inferred that at 1.8, the time would be around 12.5 sec, so at 1.5, the time would be between 8.3 and 12.5 sec.

16. Answer: J.

Concept: *S102 Experimental Design/Parameters*

The text and table of Experiment 3 state that students used different resistors and measured the time to reach 6 V, so the purpose of the experiment was likely to see how resistance affected time.

17. Answer: A.

Concept: *S305 Physics; S203 Reading a Figure*

According to the text of Experiment 1 and Figure 1, the voltmeter measured voltage across the capacitor. In order to measure voltage across a resistor, the part of the circuit with the voltmeter (circled V) should connect to the circuit just before and after the resistor.

18. Answer: F.

Concept: *S201 Reading a Table*

In Table 2, the fastest time (lowest number of seconds) is at a capacitance of 0.1 x 10^-6 F.

In Table 3, the fastest time is at a resistance of 0.25 x 10^7Ω, which can be rounded to 0.3.

19. Answer: B.

Concept: *S207 Infer from Data; S103 Argumentation and Evidence*

In Table 2, which describes experiment 2, as capacitance increased, time increased.

20. Answer: F.

Concept: *S201 Reading a Table; S102 Experimental Design/Parameters*

In Table 1, the more heat was released, the more the water temperature changed. In Table 2, as the amount of sucrose increased, heat released increased, so it can be inferred that the temperature change increased as well.

21. Answer: B.

Concept: *S204 Trends*

In Table 1, the more heat was released, the more the water temperature changed. The graph that shows this direct relationship is B, with a steady upward slope.

Tip: *do not be tricked by the fact that the information is out of order! This is a frequently missed question for this reason.*

22. Answer: G.

Concept: *S201 Reading a Table*

When 1.0 g sucrose is burned, 16.0 kJ is released. When 0.5 g sucrose is burned, 8.0 kJ is released, which is a decrease of exactly half of 16.0.

23. Answer: A.

Concept: *S201 Reading a Table*

In Table 1, the least heat was released by 1.0 g of potato (3.2), then egg (6.7), then bread (10.0), and lastly cheese (17.0 kJ). The amount of heat released from 1.0 g of sucrose is 16.0 kJ, which is more than every food except cheese.

24. Answer: H.

Concept: *S205 Extrapolation*

As the amount of potato is multiplied by 5 from 1.0 g to 5.0 g, the heat released will also be multiplied by 5, from 3.2 to 16.0. 16 is closest to 15 kJ.

25. Answer: D.

Concept: *S204 Trends*

In Figure 1, the line curves to show that when temperature decreases from 10 to 0 (the right half of the graph), density increases then decreases.

26. Answer: G.

Concept: *S201 Reading a Table*

In Table 1, all liquids have a lower density than the least dense solid (glucose; 1.56) *except* for mercury, which has the highest density on the table. Thus, the student's claim would not be supported by the data.

27. Answer: B.

Concept: *S204 Trends*

According to Figure 2, as the temperature increases, density decreases, which is shown by the steady downward slope of the line.

28. Answer: F.

Concept: *S304 Chemistry; S201 Reading a Table*

Liquids form layers based on density, with the highest density at the bottom and the lowest density at the top. Ethyl ether is 0.71, mercury is 13.59, and water is 0.9971. Thus, the mercury would be on the bottom, water in the middle, and ethyl ether on top.

29. Answer: C.

Concept: *S302 Science Math; S201 Reading a Table*

According to Figure 1, water at 4°C has a density of 1. The text states that density = mass/volume. If we have 100 g water, the density equation could be rewritten as 1 = 100/volume, and solved to find volume = 100.

30. Answer: F.

Concept: *S204 Trends*

In Study 4, which is represented by Figure 3, as time increases, the number of captures by frugivores (line with squares) decreases, as shown by the line's downward slope.

31. Answer: D.

Concept: *S204 Trends*

If more birds are captured, it is likely that more birds are present. Since the number of captures for insectivores (line with diamonds) decreased after fragmentation, fragmentation probably caused a decrease in insectivore populations. However, the hummingbirds (line with triangles) increased, so fragmentation probably caused an increase in hummingbird populations.

32. Answer: G.

Concept: *S205 Extrapolation*

In Figure 1, the 70 m point is around -3 and the 80 m point is around -2, so a 75 m point would likely be around -2.6.

33. Answer: C.

Concept: *S302 Science Math; S101 Find in Text*

In Study 2, there was an average change in AGTB of 0. It is possible that the AGTB of every plot was 0, or it is possible that the AGTB averaged out to 0, such that some plot increased and some plots decreased.

34. Answer: J.

Concept: *S103 Argumentation and Evidence; S207 Infer from Data*

The first paragraph of the text states the researchers predicted fragmentation would cause a decrease in AGTB and animal populations. Study 4 (Figure 3) shows an increase in hummingbird populations, which is least consistent with the researchers' prediction.

35. Answer: C.

Concept: *S302 Science Math; S202 Reading a Graph*

In Year 2, 80 insectivores (line with diamonds) were captured every 1,000 hr. Thus, in 10,000 hr (10 times 1,000), 800 insectivores were captured (10 times 80).

36. Answer: H.

Concept: *S206 Correlation*

In Figure 1, the core soils that have close to 85 ohms of resistivity and 22 mL/g CO_2 are yellow till and gray till C. Yellow till has very different percentages of sand, silt, and clay. Gray till C has very similar percentages of sand, silt, and clay, so the sample is likely gray till C.

37. Answer: D.

Concept: *S306 Earth/Space Science; S203 Reading a Figure*

Since soil is laid down over time, the deepest layers are the oldest. Of the four answer choices, gray till D is the deepest below the surface and therefore the oldest.

38. Answer: G.

Concept: *S203 Reading a Figure*

In Figure 1, the sand and gravel layer has the highest resistivity (almost 150), clearly higher than the resistivities of the till layers.

39. Answer: C.

Concept: *S206 Correlation*

In Figure 1, the resistivity of bedrock is around 50, which is closest to the resistivity of olive green and gray till.

40. Answer: J.

Concept: *S205 Extrapolation*

In Figure 1, the CO_2 is highest for gray till A around 35 mL/g, so for present day CO_2 levels to be higher than any measured, they would have to be higher than 35.

ACT 59F (2003)

English

1. Answer: B.

Concept: *E201 Relevancy: Adding, Deleting, and Replacing Information*

The question states specifically that the correct choice will be "most relevant to the information provided in this first paragraph," so it must be read in context. The sentence following lists different types of people which might be seen on the subway. This information only supports answer choice **B**, as it has nothing to do with speed, cost, or calmness.

2. Answer: F.

Concept: *E102 Commas*

The commas in this sentence are confusing, so identifying the subject and predicate can help determine where breaks are necessary. The subject is a list of different types of people from "A musician" to "stockbrokers in crisp, charcoal gray suits." The predicate is "get on at Wall Street." Commas in this sentence are only needed to separate list articles. The end of a list does not need another comma, as there is no new article, so answer choice **G** is incorrect. "Charcoal gray" is a phrase, not two separate adjectives, so separating them is incorrect (unless the suits are literally made of charcoal). Similarly, there is no need to separate "suits" from its descriptor "charcoal gray."

3. Answer: D.

Concept: *E106 Apostrophes: Possessive, Plural, Contractions*

The difference between the possessive "whose" and the conjunction "who's" ("who is") is the key here. Replace the underlined portion with "who is" and it should be apparent that "who's" is the correct answer.

4. Answer: G.

Concept: *E202 Word Choice: Correct Word*

Prepositions are difficult because there isn't a hard and fast rule to follow. Simply substitute each answer choice because only one will make sense in these situations. In this case, only "as" correctly relates the information about the girls and the teenager with the cat.

5. Answer: B.

Concept: *E103 Independent Clauses: Period, Semicolon, Comma and FANBOYS*

Separating Independent Clauses
1. Period
2. Semicolon
3. Comma FANBOYS

It's important to recognize that this sentence is compound. As soon as the reader sees "I think," it should be apparent that a new sentence has begun and a method of separating these sentences is necessary. The only answer choice which correctly separates the two independent clauses is answer choice **B**, which uses a comma and the conjunction "and."

6. Answer: J.

Concept: *E204 Short and Simple*

Any answer choice other than **J** redundantly states information mentioned earlier in the sentence: the word "maybe." Any answer choice other than **J** repeats the "possibility" which is already conveyed with the word "maybe."

7. Answer: A.

Concept: *E205 Transition Words/Phrases; E204 Short and Simple*

The options provided all add unnecessary transitions. While it may be difficult to determine when a transition is necessary, one might notice that all of the transition words *mean the same thing*. Then, it becomes clear that one can't be correct and the others incorrect, thus eliminating them all.

8. Answer: G.

Concept: *E106 Apostrophes: Possessive, Plural, Contractions*

It's = it is
Its = possessive

Tip*: "* **its'** *" doesn't exist!*

The reader should replace the underlined portion with each answer to see which makes the most sense. In this question, the sentence must read "It is impossible," which is the only thing that makes sense.

9. Answer: C.

Concept: *E204 Short and Simple*

All the other options here are wordy to the point of just being confusing: don't be fooled! If a one-word answer sounds correct, it often is.

10. Answer: H.

Concept: *E101 Verbs: Agreement/Tense*

Note the *NOT* in the question! Answer choice **H** is the only unacceptable answer because the existing past-tense verb "watched" is the active verb of the sentence. "Playing" is only a modifier/descriptor of the elderly man, and thus should be either present or past tense with appropriate pronoun pairings. All of the acceptable answer choices modify the verb "playing" with restrictive information that correctly renders it dependent.

11. Answer: D.

Concept: *E202 Word Choice: Correct Word*

Preposition questions are tough! The reader must simply know that one sits "across *from,*" not "across *with,*" another person.

12. Answer: G.

Concept: *E207 Modification: Moving Modifiers*

The underlined phrase is describing the *woman.* Thus, it fits most appropriately right alongside her to avoid confusion.

13. Answer: A.

Concept: *E202 Word Choice: Correct Word*

The question here specifically asks for a choice emphasizing "the rapid speed," so the verb "hurtled" (**A**) is the most fitting option. It is a strong action verb with much more emphasis than "continued," "proceeded," or "moved," which are hardly descriptive.

14. Answer: H.

Concept: *E201 Relevancy: Adding, Deleting, and Replacing Information*

If the sentence is read, it should take little elimination to determine which answers are irrelevant. There is no physical description, and a quick reference to the opening sentence of the essay will rule out **G**, nor is there an "explanation for the narrator's actions." If it wasn't apparent immediately, answer choice **H** is the only one supported by the essay.

15. Answer: C.

Concept: *E210 Writer's Goal*

In "yes-or-no" questions, keep in mind that what matters is the *supporting evidence*. In this case, answer choice **C** is correct because it accurately portrays the essay. The others, while referencing the passage, do not provide sound reasoning based off of these references. The evidence provided in **A** does not support the "yes," so it is wrong. The support of **B** is simply untrue and so is **D**.

16. Answer: F.

Concept: *E104 Nonessential Information: Commas, Dashes, Parentheses*

The clause "known as the Navajo code talkers" is functionally nonessential to the sentence, and thus does not affect its structure. Nonessential clauses require two commas, before and after the clause, to indicate that it is nonessential.

17. Answer: C.

Concept: *E102 Commas*

It is helpful for the reader to understand that the independent clause of this complex sentence *ends* at "1945." The clause beginning with "transmitting information" is a dependent clause that is conveying more information on the Navajo code talkers. There should be no commas or other punctuation in the underlined portion, as there is nothing to separate. The preposition "on" does not need a comma before or after it. A colon at the end is incorrect because the clause prior to it is dependent. Answer choice **D** would split up the entire sentence, making the first independent clause dependent, which is always wrong.

18. Answer: G.

Concept: *E101 Verbs: Agreement/Tense*

"Had" correctly places the action in the past tense, as the action began in the past *and ended in the past*. There is no indication that any of the information in continuing in the present, or even beyond 1945.

19. Answer: A.

Concept: *E202 Word Choice: Correct Word*

These adjectives each have different meanings. If the reader is uncertain about them, simply see if any of them can be disregarded to help narrow down the options. Since the adjective is describing "machines" it should be easy to eliminate "thorny" and "gawky." Now, consider the phrase "strenuous exercise." Answer choice **C** would indicate that the machines were somehow demanding on the coders *physically*, when the passage seems to indicate that they were difficult to use because they were complex and slow.

20. Answer: J.

Concept: *E103 Independent Clauses: Period, Semicolon, Comma and FANBOYS*

Separating Independent Clauses
1. Period 2. Semicolon 3. Comma FANBOYS

The word "whereas" is often misused, so don't be daunted by its presence. Instead, consider and rule out the simpler answers. There are two independent clauses in need of separation: answer choices **G** and **F** have no comma, so they can be ruled out. While answer choice **H** has a comma, it has no conjunction to go with it. Although "whereas" is not in FANBOYS, it serves a similar purpose and is correct in this usage.

21. Answer: D.

Concept: *E205 Transition Words/Phrases*

Transition words serve a purpose - they are not there for show! "Nevertheless" implies exception; "similarly" implies comparison, and "still" implies some sort of contrast. Check the context of the entire sentence and it should be clear that none of these transition words apply.

Note: *it is of course possible to put a transition word here, but none of the answer choices are appropriate!*

22. Answer: H.

Concept: *E102 Commas*

Big 3 Comma Rules
1. No commas between subject and verb 2. No commas before or after prepositions 3. No commas between describing words and the things they describe

No comma is necessary in the underlined portion because nothing is being separated (that is, neither clauses nor lists). Also, there should never be a comma before or after a preposition! Only answer choice **H** abides by this rule.

23. Answer: C.

Concept: *E105 Pronouns: Agreement/Case; E101 Verbs: Agreement/Tense*

The antecedent to the underlined pronoun is "the Navajo language." As such, a singular pronoun ("it") is necessary. This narrows down the answer choices to **B** and **C**. The verb "make" must agree with "a structure and sounds," which is plural. So, **C** is correct.

24. Answer: F.

Concept: *E202 Word Choice: Correct Words*

Another confusing preposition! Again, the reader must be familiar with the language in order to know that a person gets "exposure *to*" something, not "from," "with," or "of" it in this context. (One could suffer "from exposure," as a physical ailment, but that is not relevant here.)

25. Answer: B.

Concept: *E103 Independent Clauses: Period, Semicolon, Comma and FANBOYS*

Separating Independent Clauses

1. Period
2. Semicolon
3. Comma FANBOYS

This is another *NOT* question, so be careful not to pick the first right answer! Remember that on the ACT a semicolon and a period are functionally the same, so they are both correct. Answer choice **B** is clearly incorrect because two independent clauses cannot be separated with nothing!

26. Answer: J.

Concept: *E105 Pronouns: Agreement/Case*

In this sentence, the antecedent to the pronoun is somewhat unclear because it hasn't been stated since the beginning of the paragraph. Because of the ambiguity, it's better to just state the intended subject instead of using a pronoun.

27. Answer: A.

Concept: *E201 Relevancy: Adding, Deleting, and Replacing Information*

Check the paragraph: is there any reason to mention the "size" of the Navajo people? There is absolutely no reason to mention it! If there is an answer choice which excludes that information, it is correct. In this case, answer choice **A** removes the information that has no relation to the rest of the passage.

28. Answer: J.

Concept: *E204 Short and Simple*

It is simply redundant to state that the peril was "dangerous," "hazardous," or "risky." Omitting the underlined portion is correct.

Tip: *Remember to always give special attention to options for omission, as they are often correct.*

29. Answer: C.

Concept: *E103 Independent Clauses: Period, Semicolon, Comma and FANBOYS*

The compound predicate here can be combined with only the conjunction "and." The sentence is not entirely compound as it does not repeat or introduce a subject for the second predicate, so no comma is needed as there is no new independent clause.

30. Answer: F.

Concept: *E203 Word Choice: Tone; E204 Short and Simple*

The phrase "secret work" is concise and accurate, while the other options contain expressions which aren't particularly proper or are redundant. "Hush-hush" and "under wraps" are idioms better kept for creative passages, rather than informative.

31. Answer: D.

Concept: *E102 Commas*

Tip: *find the sentence!*

This question might strike the reader as a little tricky. Consider how this sentence would best be rearranged. "Everybody listens when storyteller Smith practices her art." The subject and predicate of this sentence is "everybody listens." In the passage, the information is inverted so that the subject-predicate construction follows the introductory (dependent) clause. Thus, it is necessary to recognize that the information prior to "everybody listens" needs to be offset by a comma after "art," but nowhere else.

32. Answer: F.

Concept: *E205 Transition Words/Phrases*

The transition "indeed" is appropriate here because it expands upon the previous point. The other options bear implications which do not fit this context.

33. Answer: B.

Concept: *E105 Pronouns: Agreement/Case*

As the antecedent is "the griots," a group of people, "who" is appropriate because it refers to people rather than objects. "Whom" needs a paired preposition. Answer choices **A** and **D** would incorrectly assign the griots with the relative pronouns "where" and "that."

34. Answer: J.

Concept: *E103 Independent Clauses: Period, Semicolon, Comma and FANBOYS*

Separating Independent Clauses

1. Period
2. Semicolon
3. Comma FANBOYS

It is necessary for the reader to recognize that there are two independent clauses here that need proper separation. Only answer choice **J** incorrectly connects the two clauses with only a comma. Answer choice **H** may seem like it is incorrect, but it actually correctly removes the subject "she" and thus makes the following clause dependent.

35. Answer: C.

Concept: *E201 Relevancy: Adding, Deleting, and Replacing Information*

Consider what the phrase in question means out of context, as well as in context. It is by no means an essential transition, as in **A**, nor a comparison as in **B**. Answer choice **D** can be ruled out because the information is completely crucial! Answer choice **C** correctly describes its purpose.

36. Answer: H.

Concept: *E204 Short and Simple*

The redundancy in this sentence is the inclusion of both her being "in the field of education" and public schools, as one can hardly be one without the other.

37. Answer: A.

Concept: *E104 Nonessential Information: Commas, Dashes, Parentheses*

This phrase serves as further description of "Cindy Ellie," and thus is only a modification and not a new clause. As such, only a comma is needed.

38. Answer: J.

Concept: *E201 Relevancy: Adding, Deleting, and Replacing Information*

Remember that in "yes-or-no" questions it is the supporting evidence which determines the correctness of the answer, not the "yes" or "no." It should be clear that answer choice **J** is the best option because the reasoning behind the others is either untrue (**H**) or not as relevant. Although answer choice **F** may seem attractive, and there is nothing necessarily wrong with it, answer choice **J**'s support is correct in stating that it "does not logically fit at this point in the essay."

39. Answer: D.

Concept: *E104 Nonessential Information: Commas, Dashes, Parentheses*

It is necessary for the reader to note that the portion "who had… in Gambia" is a nonessential clause because it can be removed without affecting the independent clause of the sentence. Nonessential clauses are always nested between commas, so a single comma must follow "Alex Haley" to match the one following "Gambia."

40. Answer: G.

Concept: *E204 Short and Simple*

While the other options listed are grammatically correct, it is always best to choose the *shortest* correct answer. Because "for" is just as correct as any of the other answer choices and states it in the simplest, most concise manner, it is correct.

41. Answer: C.

Concept: *E103 Independent Clauses: Period, Semicolon, Comma and FANBOYS*

Separating Independent Clauses

1. Period
2. Semicolon
3. Comma FANBOYS

The word "This" indicates a new independent clause has begun. It must be separated from the previous sentence correctly. Only answer choice **C** does so.

42. Answer: F.

Concept: *E201 Relevancy: Adding, Deleting, and Replacing Information*

The most (and indeed only) relevant quote provided is answer choice **F**. It provides an analogy appropriate to the situation of a "belated discovery," whereas the others do not fit this section at all.

43. Answer: D.

Concept: *E204 Short and Simple*

It is redundant to state that she could speak "for twelve hours straight" and "consecutively," as that is already implied by the word "straight." Answer choices **B** and **C** suffer the same problem. Redundancy on the ACT is always incorrect, so it is best to omit entirely.

Tip: *Remember to always pay attention to options for omission, as the ACT loves them!*

44. Answer: F.

Concept: *E102 Commas*

There's no need for a comma here as there is no change of clause in the underlined portion. "It's" is short for "it is," which is correct here.

45. Answer: D.

Concept: *E210 Writer's Goal*

Remember to focus on the supporting details. In this case, answer choice **D** is the only option which addresses both the story *and* the question. The other answer choices fail to accurately do both.

46. Answer: G.

Concept: *E105 Pronouns: Agreement/Case*

The question here is what the pronoun is referring to. Later in the sentence it states "what *they're* really interested in are..." which indicates that there is a plural noun present. Since the correct pronoun will not refer to Joe, it must be **G**, "children." "They" or "some of them" would mean that the sentence is using pronouns without an antecedent noun which is always incorrect.

47. Answer: C.

Concept: *E107 Colons and Dashes*

The colon is used here to separate an independent clause from a list of examples. Answer choice **D** is incorrect because the extra comma at the end incorrectly separates the article "dirt" from the parenthetical description (which is part of the "dirt" list article).

48. Answer: F.

Concept: *E202 Word Choice: Correct Word*

These sorts of prepositional phrase questions can be difficult to pin down because there are no easy rules to reference. The reader must know that the construction "as if" is correct in this scenario. Inserting the other phrases should sound incorrect.

49. Answer: B.

Concept: *E208 Moving Sentences*

Note first, the question states "after" the correct sentence. This is important. The sentence states that the narrator has "doubts." Always read for context when inserting a sentence - both the sentence before and after will be relevant. In this case, the only obvious answer is Sentence 2 where the narrator says

the parents call the baseball "organized." Sentence 3 indicates that the children are anything but organized. Therefore, answer choice **B** is correct.

50. Answer: F.

Concept: *E205 Transition Words/Phrases*

The transition word "since" loosely means "because." This implication of causation is correct given the cause-and-effect relationship of the batter and the stationary tee. Note also: all the other answers have *very* similar connotations, which should be a strong indicator that they are wrong as there can only be one correct answer!

51. Answer: C.

Concept: *E103 Independent Clauses: Period, Semicolon, Comma and FANBOYS*

This is a *NOT* question, so don't forget that three of them are correct. Answer choice **C** would mean that the subject of the sentence ("the umpire") never actually does anything! Answer choices **A**, **B**, and **D** correctly state that the umpire "gives" the players chances, but answer choice **C** never gets there because the comma after "umpire" is never resolved later in the sentence!

52. Answer: J.

Concept: *E203 Word Choice: Tone*

To determine what is lost, first determine what they contribute. "Lots of them do" indicates that what the batters fail to do happens frequently. While admiration for the umpire may be *implied* by the sentence (and the word "patient"), the information removed would not affect that information. Answer choices **G** and **H** should seem wildly incorrect.

53. Answer: A.

Concept: *E204 Short and Simple*

The other two grammatically correct choices in this question are wordy and add no meaning to the sentence which is not already provided by answer choice **A**. The shorter option always wins between two similar choices.

54. Answer: F.

Concept: *E205 Transition Words/Phrases*

Even though it is in the middle of the sentence, it is still a transition word. Therefore, read the sentence prior to determine its context. It is important to consider what each transition means. "Instead" implies replacement; "likewise" is a similarity through comparison; "meanwhile" is a simultaneous action. "Therefore" correctly implies a correlation of causation.

55. Answers: A.

Concept: *E201 Relevancy: Adding, Deleting, and Replacing Information*

What does the proposed addition have to do with the rest of the sentence? Answer: It doesn't! There is no reason to add it. The fact that **B-D** are all synonymous and grammatically valid should be a strong clue that one can't be correct, because they would all be.

56. Answer: J.

Concept: *E102 Commas*

No clauses or articles are being separated here, so there is no need for an additional comma. Thus, answer choice **J** is correct.

57. Answer: C.

Concept: *E105 Pronouns: Agreement/Case*

"It" is the correct pronoun here, not "that,' because there is no need for a relative pronoun, so **B** and **D** are incorrect. The "What" is incorrect without an additional "is" after "about" to keep the clause functionally the same. Only "It's about" serves this purpose out of the given options.

58. Answer: G.

Concept: *E106 Apostrophes: Possessive, Plural, Contractions*

Although it's an odd one, the word "grown-ups" is plural, so a plural-possessive needs an apostrophe *after* the "s." The comma in answer choice **J** is only a distraction!

59. Answer: C.

Concept: *E204 Short and Simple*

"They're not" is concise and adequately communicates the exception stated in the sentence. The other options are wordy and confusing, adding no new thought to the sentence.

60. Answer: J.

Concept: *E210 Writer's Goal*

Don't overvalue the "yes-or-no" portion of each answer: the supporting evidence is what determines the correct choice. Only answer choice **J** addresses both the question and the passage correctly. The essay only mentions Joe's son in passing as a way to bring up the topic of T-ball games in general.

61. Answer: A.

Concept: *E202 Word Choice: Correct Word*

The word "slowly" is immediately before the underlined portion, so it should be easy to determine what type of description is needed. Answer choice **A** is the only option which does not imply a sudden or immediate loss of feathers.

62. Answer: G.

Concept: *E201 Relevancy: Adding, Deleting, and Replacing Information; E204 Short and Simple*

Notice first that there are three significantly longer sentences and one that is short and concise. This should be a clue! Two of the answer choices explain what the word "diurnal" means, so don't be confused by it or allow it to sway the answer choice. Whether or not raptors are diurnal is simply not relevant and can be eliminated. Thus, answer choice **G** is correct.

63. Answer: C.

Concept: *E202 Word Choice: Correct Word*

The correct answer will *NOT* be an acceptable substitute for "whole." In this context, the sentence is saying that the "bird's body mistakenly believes the feather is unbroken." The only answer choice which does not correlate would be "total," answer choice **C**. "Total" would be similar to the word "entire" (i.e. totally and entirely).

64. Answer: G.

Concept: *E201 Relevancy: Adding, Deleting, and Replacing Information*

The most relevant option is the one which supports the statement of "pain" following the underlined portion. The best option is answer

choice **G**, as the others would not imply any sort of difficulty in removing them.

65. Answer: A.

Concept: *E105 Pronouns: Agreement/Case*

The singular antecedent of the needed pronoun is "a quill stub," which mandates a singular pronoun. This rules out answer choice **B** and **C** which are plural. The relative "that" is also incorrect, as there is no introduction of a restrictive clause. Thus, leaving only the simple pronoun "it."

66. Answer: H.

Concept: *E103 Independent Clauses: Period, Semicolon, Comma and FANBOYS*

Separating Independent Clauses
1. Period
2. Semicolon
3. Comma FANBOYS

The dash indicates that the information that follows is an explanation. As it stands in the passage, it is also a dependent clause. The correct answer, which will be grammatically *incorrect*, will separate the two clauses incorrectly. Answer choice **H** places a period where the hyphen is without making the following clause independent with a correct subject-predicate construction, and is therefore wrong.

67. Answer: D.

Concept: *E101 Verbs: Agreement/Tense*

The incorrect answers here are confusing. Answer choice **D** is the only possible option because without it there would never be an independent clause! The subject ("all flighted birds") must connect with its predicate ("have ten primary flight feathers"), which only occurs in answer choice **D**.

68. Answer: H.

Concept: *E108 Adjectives and Adverbs*

The two underlined words are *both* adverbs that are modifying the verb "shaped." As such, the correct form of those adverbs are "slightly" and "differently," which is answer choice **H**.

69. Answer: B.

Concept: *E203 Word Choice: Tone*

Consider the implications of the removed words "carefully" and "small." These most support the idea of delicacy as stated in answer choice **B**. The words do not address limitations, differentiation, or ease as the other options imply.

70. Answer: F.

Concept: *E202 Word Choice: Correct Word*

Notice that the word "will" is not underlined, nor is the preposition "to," which are essential to identifying the correct answer. These subtleties make a big difference in choosing the correct answer. The word "will" must be followed by "be," which eliminates **H** and **J**. The preposition with "equally long" would be "as" (not "to"), so **G** is incorrect.

71. Answer: A.

Concept: *E205 Transition Words/Phrases*

"Next" correctly shows a sequence of events. While "Finally" also shows sequence, it improperly suggests that this is the final step, which it is not.

72. Answer: J.

Concept: *E101 Verbs: Agreement/Tense; E206 Modification: Dangling Modifiers*

The subject-verb agreement is key here. As it is written, the subject of the sentence is "glue," which also shifts the sentence into passive voice. The real problem, however, is that this causes "glue" to be the one doing the "sliding" at the start of the sentence, instead of the rehabilitator. Only answer choice **J** correctly connects the subject (the rehabilitator) with the verb (sliding).

73. Answer: B.

Concept: *E103 Independent Clauses: Period, Semicolon, Comma and FANBOYS*

Be careful: this is a *NOT* question. The question states that the correct answer will be an unacceptable way to separate two independent clauses. **A** is correct because a semicolon is the same as a period on the ACT. **C** uses a comma and a conjunction, which is correct. Answer choice **D** simply makes the second clause into what is called a restrictive clause by using "that" and removing the subject. Only answer choice **B** would be incorrect because "eventually" is between nested commas which means the sentence would have to function without the commas and the word in between them.

74. Answer: G.

Concept: *E106 Apostrophes: Possessive, Plural, Contractions*

If the sentence doesn't say "it is," then the apostrophe is never correct (**F** and **J**). In no circumstance is it appropriate to say "to have grow" in English, so **H** is also incorrect (and doubly so for **J**).

75. Answer: C.

Concept: *E201 Relevancy: Adding, Deleting, and Replacing Information*

One last time for this test: focus on the *support*, not the "yes or no" portion of the answers. The incorrect answer choices focus too much on the rehabilitators, when in fact the passage is about "Fixing Raptor Feathers," as the title states. Although a significant portion of the text explains how the rehabilitators help with this problem, that doesn't mean that the rehabilitators are the new focus. Thus, answer choice **C** is correct.

Math 59F

1. Answer: B.

Concept: *M106 Sequence*

The sum of an arithmetic sequence is
$\frac{n}{2}(a_1 + a_n)$.

In this problem, $n = 12$, $a_1 = 1$, $a_n = 12$

$$\left(\frac{12}{2}\right)(1 + 12) = 6 \times 13 = 78$$

If you don't know the formula, you have to do it the long way:

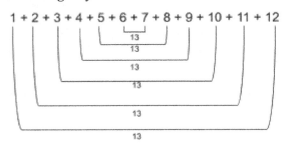

$1 + 2 + 3 + 4 + 5 + 6 + 7 + 8 + 9 + 10 + 11 + 12$

$1 + 12 = 13$
$2 + 11 = 13$
$3 + 10 = 13$
$4 + 9 = 13$
$5 + 8 = 13$
$6 + 7 = 13$

$\overline{\Sigma = 6 \times 13 = 78}$

B. 78

Tip: *Know how to add up a long list of consecutive or sequential numbers.*

---

2. Answer: J.

Concept: *M110 Percent*

$40 + 22\%$

$40 + 40(.22)$

$40(1.22) = 48.80$

J. 48.80

3. Answer: B.

Concept: *M109 Rate & Proportion*

First, cross multiply:
$$\frac{112}{800} = \frac{x}{1400}$$

$(112)(1400) = 800x$
$\div 800 \qquad\qquad \div 800$

$$\frac{112 \times 1400}{800} = x$$

$196 = x$

B. 196

4. Answer: G.

Concept: *M202 Solving Equations*

$7 + 3x = 22$
$-7 \qquad\quad -7$

$3x = 15$
$\div 3 \quad\; \div 3$

$x = 5$

$2x = 2 \times 5 = 10$

Trap: *Answer F is x=5, but you are solving for 2x!*

G. 10

5. Answer: C.

Concept: *M212 Linear Function: Rate*

$$\frac{30}{day} + \frac{28.5}{mile}$$

$$28.5c = \$.285$$

$$5\ days \times \frac{30}{days} + (350\ miles)(.285\ miles)$$
$$150 + 99.75 = 249.75$$

C. $249.75

6. Answer: F.

Concept: *M303 Quadrilaterals*

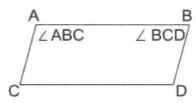

∠ABC and ∠BCD are supplementary

F. *add up to* 180°

7. Answer: B.

Concept: *M104 Fractions*

Use the TI-84/83 LCM (least common multiple) function:

MATH>NUM>LCM(15,12)ENTER=60
LCM(60,8)=120

Note: *you can only do two at a time!*

Old school solution:

15   12   8
5 (3 3)(4 4) 2

$LCM = 5 \times 4 \times 3 \times 2 = 120$

B. 120

8. Answer: H.

Concept: *M201 Algebraic Operations; M205 Exponents & Roots*

$(2x^4 y)(3x^5 y^8)$

$(2 \times 3)(x^{4+5})(y^{1+8})$

H. $6x^9 y^9$

9. Answer: C.

Concept: *M101 Word Problems - Translation & Vocabulary; M204 Absolute Value*

First off, it's a #9, so it <u>has</u> to be easy. Second, the word *difference* means subtract. The only answer choice with <u>subtraction</u> is C!

The absolute value is used because you don't know which ticket is more expensive, and the *difference* should not be a negative value.

C. $|12a - 18s| = 36$

10. Answer: F.

Concept: *M205 Exponents & Roots*

<u>Plug in a number</u> $x > 1$, so make $x = 2$.

F. $\sqrt{2} = 1.414$ Winner!
G. $\sqrt{2 \times 2} = 2$
H. $\sqrt{2 \times 2} = 2$
J. $2 \times \sqrt{2} = 2.828$
K. $2 \times 2 = 4$

F. $\sqrt{x}$

11. Answer: B.

Concept: *M214 Functions f(x)*

This style of question used to be on both the ACT and SAT (especially the SAT), but isn't very common anymore.

$$(a, b) \blacklozenge (c, d) = \frac{ac + bd}{ab - cd}$$

$$(2, 1) \blacklozenge (3, 4) = \frac{(2 \times 3) + (1 \times 4)}{(2 \times 1) - (3 \times 4)}$$

$$= \frac{6 + 4}{2 - 12}$$

$$= \frac{10}{-10}$$

$$= -1$$

B. -1

12. Answer: G.

Concept: *M302 Triangles; M301 Lines & Angles*

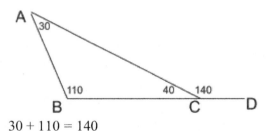

$30 + 110 = 140$

$\angle C = 180 - 140 = 40$

G. 140°

13. Answer: E.

Concept: *M302 Triangles*

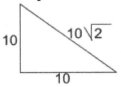

E. $10\sqrt{2}$

Tip: *Know the relative side lengths of 45-45-90 and 30-60-90 right triangles! Always on the test.*

---

14. Answer: H.

Concept: *M503 Probability; M110 Percent*

400 bags, 25% are red, 75% are not red.

$$75\% = \frac{3}{4}$$

H. $\frac{3}{4}$

15. Answer: D.

Concept: *M201 Algebraic Operations*

$$x^2 - 2x + 6 + (?) = 3x^2 + 7x$$

Isolate the unknown value:

$$3x^2 + 7x - (x^2 - 2x + 6) = ?$$

$$3x^2 - x^2 + 7x + 2x - 6 =$$

$$2x^2 + 9x - 6$$

D. $2x^2 + 9x - 6$

16. Answer: G.

Concept: *M210 Systems of Equations; M207 Linear Functions: y=mx+b*

Put into slope-intercept form:

$$8x + 9y = 3$$
$$\underset{-8x}{} \qquad \underset{-8x}{}$$

$$9y = -8x + 3$$
$$\underset{\div 9}{} \qquad \underset{\div 9}{}$$

$$y = \frac{-8}{9}x + \frac{1}{3}$$

Parallel lines have the <u>same</u> slope.

G. $-\dfrac{8}{9}$

> Tip: *Know how to convert from standard form to slope-intercept form quickly; the ACT loves this question!*

17. Answer: D.

Concept: *M208 Coordinate Geometry & XY-plane*

The midpoint is simply the average of the x's and y's.

> Trick: *Notice the answer choices with x are all equal, but the y's are different. Because of this, you <u>only</u> need to do the y's.*

$$\frac{6 + 4}{2} = \frac{10}{2} = 5$$

D. $(6, 5)$

18. Answer: G.

Concept: *M201 Algebraic Operations*

$$y = x^2$$

$$-y = -x^2$$

G. $-x^2$

19. Answer: D.

Concept: *M214 Functions f(x)*

$$h(x) = 4x^2 - 5x$$

$$\begin{aligned} h(-3) &= 4(-3)^2 - 5(-3) \\ &= 4 \times 9 + 15 \\ &= 36 + 15 \\ &= 51 \end{aligned}$$

D. 51

20. Answer: F.

Concept: *M302 Triangles*

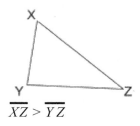

$$\overline{XZ} > \overline{YZ}$$

> Tip: *The angle opposite the longer side has a greater degree measure.*

F. *The measure of ∠X is always less than the measure of ∠Y.*

21. Answer: C.

Concept: *M204 Absolute Value*

$|7(-3) + 2(4)|$

PEMDAS → treat absolute value as a grouping symbol (parentheses).

Do the math <u>inside</u> first, then take the absolute value.

$|-21 + 8| = |-13| = 13$

Trap: *Many students mistakenly make everything positive and then do the operation, making this problem* $|23 + 8| = 29$, *answer E.*

C. 13

22. Answer: G.

Concept: *M204 Absolute Value*

$x > |y|$
$x > |-4|$
$x > 4$

G. $x > 4$

23. Answer: C.

Concept: *M303 Quadrilaterals*

$Perimeter = 72$

$2x + 2(12) = 72$

$2x + 24 = 72$
$-24 \quad -24$

$2x = 48$
$\div 2 \qquad \div 2$

$x = 24$

C. 12, 24, 24

24. Answer: K.

Concept: *M108 Ratio; M302 Triangles*

Similar triangles have congruent angles and sides in ratio.

The smaller side is 5 ("matches" 2).

$2 : 5$

Cross multiply:

$$\frac{2}{5} = \frac{5}{x}$$

$2x = 25$
$\div 2 \qquad \div 2$

$x = 12.5$

K. 12.5

25. Answer: A.

Concept: *M208 Coordinate Geometry & XY-plane; M303 Quadrilaterals*

Square with side 3. Vertex at (3,0).
This problem is ultra simple: add 3 to the x and y value of the coordinate pair.

$3 + 3 = 6$

$(6, 0)$ is 3 units from $(3, 0)$.

A. $(6, 0)$

26. Answer: K.

Concept: *M305 Circles*

Consider each answer choice:

F. $\angle$TUM is 65°.

$\triangle$TMU is isosceles, so $\angle$TUM and $\angle$UTM are congruent. Calculate their measures by:

$50^o + 2(x) = 180$
$-50 \qquad -50$

$2x = 130$
$\div 2 \qquad \div 2$

$x = 65$

So, F is true.

G. $\overline{TU}$ to $\overline{RS}$. TRUE.
Chords formed by two intersecting diagonals <u>are</u> parallel.

H. Arc TXU measures 50°. TRUE.
Vertical angles!

J. $\overline{RM} \cong \overline{TM}$. TRUE.
All radii are congruent.

K. $\overline{RS} \cong \overline{SM}$. FALSE.
$\overline{RS}$ is a chord that forms at the base of an isosceles triangle.

Since $\angle$RMS measures 50°, the base and sides are <u>not</u> congruent.

K. $\overline{RS} \cong \overline{SM}$

27. Answer: A.

Concept: *M207 Linear Functions: y=mx+b*

Linear Profit Model:
(selling price − cost of each item)(number of items) − cost

$(20, 000 - 7, 000)(x) - 10, 000, 000$

A. $(13, 000)x - 10, 000, 000$

28. Answer: G.

Concept: *M216 Quadratics & Parabolas; M217 Factoring & FOIL*

$2x^2 + 6x = 36$
$\div 2 \qquad \div 2$

$x^2 + 3x = 18$
$-18 \qquad -18$

$x^2 + 3x - 18 = 0$

Factor:
$(x + 6)(x - 3) = 0$

Trick: Backsolve by putting answers into the equation.

G. $- 6 \; and \; 3$

29. Answer: C.

Concept: *M212 Linear Function: Rate*

You know this is a linear function problem because it is a <u>constant rate.</u>

Plug in values of t and x into equations. Start with $t = 0$ to find $x = 10$.

A. $10 = 0 + 10$ YES
B. $10 = 4(0) + 6$ NO
C. $10 = 4(0) + 10$ YES
D. $10 = 10(0) + 4$ NO
E. $10 = 14(0)$ NO

Only A and C remain. Now put in $t = 1$ and find $x = 14$.
A. $14 = 1 + 10$ NO
C. $14 = 4(1) + 10$ YES

Note: *This is a question that many students get incorrect. Know how to do this one. It is easy and very common.*

C. $x = 4t + 10$

30. Answer: J.

Concept: *M501 Mean, Average*

To solve, you can PLUG IN your own numbers.

$$\frac{(1 + 2 + 3 + 4)}{4} = \frac{10}{4} = 2.5$$

To increase by 2, add $2 + 2.5 = 4.5$
Let x be the increase.

Solve for x:

$$\frac{10 + x}{4} = 4.5$$
$$\times 4 \qquad \times 4$$
$$10 + x = 18$$
$$- 10 \qquad - 10$$
$$x = 8$$

J. 8

31. Answer: D.

Concept: *M305 Circles*

$r = 9$

$Area = \pi r^2$

$Area = \pi(9)^2 = \pi(81) = 254.34$

D. 254

32. Answer: G.

Concept: *M302 Triangles*

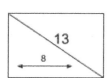 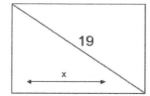

Similar means proportional.

Cross multiply:

$$\frac{8}{13} = \frac{x}{19}$$

$$152 = 13x$$
$$\div 13 \qquad \div 13$$

$$11.69 = x$$

G. 12

33. Answer: D.

Concept: *M308 Multiple Figures; M302 Triangles*

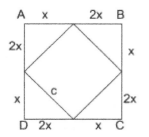

$Area\ of\ ABCD = (x + 2x)^2 = (3x)^2 = 9x^2$

Use <u>Pythagorean Theorem</u> to find the shaded area.

$$x^2 + (2x)^2 = c^2$$

$$x^2 + 4x^2 = c^2$$

$$5x^2 = c^2$$

$Shaded\ area = c^2 = 5x^2$

$$\frac{Shaded\ area}{Area\ of\ square} = \frac{5x^2}{9x^2} = \frac{5}{9}$$

D. $\dfrac{5}{9}$

34. Answer: K.

Concept: *M404 Law of Sines/Cosines*

Let's look at each answer choice:

F is wrong because Pythagorean only works for *right triangles*.

G is wrong because area wouldn't provide the length of the hypotenuse.

H and J are obviously wrong because the only angle that is given is not 30-60-90 or 45-90.

K. The law of cosines: For any ABC, where a is the length of the side opposite ∠A, b is the length of the side opposite ∠B, and c is the length of the side opposite ∠C, a2 = b2 + c2 – 2bc cos(∠A)

> Tip: *Be familiar with the Law of Sines and Cosines. See video lesson on 3RPrep YouTube Channel.*

35. Answer: A.

Concept: *M207 Linear Function: y=mx+b*

$2x + y = 4$

Solve for intercepts:

x	y
0	$y = 4$
$2x = 4$ $\div 2 \quad \div 2$	0

Intercepts: $(0, 4)$ $(2, 0)$

Graph:

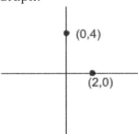

A.

Tip: *Know how to graph a line in standard form quickly by solving for the intercepts. Do not waste time converting to slope-intercept.*

36. Answer: F.

Concept: *M301 Lines & Angles*

A line separates a plane into two parts. None of the others do. <u>Geometry knowledge!</u>

F. *A line*

Tip: *a plane goes on forever in all directions and a line goes on forever in two directions. Therefore, on a line can bisect a plane!*

37. Answer: D.

Concept: *M304 Polygon*

Solution: 1. Draw & Count
               2. Know the formula!

1.

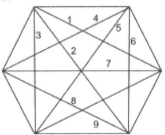

2. $\dfrac{n(n - 3)}{2} = \dfrac{6(6 - 3)}{2} = 9$

38. Answer: G.

Concept: *M215 Equation of a Circle*

Tip: *The equation of a circle, $(x - h)^2 + (y - k)^2 = r^2$, where (h, k) is the coordinate pair of the center of the circle and r is the radius. Memorize this; it appears on almost every test.*

Here, the center of the circle is at $(4,0)$. The circle is *tangent* to the y-axis, so the radius is 4 units. So, pick the correct equation, G.

G. $(x - 4)^2 + y^2 = 16$

39. Answer: A.

Concept: *M104 Fractions*

Trick: *Use your calculator to turn each fraction into a decimal and list them in order.*

$\dfrac{5}{3} = 1.67$

$$\frac{7}{4} = 1.75$$

$$\frac{6}{5} = 1.2$$

$$\frac{9}{8} = 1.125$$

A. $\dfrac{9}{8} < \dfrac{6}{5} < \dfrac{5}{3} < \dfrac{7}{4}$

40. Answer: F.

Concept: *M215 Conic Sections*

The perimeter of an ellipse is <u>not</u> a common question. Notice that they give you the equation! It is a simple plug and chug.

$w = 3 \quad h = 4$

$$P = \frac{\pi}{2}\sqrt{2(4^2 + 3^2)}$$
$$P = \frac{\pi}{2}\sqrt{2(16 + 9)}$$
$$P = \frac{\pi}{2}\sqrt{2(25)}$$
$$P = \frac{5\pi}{2}\sqrt{2}$$

F. $\dfrac{5\pi}{2}\sqrt{2}$

41. Answer: C.

Concept: *M104 Fractions; M103 Properties of Integers*

$$\frac{A}{30} + \frac{B}{105} = \frac{7A + 2B}{x}$$

Trick: *Use your Ti-83/84 to find the LCM or common denominator. lcm*(30, 105) = 210.

C. 210

42. Answer: H.

Concept: *M212 Linear Function: Rate; M506 Table*

36 months at 10% interest is $32.27 <u>per</u> $1000 borrowed

$$\frac{\$6500 \text{ } borrowed}{\$1000} = 6.5$$
$6.5 \times \$32.27 = 209.755$

H. $209.76

43. Answer: D.

Concept: *M212 Linear Function: Rate; M506 Table*

The *maximum* amount borrowed will be the result of dividing the 5% interest payment into her maximum monthly payment.

$$\frac{300}{18.87} = 15.898$$

Don't stop here: 15.898 is the number *in thousands* that she can borrow.

$15.898 \times 1000 = \$15,898$

D. $15,000

44. Answer: G.

Concept: *M506 Table; M501 Average*

To find 9%, you must average 8% and 10%.

8%, 60 month is $20.28
10%, 60 month is $21.24

$$\frac{20.28 + 21.24}{2} = 20.76$$

G. $20.76

45. Answer: B.

Concept: *M404 Law of Sines/Cosines; M302 Triangles*

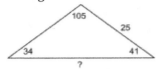

$$\frac{25}{sin(34)} = \frac{x}{sin(105)}$$

Solve for *x* by multiplying out $sin(105)$:

B. $\dfrac{25sin(105)}{sin34}$

46. Answer: J.

Concept: *M219 Complex Numbers; M217 Factoring & FOIL*

$i^2 = -1$

$$(4 + i)^2 = (4 + i)(4 + i)$$
$$= 16 + 4i + 4i + i^2$$
$$= 16 + 8i - 1$$
$$= 15 + 8i$$

J. $15 + 18i$

47. Answer: E.

Concept: *M203 Inequalities; M103 Properties of Integers*

$2r + s = 15, \ s > 10$

If $s > 10$, make $s = 11$.

Substitute and solve.
$$2r + 11 = 15$$
$$\quad -11 \quad -11$$

$$2r = 4$$
$$\div 2 \quad \div 2$$

$$r = 2$$

R cannot be greater than 2; that would make $x < 10$. Thus, *r* must be less than or equal to 2.

E. $r \leq 2$

48. Answer: K.

Concept: *M103 Properties of Integers; M205 Exponents & Roots*

To solve, simply plug in your own numbers using a positive number for *x* and a negative number for *y*.

Pick $x = 3$ and $y = -3$.

F. $-3 - (3) = -6$ NO.

G. $3 + (-3) = 0$ NO.

H. $(3^3)(-3) = -81$ NO.

J. $\dfrac{(3^2)}{(-3)} = -3 \ No.$

K. $\dfrac{3}{(-3)^2} = \dfrac{1}{3} \ Yes!$

K. $\dfrac{x}{y^2}$

49. Answer: A.

Concept: *M206 Logarithm*

$log_2 8 = 3$
$2^3 = 8$

A. 3

50. Answer: F.

Concept: *M401 SOHCAHTOA*

Solve for $\overline{AC}$:

$(AC)^2 + 2^2 = 5^2$

$AC^2 + 4 = 25$
${}_{-4}{}_{-4}$

$AC^2 = 21$

$AC = \sqrt{21}$

$$S\frac{O}{H}\ C\frac{A}{H}\ T\frac{O}{A}$$

$\tan B = \dfrac{\sqrt{21}}{2}$

F. $\dfrac{\sqrt{21}}{2}$

51. Answer: D.

Concept: *M209 Variation: Direct/Inverse*

$50 + fee

Let y represent the fee which varies directly with the square root of time. Let x represent the time:
$y = k\sqrt{x}$

Solve for k:
$\$90 = \$50 + k\sqrt{16}$
${}_{-40}{}_{-40}$

$40 = 4k$
${}_{\div 4}{}_{\div 4}$

$10 = k$

Substitute:
$y = \$50 + 10(\sqrt{36})$
$y = 50 + 10 \times 6$
$y = 50 + 60$
$y = 110$

D. $110

52. Answer: H.

Concept: *M401 SOHCAHTOA*

$$S\frac{O}{H}\ C\frac{A}{H}\ T\frac{O}{A}$$

$\sin(d) = .8$

$\sin(d) = \dfrac{opp}{hyp} = \dfrac{AC}{6}$

$\dfrac{AC}{6} = .8$
${}_{\times 6}{}_{\times 6}$

$AC = 4.8$

$AC^2 + CD^2 = 6^2$

$(4.8)^2 + CD^2 = 36$

$23.04 + CD^2 = 36$
${}_{-23.04}{}_{-23.04}$

$CD^2 = 12.96$

$CD = \sqrt{12.96}$

$CD = 3.6$

H. 3.6

> Note: *this is a 3-4-5 triangle!*

53. Answer: D.

Concept: *M204 Absolute Value*

To solve, plug in sample integers.

A. For *always*, use A=1, B=1
$|1 + 1| = |1 - 1|$
$2 = 0$ NOT TRUE.

B. Same as A. NOT TRUE.

C. $|0 + 0| = |0 - 0|$

0 = 0 True, but not the <u>only</u> case.

D. $|0 + 1| = |0 - 1|$
$1 = 1$
or
$|1 + 0| = |1 - 0|$
$1 = 1$
True!

E. Obviously wrong since C and B are not true.

D. *only when a = 0 or b = 0*

54. Answer: K.

Concept: *M216 Quadratics & Parabolas*

$L = x \times x = x^2$
$R = x \times y$
$S = y \times y = y^2$

Count the number of L, R, S

$2(L) + 13LR + 15(S)$

Substitute:

$2x^2 + 13xy + 15y^2$

K. $2x^2 + 13xy + 15y^2$

55. Answer: C.

Concept: *M207 Linear Functions: y=mx+b*

$y = (A + 1)x + 8$

Pass through $(2, 6)$

Substitute and solve for $(A + 1)$, the slope:

$6 = (A + 1)2 + 8$
$-8 \qquad\qquad -8$

$-2 = (A + 1)2$
$\div 2 \qquad\qquad \div 2$

$-1 = (A + 1)$

C. -1

56. Answer: K.

Concept: *M216 Quadratics & Parabolas*

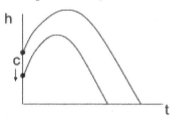

To solve: If you alter the c-term, the graph of the parabola changes at the *h*-intercept, the maximum, and the *t*-intercept.

K. *I, II, and III*

57. Answer: E.

Concept: *M207 Linear Functions: y=mx+b;*
M210 Systems of Equations

$x = -3 \quad y = x - 3$

Substitute:
$y = (-3) - 3$

$y = -6$

E. $(-3, -6)$

58. Answer: K.

Concept: *M304 Polygon*

See lesson M304 on angles of polygons.
A pentagon has 540 degrees.

$540 - 50 = 490^o$

K. 490

59. Answer: E.

Concept: *M101 Word Problems - Translation*
& Vocabulary

$3c = b, \ so \ c = \dfrac{b}{3}$

What is $c + 3$?

$\dfrac{b}{3} + 3$

E. $\dfrac{b}{3} + 3$

60. Answer: K.

Concept: *M305 Circles*

$radius = R, \ circumference = 2\pi R$
$3 \ laps \ = \ 3 \times (2\pi R) = 6\pi R$

K. $6\pi R$

Reading 59F

1. Answer: D.

Concept: *R104 Big Picture*

It is clear that there is only one narrator discussing his own life, so **A** and **B** can be eliminated. Answer choice **D** is a more accurate representation of the passage, since the boy is not agonizing over mixed messages as in answer choice **C**.

2. Answer: F.

Concept: *R301 Main Idea/Function: Passage*

Answer choice **F** is the most clear right answer. However, if it isn't apparent, a skim through the answer choices and the first/last paragraphs of the passage reveal that **G** and **H** are incorrect, since they mention reflection occurring only at the beginning and the end. Answer choice **J** is easily eliminated because there is no dialogue.

3. Answer: C.

Concept: *R104 Big Picture*

Since the overall purpose of the passage is to illustrate the narrator's family trait with examples, answer choice **C** is the only choice that fits.

4. Answer: G.

Concept: *R203 Inference/Assumption*

Refer to the passage where the narrator begins his description of the basketball court project. He talks about making plans in lines 22-27, getting to work, and then being discouraged when his grandfather delivers the wrong size hoops. This shows he is enthusiastic at first, until he realizes his grandfather's error. Although answer choice **J**

is close, the choice implies the narrator loses his enthusiasm at the start.

5. Answer: A.

Concept: *R203 Inference/Assumption*

Although the answer is not explicitly stated, there is plenty of textual evidence. In line 24, the grandfather is described as "always interested in plans." After the hoops are delivered, the grandfather is described as "sensitive," especially about "the flawed part" of their work (lines 44-46). The only answer choice that reflects this sudden change from optimistic to defensive is **A**.

6. Answer: H.

Concept: *R201 Detail; R101 Line Number*

Refer to the lines in question and answer choice **H** should seem incredibly obvious. Answer choices **F** and **J** would both mean that the ridicule and the tilting shelves had actually happened, when in fact they were hypothetical. Answer choice **G** is simply never mentioned.

7. Answer: A.

Concept: *R201 Detail; R102 Paragraph Number*

Refers to the lines in question. If answer choice **A** is not immediately apparent (for it is the only one mentioned), eliminate the other answer choices. They didn't blame anyone for the problem, but especially not the narrator, so **B** is incorrect. **C** suggests praise, but there is no praise mentioned. Answer choice **D** would mean that there wasn't a problem with the crutches, but there was.

8. Answer: G.

Concept: *R203 Inference/Assumption; R101 Line Number*

Lines 36-46 describe the narrator's grandfather's hurt feelings and defensiveness. Although there are no quotations, these are clearly meant to be responses by the grandfather, which makes **H** and **J** incorrect. If the reader isn't sure about whether the information is opinion or fact, the grandfather should not sound apologetic (**F**); thus, answer choice **G** is correct.

9. Answer: B.

Concept: *R203 Inference/Assumption*

Once again, the question asks for an inference, but the support for the inference is in the passage! The narrator discovers his error at the end of the passage and mentions that he was "relieved to find it," that it makes him feel connected to his grandfather. From this, it can be inferred that he feels comforted, which indicates answer choice **B**. Answer choice **D** is trying to trick because it says "relief," but the second half of the choice is obviously wrong.

10. Answer: H.

Concept: *R103 Keyword*

Lines 78-82 explain the difference between the two phrases. The author states "diminished excellence is a condition of the world," whereas "flawed competence comes out of character." This suggests that diminished excellence is part of the environment and flawed competence comes out of the individual.

11. Answer: A.

Concept: *R204 Main Idea/Function: Paragraph; R102 Paragraph Number*

Refer back to the first paragraph, which describes longitude and how it can be found at sea. The rest of the passage is about the challenges and history of finding latitude at sea, so the first paragraph is introducing the topic and orienting the reader (**A**).

12. Answer: F.

Concept: *R204 Main Idea/Function: Paragraph; R102 Paragraph Number*

Double-check the lines in question and put into context. The lines mention that the challenge of longitude lasted over four centuries and the large prize offered for the solution. Both of these details emphasize how big the longitude problem is.

13. Answer: C.

Concept: *R201 Detail; R203 Inference/Assumption*

Since Harrison is the inventor of the clock that finally solved the longitude problem, it can be "reasonably inferred," as the question asks, that nobody had solved the problem of clocks at sea.

14. Answer: J.

Concept: *R203 Inference/Assumption; R101 Line Number*

By looking at the mentioned lines, the example is found immediately after the author mentions that there is no practical method of calculating longitude, so it can easily be inferred that the example illustrates the consequences of this challenge.

15. Answer: A.

Concept: *R201 Detail*

Reread the given lines to find the correct information. The last lines of the paragraph, 23-25, states that "one degree shrinks from sixty-eight miles at the Equator to virtually nothing at the poles." This is correctly reflected in answer choice **A**.

16. Answer: G.

Concept: *R201 Detail*

Skim the passage to find the detail about the metals in Harrison's clock. The passage mentions that the clock had a combination of different metals that counteracted changes in temperature (lines 69-72), which matches answer choice **G**.

17. Answer: D.

Concept: *R203 Inference/Assumption*

Although the passage doesn't mention specific competitors of Harrison's, the passage does mention, in lines 76-79, that the commissioners of the prize wanted to award the prize to astronomers, who would fall within the category of "the scientific community."

18. Answer: H.

Concept: *R201 Detail*

Skim the passage to find the specific detail the question requires. Lines 74-82 describes Harrison's challenge with "every success of his parried by members of the scientific elite." However, Harrison's "approach triumphed in the end" (lines 80-81), and he got the reward.

19. Answer: D.

Concept: *R203 Inference/Assumption*

Refer back to the given lines. This part mentions that Harrison's followers made "modifications" that "enabled it to be mass produced and enjoy wide use," suggesting they wanted to make his design more practical.

20. Answer: G.

Concept: *R201 Detail*

The final paragraph is the only place where the *current* instruments for determining longitude ("satellites") are mentioned.

21. Answer: C.

Concept: *R104 Big Picture; R203 Inference/Assumption*

The answer to this question is not explicitly stated in the passage, but it can be inferred. In the last paragraph, the author quotes her mother, who calls herself a designer, and says that her work gives her happiness. The only answer that makes sense is answer choice **C**, "self-worth."

22. Answer: G.

Concept: *R203 Inference/Assumption*

Whenever the question asks for an inference, there is still support in the passage. In this case, skim the passage for a mention of how she described the dinner-dances, and the line (25-26) that states she looked forward to the dinner-dances with "long anticipation" Thus, answer choice **G** is correct.

23. Answer: A.

Concept: *R204 Main Idea/Function: Paragraph; R102 Paragraph Number*

Reread the paragraph in question2. It states that "the window shopping and dinner-dances stopped," that downtown was "grimy" now. Answer choice **A** correctly states that this paragraph is contrasted with the earlier scene depicted when the family went window shopping and the narrator was "drunk with wonder" at the shop displays.

24. Answer: G.

Concept: *R104 Big Picture*

This question is perhaps best answered through elimination. The lines in question refer to the entire end of the passage, so hopefully a reread of the entire section isn't necessary. This portion describes how Oka-chaan began working for wealthier women, the attitude of those women, the father's response to these women and his anger, and Oka'chaan's defense of her work. Only answer choices **G** and **J** are relevant here, but it would be strange to suggest that the father were in any way the "primary focus" as the question suggests. Oka-chaan's strength in dealing with the women she works for and the father is clearly the focus, so **G** is correct.

25. Answer: D.

Concept: *R203 Inference/Assumption; R101 Line Number*

Reread the given line, along with the lines before and after. The narrator's father is tying his tie and explaining the importance of the dimple. The narrator states that she saw this time of year as "magical," which correlates to the adjective "arcane" in line 54. There's no indication that there is anything negative about this information, eliminating **A**. The lines clearly from the perspective of the

daughter, so **B** is incorrect. The reader shouldn't have any reason to believe that the daughter thought her father was silly, as she clearly revered him and their time together.

26. Answer: G.

Concept: *R203 Inference/Assumption; R101 Line Number*

The lines in question are a description of how the wealthy woman spoke to Oka-chaan, but the correct answer will be an *inference of the narrator's view* of that situation. Based on that description, it should seem clear that the narrator was "recognizing that her mother was being demeaned" by this woman, as stated in **G**. There's no indication that the narrator felt unsure about anything as in **F**. Answer choice **H** is a trick that includes the word "distance" to match the question, but is irrelevant. **J** is the only other possible answer, but there is not enough supporting evidence in the passage to suggest the narrator was doing anything other than *watching* this interaction.

27. Answer: D.

Concept: *R203 Inference/Assumption*

The portion in question was in the lines above, so hopefully another read won't be necessary. In lines 81-83, the father talks about the customer's contempt and the mother "kneeling...like a servant." Although it is not directly stated, it can be inferred that the mother's sewing business is embarrassing to him, or "threatens his sense of dignity": answer choice **D**.

28. Answer: G.

Concept: *R104 Big Picture; R102 Paragraph Number*

Let's eliminate some answers. Answer choice **F** is clearly incorrect as the only mention of finances is the father's mentioning that they *don't need the money* (lines 79-80). Answer choice **H** can be eliminated because the parents don't mention the children at all in their argument. Clearly only the father was angry at the woman, while Oka-chaan is *not* worried about the woman's behavior towards their family. Thus, answer choice **G**, which may have seemed obvious from the start, is the only possible answer.

29. Answer: D.

Concept: *R202 Vocabulary in Context; R101 Line Number*

Always double-check vocabulary in context! In this case, the "architectural wonders" are "crafted from fresh produce and pungent sausage."

30. Answer: H.

Concept: *R201 Detail*

Lines 43-44 describe the father as he "trod unmincingly on Okaa-chan's feet and guided her into the walls," which can only be describing clumsiness (**H**).

31. Answer: D.

Concept: *R204 Main Idea/Function: Paragraph; R102 Paragraph Number*

Reread the given lines. The text emphasizes the ideas of difference and uniqueness at almost every line of this quotation. The only answer choice that suggests uniqueness is **D**.

32. Answer: F.

Concept: *R104 Big Picture*

Although this question refers to specific names mentioned in the passage, it can easily be inferred that these figures are mentioned to support the overall idea of the passage, which is that people with diseases/disabilities find unique ways of learning and overcoming them. Although answer choice **F** is curiously worded, the other answer choices are either obviously wrong (**G**) or address only narrow details in the passage (**H** and **J**).

33. Answer: B.

Concept: *R203 Inference/Assumption*

In this case, the answer is clearly stated in the passage. Lines 43-45 state that Luria had a "new view of the brain, a sense of it not as programmed and static, but rather as dynamic and active." Thus, the old view must have been "unchanging," which is closest to answer choice **B**, "static."

34. Answer: J.

Concept: *R202 Vocabulary in Context; R101 Line Number*

Always double-check for vocabulary in context. "The minus of a handicap" is "transformed... into the plus of compensation." This *transformation* of something going from a minus to a plus can best be translated as an "adaptation," as in the sense of someone adapting to a bad situation to make it better. Thus, **J** is correct.

35. Answer: A.

Concept: *R204 Main Idea/Function: Paragraph; R102 Paragraph Number*

This paragraph describes how the brain adapts and how the "norm" should be less rigidly defined. Answer choice **B** doesn't make sense and **C** is unrelated to the paragraph. Answer choice **D** can be eliminated because he doesn't talk about *which* of his subjects helped him reach these conclusions, so **A** is the only remaining choice.

36. Answer: H.

Concept: *R104 Big Picture*

This question is difficult, but the answer is almost explicitly stated in lines 70-76. The narrator states that when physicians study disease, they must also "study... identity, the inner worlds that patients... create." Answer choice **F** is clearly incorrect and **G** is not mentioned. From answer choices **H** and **J**, the narrator actually states that the "realities of patients... cannot be comprehended wholly from the observation of behavior." Thus, it cannot be "known" (**J**), but it can be "examined," as in answer choice **H**.

37. Answer: C.

Concept: *R203 Inference/Assumption*

The narrator states that he made the decision to take off his "white coat" because he realized that patients' personal realities can't be "comprehended wholly from observation... from the outside." Because of this, he leaves the hospital and begins making house calls to his patients. Answer choice **A** and **D** should appear completely wrong and unsupported by the passage. From the remaining choices, answer choice **B** is absurdly vague while **C** correctly pertains to the author's interest.

38. Answer: G.

Concept: *R204 Main Idea/Function: Paragraph; R102 Paragraph Number*

Reread the given paragraph. The author talks about how "defects, disorders, diseases" can bring out "powers, developments." This means that situations previously considered as problems can lead to interesting, unique, developments. The closest answer choice based on this information is **G**.

39. Answer: D.

Concept: *R202 Vocabulary in Context; R102 Paragraph Number*

For vocabulary in context, always refer back just in case. That being said, "ravage" really only has one meaning, which is "destroy." "Ravages" is simply the noun form.

40. Answer: H.

Concept: *R202 Vocabulary in Context; R102 Paragraph Number*

Refer to the vocabulary in question! The passage states that "the miracle is is how *they* all cooperate." "They" must be referring to the "hundreds of tiny areas crucial for every aspect of perception and behavior" in the brain. The only answer choice that describes the many different parts of the brain working together is answer choice **H**.

Science 59F

1. Answer: C.

Concept: *S203 Reading a Figure*

In Figure 2, all of the bars extend through two grades except two: chlorite in only low grade and kyanite in only medium grade.

2. Answer: J.

Concept: *S203 Reading a Figure*

In Figure 1, Facies G covers around the area over 175°C, a pressure above 10, and a depth below around 35. Thus, a pressure of 11 kb and temperature of 600°C is most likely of all the listed choices to create Facies G, because the other choices have too low pressure.

3. Answer: C.

Concept: *S204 Trends*

In Figure 1, pressure is on the left y-axis and increases downwards while depth is on the right y-axis and increases downwards as well. Thus, both pressure and depth increase together.

4. Answer: J.

Concept: *S203 Reading a Figure*

In Figure 2, all of the bars extend through one or two grades, except plagioclase, which extends through all grades. It is impossible to eliminate a grade by the presence of plagioclase.

5. Answer: A.

Concept: *S207 Infer from Data*

The question is asking for the rock on Figure 1 at Earth's surface, which is a depth of 0 km.

Only Facies A and B occur at the surface. Molten rock would refer to a higher temperature, further supporting Facies A.

6. Answer: J.

Concept: *S101 Find in Text*

According to the first sentence of each of the scientists, Scientist 1 believes the object was a comet and Scientist 2 believes the object was an asteroid. These are two different objects.

7. Answer: B.

Concept: *S101 Find in Text*

Scientist 2 states that an asteroid of this size would break apart at 8 km, but a comet would have exploded at a much higher altitude.

8. Answer: G.

Concept: *S101 Find in Text; S304 Chemistry*

Scientist 1 states that ices and dust are vaporized in the explosion, which means they changed to gases.

9. Answer: D.

Concept: *S101 Find in Text*

Scientist 2 states that large fragments couldn't be recovered "due to the area's boggy soil," which describes the soil conditions in the area.

10. Answer: H.

Concept: *S101 Find in Text*

Scientist 2 states that "the asteroid flattened," then "decelerated rapidly." If the asteroid had not flattened, it would have decelerated more gradually.

11. Answer: A.

Concept: *S104 Inference*

Answer choice **A** is the only reasonable explanation for the damage caused by the explosion. Answer choice **B** would explain a lack of damage. **C** and **D** do not fit with Scientist 2's description of the height of the explosion of two possible objects (8 km or higher).

12. Answer: G.

Concept: *S103 Argumentation and Evidence*

The paragraph at the start of the passage states that the object was between 10 and 100 m in diameter. If comets were much larger than 100 m in diameter, it would be unlikely that Scientist 1 is correct that a comet was the object that caused the explosion.

13. Answer: A.

Concept: *S201 Reading a Table*

In Table 3, the hand-planted seeds column is next to the ant-planted seeds column. Ant-planted seeds mark higher for seeds that germinated, plants alive after 1 year, and plants alive after 2 years.

14. Answer: G.

Concept: *S301 Inquiry Process; S102 Experimental Design/Parameters*

A controlled variable is one that is kept the same between the different groups in the experiment. Each site had two seed dishes, so the number of seed dishes was controlled.

15. Answer: C.

Concept: *S201 Reading a Table*

In Table 1, the percentage of seed mass composed of elaiosome (last column) was the same for both species (6.2).

16. Answer: G.

Concept: *S102 Experimental Design/Parameters*

Study 2 describes Site 3 as having *both* plants absent. This would allow the scientists to study the behavior of ants in an area without the plant species.

17. Answer: C.

Concept: *S102 Experimental Design/Parameters*

Answer choice **C** is the only reasonable answer. Study 2 includes only the seed dishes. Seeds from both plants were present at both sites, but they may have been removed by animals other than ants.

18. Answer: J.

Concept: *S207 Infer from Data*

According to Table 2, more seeds were removed from the species that was absent in the area, so it can be inferred that abundance of a plant species affects which seeds the ants choose.

19. Answer: A.

Concept: *S204 Trends*

In Tables 1 and 2, for each brand of tape, the average force required to tear the tape off was always higher for a wider tape. Thus, as the tape's width increases, the force required increases.

20. Answer: G.

Concept: *S205 Extrapolation*

In Table 2, Brand X required 1.6 N for 1.0 cm tape, 3.2 N for 2.0 cm tape, and 5.0 for 3.0 cm tape. Following this pattern, for each additional cm of tape, another 1.6-1.8 N are needed. 4 cm of tape would require around 6.8 N, so 7.0 N is the closest answer.

21. Answer: A.

Concept: *S201 Reading a Table*

Table 1 describes tape on paper and Table 2 describes tape on plastic. Brand X requires more force for paper than plastic. Brand Y is the same for both materials. Brand Z is roughly the same, since 1.0 cm is 1.9 N and 2.0 cm is 3.9 N for paper, and 1.5 cm is 2.8 N for plastic.

22. Answer: G.

Concept: *S201 Reading a Table; S102 Experimental Design/Parameters*

In both Tables 1 and 2, Brand Y is only used at 2.0 and 2.5 cm.

23. Answer: A.

Concept: *S102 Experimental Design/Parameters; S305 Physics*

In Figure 1, the spring scale is measuring the force acting on the clamp, which is acting on the tape.

24. Answer: F.

Concept: *S205 Extrapolation*

The given sample was 2.5 cm wide and had 4.9 N for paper and 4.1 N for plastic. On Table 1, which describes paper, 2.5 cm wide and 4.9

N could fit brand X or Z. On Table 2, which describes plastic, 2.5 cm and 4.1 N fits X only.

25. Answer: B.

Concept: *S201 Reading a Table; S305 Physics*

Heat flows from higher temperature to lower temperatures. The only trial in Table 1 that had T2 hotter than T1 was Trial 6.

26. Answer: F.

Concept: *S201 Reading a Table; S207 Infer from Data*

The best insulator would have the lowest heat flow. In Table 1, trials 7-10, the lowest heat flow was with wood.

27. Answer: D.

Concept: *S201 Reading a Table; S207 Infer from Data*

In Table 1, Trials 1 and 5 use the same material (glass wool). In Trial 1, the heat goes from 50°C to 20°C at a rate of 0.025. In Trial 5, the heat goes from 100°C to 70°C at a rate of 0.025. The rate is the same, despite different temperatures, and the difference in temperatures is the same (30°C).

28. Answer: H.

Concept: *S201 Reading a Table*

In Table 2, Trials 6-11, brick has a higher conductivity (0.500) than glass wool (0.025). Brick has a higher conductivity (0.500) than wood (0.072). Steel has a higher conductivity (31) than concrete (0.540). Steel does NOT have a higher conductivity (31) than aluminum (140).

29. Answer: A.

Concept: *S203 Reading a Figure; S201 Reading a Table*

In Table 1, Trials 1 and 3, the differences are in configuration and heat flow. Configuration A has a higher heat flow than Configuration C. Configuration A has less distance between the walls than Configuration C.

30. Answer: H.

Concept: *S304 Chemistry; S201 Reading a Table*

In Table 2, the highest quantity of NaCl is labeled "Solution was boiling." Once a solution is boiling, the liquid will not get any hotter. Any additional heat will cause it to evaporate.

31. Answer: A.

Concept: *S204 Trends*

In Table 2, as NaCl increased (first column), the temperature (second column) increased as well.

32. Answer: G.

Concept: *S205 Extrapolation*

In Table 2, 0.050 NaCl was 34 and 0.075 was 50. 0.060 would be between 34 and 50, so 42 would be the best answer.

33. Answer: D.

Concept: *S102 Experimental Design/Parameters*

In Experiment 1, the experiment used Mg ribbon, cut ribbon, and powder. Experiments 2 and 3 only use Mg powder. The forms of Mg differ by surface area.

34. Answer: F.

Concept: *S201 Reading a Table; S202 Reading a Graph*

In Figure 1, Mg powder makes the most heat. In Table 1, 0.50 Fe makes the most heat with the least material. In Table 2, 0.125 NaCl makes the most heat.

35. Answer: D.

Concept: *S304 Chemistry*

D is the only reasonable answer that would reduce the coating on the surface of Mg. A and C would cause slower reactions, and B shows NaCl and Fe interacting together, which didn't occur in any of the experiments.

36. Answer: F.

Concept: *S202 Reading a Graph*

The acceleration factor shows how fast the reaction was. In Figure 2, Enzyme A (solid line) reaches a peak acceleration factor around a pH of 5.

37. Answer: B.

Concept: *S202 Reading a Graph*

In Figure 2, Enzyme A (solid line) and Enzyme B (dashed line) have the same acceleration factor at the point of intersection, which is around a pH of 6.7.

38. Answer: J.

Concept: *S202 Reading a Graph; S207 Infer from Data*

In Figure 3, acceleration factor increases with substrate concentration. In Figure 4, acceleration factor increases with enzyme concentration. Thus, acceleration factor depends on both substrate and enzyme concentration.

39. Answer: A.

Concept: *S204 Trends; S202 Reading a Graph*

In Figure 4, the line for A is higher than line B at all enzyme concentrations, so the scientist is incorrect.

40. Answer: G.

Concept: *S304 Chemistry; S202 Reading a Graph*

In the figure, trypsin (solid line) works at a higher pH than pepsin (dashed line). Higher pH is less acidic, so trypsin works in a less acidic environment than pepsin. Thus, the small intestine must be less acidic than the stomach.

Printed in Great Britain
by Amazon

22749324R00132